"This book will be very useful to educators. Intentional cell phone use in educational settings is virtually nonexistent, and yet the phones themselves are the fastest growing form of communication technology in the world. A practical guide to helping educators with sensible, useful, and safe strategies, practices, policies, and learning theories—along with lesson and unit ideas across the K–12 spectrum—should prove very interesting to a large number of early adopters and innovators."

—**Jim Lerman**, author, *Retool Your School, 101 Best Web Sites for Teacher Tools and Professional Development, 101 Best Web Sites for Elementary Teachers*, and *101 Best Web Sites for Secondary Teachers*

"Nielsen and Webb provide wonderfully detailed examples of how to use cell phones to help students learn key content and skills through innovative activities. Through sample lesson plans and a variety of research-based strategies, the authors show why and how we can engage students using simple cell phones and web resources. Their use of ubiquitous devices to create a positive learning environment, develop new knowledge, and apply what they have learned is inspiring!"

—**Elizabeth Ross Hubbell**, co-author, *Using Technology with Classroom Instruction That Works* and *Classroom Instruction That Works, Second Edition*

"Many administrators and schools ban the use of cell phones because they are not knowledgeable on effective integration and instructional strategies. *Teaching Generation Text* will serve as an essential resource to change minds and help move thinking from banning to embracing these powerful learning tools. This book will provide relevant information crucial to engaging students and making them active participants in the learning process through the use of technology that they have grown accustomed to."

—**Eric Sheninger**, principal, New Milford High School

"Thought provoking and desperately needed, this book challenges conventional thinking that restricts learning and learners. It is time to liberate our classrooms. This book provides administrators a roadmap towards that liberation and a new, better day for learning achieved by harnessing the power of cell phones to bridge the digital divide and engage learners."

—**Ryan Bretag**, administrator at Glenbrook North High School, Illinois

"Nielsen's vision for learning inspires optimism. It gives voice to learners, values individuality, and embraces flexibility. She takes us beyond progressive thinking into the realm of true educational innovation. If you value learning, read this book."

—**Michelle Luhtala**, library department chair and edWeb.net Emerging Tech Facilitator

"Many schools work hard to keep wireless phones and other electronic devices out of their schools because they think they will distract students from learning. By sharing research and practical applications, Nielsen shows why schools and parents should embrace the skills and creativity of 'generation text' to actually enhance their learning through the use of these devices."
—**Curt Rees**, elementary school principal in Wisconsin

"Cell phones are the most ubiquitous electronic device we have and it's about time educators jumped into the fray with practical teaching and learning strategies to harness their potential. That's exactly what authors Nielsen and Webb accomplish in this well-written book. Chock full of practical ideas obviously written by people who have spent considerable time working with educators and students, *Teaching Generation Text* will jumpstart the cell phone-in-classrooms movement."
—**Pamela Livingston**, author, *1-to-1 Learning: Laptop Programs That Work*

"During a time when there is so much controversy about students and the ubiquitous cell phone in schools, there are few sources that provide techniques for teachers to use in schools where the PDAs are embraced. A book that provides this information will provide a refreshing read about positive ways to improve learning by using a resource that most students already bring to school."
—**Jane E. Pollock, Ph.D.**, Learning Horizon, Inc.; author of many books including *Classroom Instruction That Works*

"The twenty-first century is dictating that educators develop new paradigms regarding instruction. Students are utilizing new technologies to learn, to communicate, to develop relationships—school systems must become agile, flexible, and 'smart' to reach the modern day learner. Our school system is addressing the needs of the 'whole, new child.' Included in this plan is the effective use of technology. *Teaching Generation Text* will redefine classroom instruction, empower teachers to develop instructional techniques that are not limited to the traditional classroom, and will most definitely energize and engage the twenty-first-century learner."
—**Edward D. Longfield**, superintendent, Manitou Springs School District 14

"As we attempt to engage students in our busy world, using cell phones has potential to be fun, efficient, and user friendly. *Teaching Generation Text* teaches educators and leaders how to keep up with the times and engage learners utilizing a tool our students already own and love."
—**Kurt Clay**, principal, Delta High School

JOSSEY-BASS TEACHER

Jossey-Bass Teacher provides educators with practical knowledge and tools to create a positive and lifelong impact on student learning. We offer classroom-tested and research-based teaching resources for a variety of grade levels and subject areas. Whether you are an aspiring, new, or veteran teacher, we want to help you make every teaching day your best.

From ready-to-use classroom activities to the latest teaching framework, our value-packed books provide insightful, practical, and comprehensive materials on the topics that matter most to K–12 teachers. We hope to become your trusted source for the best ideas from the most experienced and respected experts in the field.

Teaching Generation Text

USING CELL PHONES
TO ENHANCE LEARNING

Lisa Nielsen and Willyn Webb
Foreword by Marc Prensky

JOSSEY-BASS
A Wiley Imprint
www.josseybass.com

Library of Congress Cataloging-in-Publication Data

Nielsen, Lisa.
  Teaching generation text: using cell phones to enhance learning / Lisa Nielsen and Willyn Webb.—1
    p. cm.
  Includes index.
  ISBN 978-1-118-07687-3 (pbk.) ISBN 978-1-118-11888-7 (ebk.); ISBN 978-1-118-11887-0 (ebk.); ISBN 978-1-118-11886-3 (ebk.)
    1. Educational technology. 2. Cell phones. 3. Education—Effect of technological innovations on.
  4. Mobile communication systems—United States. 5. Telephone in education. I. Webb, Willyn H. II. Title.
  LB1028.3.N557 2011
  371.33—dc23
  2011017843

Printed in the United States of America
FIRST EDITION
PB Printing 10 9 8 7 6 5 4 3 2 1

ABOUT THE AUTHORS

Lisa Nielsen and Willyn Webb are experts in the use of cell phones in education. They speak to audiences around the globe at conferences, via webinars, on radio programs, and through their online classes at Touro College (New York) and Colorado Mesa University for educators interested in using cell phones for learning.

Lisa Nielsen works with schools in New York City to innovate learning with technology. Her popular blog, *The Innovative Educator*, was named a top-twenty education blog by Discovery Education. She also writes for *Tech & Learning, ISTE Connects, Leading & Learning, edReformer, The Huffington Post*, and *mindSHIFT*.

Nielsen is an outspoken and passionate advocate of learning innovatively. She is frequently covered by local and national media for her views on "thinking outside the ban" to harness the power of technology for learning, and in her writing and speaking she shares real-life anecdotes about taking the risks necessary to do what is in the best interests of twenty-first-century students. For more on Lisa's work, visit www.educatinginnovatively .com or follow her on Twitter @InnovativeEdu.

Willyn Webb is a licensed professional counselor, administrator, educator, author, college professor, wife, and mother of three girls. She was a pioneer in bringing the language and interventions of solution-focused therapy to the classroom with her *Solutioning* books. She has also published children's books and a play. She has been spreading the word about harnessing the power of cell phones in the classroom through articles in national magazines and in presentations at the International Society for Technology in Education (ISTE), Tech Forum, and many other venues.

Webb has over twenty years of experience in education, most recently developing an alternative high school in Colorado where she uses cell phones, Facebook, and other technologies to build relationships, educate, and support services to others. For more on Willyn, her books, and her speaking go to www.willynwebb.com or follow her on Twitter @WillynWebb.

This book is dedicated to all the innovative educators out there who are excited to be the pioneers in harnessing the power of technology to effectively engage learners. We truly hope that you find what you read here a worthwhile investment of your valuable time.

If you do, we encourage you to keep the conversation going by joining our Facebook fan page at http://tinyurl.com/teachinggenerationtext and our Cell Phones in Education Group on Classroom 2.0 at www.classroom20.com/group/CellPhonesinEducation and following us on Twitter at @InnovativeEdu and @WillynWebb.

To Skylyn, Joyclie, and Missa, my texting teen and tweens, for inspiring me, showing me the value of cell phones for learning, and putting up with me during the writing of this book.

i <3 u!
Willyn Webb

To my beau Barry and BFFs Melanie, Penelope, and Celine for providing encouragement to think outside the ban and write a book that helps others do the same.

Lisa Nielsen

CONTENTS

Cell phones? In class??? Only a few years ago, the reaction from people I talked to about this was precisely the same as the one I got from a French woman when I told her I was bringing a highly unusual English cheese to a party in Paris: "Cheese?" she said, with her nose in the air, "to France???" Her unstated conclusion—"never!!!"—was pretty much the universal answer for cell phones in class as well.

Nevertheless, it occurred to a great many people—mostly the young—that cell phones would, indeed, make great learning devices. I heard one report of a five-year-old who, when informed by her grandfather that "when I was in school we didn't have cell phones," asked him, "Well, then, how did you get on the Internet?"

For the young, the fact that cell phones are powerful, inexpensive computers optimized for communication; full of useful add-ons such as texting, cameras, GPS, and Internet browsers; easy to download to; easily attachable to external inputs and outputs; and, most important, always in their pockets clearly makes them, when used effectively, a tremendous tool for learning.

Not long ago, however, few educators were taking that position. In fact, I remember reading a piece saying precisely the opposite—that *nothing* of value could be learned from a cell phone, including how to use it!

But the world today changes much faster than our institutions can keep up with. Even though two-thirds of the world's people (over four billion) now have a cell phone, and even though it takes only months for people to download over a billion apps for a new technology such as the iPhone, our schools still spend almost all of their sadly dwindling funds on the tools of the past. (The state of Texas, for example, spends roughly $300 million each year on textbooks.)

Ironically, the arguments offered for excluding the new, powerful, and often available devices from our classrooms—for example, that they're too distracting, not related to the purposes of education, and not needed—are the very same arguments that were offered up a century ago for excluding women from the educational decision-making process. And we all know how that fight went.

So our young people have quickly taught themselves to use these powerful devices for their own ends and have learned to take maximum advantage of every new feature offered. One of the first and most powerful tools was texting, useful because you could exchange messages completely privately, even in the middle of, for example, a noisy dance club. Celebrities' communicating on their beepers made texting popular, cell phones replaced the beepers, and the kids raced past the celebrities, writing and sending their texts at lightning speeds, even with their phones still in their pockets. In what seemed like a moment, billions of people in the world began communicating in this new way, a different language evolved, and useful services quickly sprang up (such as ChaCha, which texts you back the answer to any question, often in seconds).

But cell phones in classrooms remained, for most educators, almost entirely out of bounds—despite some sneaking around by frustrated teachers ("OK, kids, take out your 'calculators.'") In 2004, I wrote in an article entitled "What Can You Learn from a Cell Phone—Almost Anything!" that "despite what some may consider cell phones' 'limitations,' our students are already inventing ways to use their phones to learn what *they* want to know. If we educators are smart, we'll figure out how to deliver *our* product in a way that fits into our students' digital lives—and their cell phones. And instead of wasting our energy fighting their preferred delivery system, we'll be working to ensure that our students extract maximum understanding and benefit from the vast amounts of cell phone–based learning they will all, no doubt, soon be receiving."

That was not exactly a popular position. Many reacted with scorn when I began advocating "open phone tests" in schools (an idea based on the open book tests I was often given in college). In fact the words "open phone test" still draw titters from audiences, although the truth comes from the students who tell me that "most of our tests already are open phone tests—you guys just don't know it."

Today, many more educators, to their credit, have started catching on. A teacher in a fancy private girls' school in Australia decided, with her headmaster's consent, to try out the concept of open phone testing in her class. The immediate result was a front page headline in the *Sydney Morning Herald*, with long-distance calls to me in the middle of the night for comment. But people were clearly intrigued. The headmaster reported receiving large numbers of calls from places as far away as Uzbekistan. Other educators such as Lisa Nielsen, an author of this book, and the U.S. researcher Liz Kolb began to blog about positive ways to use cell phones in class. Liz's blog turned into *Toys to Tools*, the first book to embrace the idea of cell phones in class; Lisa's blog spawned this volume.

Make no mistake, however—we are still a long way from cell phones being embraced by the majority of educators as an important learning tool in our schools. The over one million children in the New York City school system, for example, are prohibited from using their cell phones in class. Many administrators and teachers remain opposed to the concept, often physically seizing the devices from students. School policies on the use of cell phones are rarely stated positively (for example, "use your phone to connect to information and the world") and are almost exclusively negative (for example, "don't do this, that, or the other thing").

That is why this book is so important. Lisa Nielsen and Willyn Webb are educators who clearly recognize the enormous potential power of these tools—when used well—for helping teachers and students. In a calm, straightforward, and easy-to-apply way, they demonstrate the tools' benefits and possibilities for helping provide our students with a better, more contemporary education. Wisely, they have focused primarily on texting— something that every phone can do. They have gathered together a wide variety of excellent suggestions and ideas from which every educator can learn and benefit (myself included!).

Although there is still valid cause for concern about a "digital divide" in education, I have always maintained that a key role for every educator is to be a "digital multiplier," that is, to ensure that the tools of their time get into the hands of *all* students, if not to own, at least to use. To the teacher worried that "half of my students don't have cell phones," I reply, "that means that 100 percent of *pairs* of students *do* have a cell phone. Let them share and learn."

If you are a teacher or administrator gingerly entering this new, twenty-first-century educational world, this book will be a valuable guide to creating lessons that are as contemporary, useful, and productive as possible, as your students share and learn through these powerful devices.

May 2011

Marc Prensky
New York City

PREFACE

W e are so glad you are a pioneering teacher, parent, administrator, or policy maker who is ready for schools to stop banning and start embracing the use of cell phones for learning. The authors of this book were motivated by their own personal stories to begin doing the same. We share each story here to give you some insight into how we started down this path.

WILLYN WEBB

Following school rules by taking students' cell phones away when they had them out in class was always uncomfortable for me. As a mother of three girls in the tween and teen age group, I was very aware of the value placed on cell phones and the amount of time spent texting. At school, a natural process began as a result of my philosophy of caring for students and treating them as my second family. I came to realize the value of text messaging as a means to increase communication efforts with students, parents, staff, and the community, and then as a means to enhance teaching and learning.

It started with attendance. When a student or student's parent could not be reached by the school phone, I grabbed my cell phone and often, not recognizing the number, the student or parent would answer. When that didn't work, by then I felt comfortable enough about having strong relationships with my students and with my administration to text students when they were absent: *how r u? we miss u at school 2day*. Attendance improved, students felt truly missed (some for the first time ever), and issues that affected their education surfaced and could be addressed.

The next step came when I had a student in my counseling office in crisis during the day; it just seemed natural to text him or her that evening: *did u find a place to stay 2nite? r u feeling better? did u talk to dad?* I experienced great success with that approach and other uses soon followed: when a student was going for a job interview, taking the driving test, or getting pregnancy test results, a text was a quick and easy way to show I cared. My new tool of texting was making a huge impact. There are a couple of students who I can honestly say would not have graduated if it were not for texting.

Little by little, texting came to be a valuable counseling and then teaching tool. I learned new and exciting uses from my students and my daughters. When my daughter texted ChaCha, a site that answers immediate questions, for the first time, I was so excited I had to stop the car to have her teach me. In my Life Skills classes, I began to use texting for homework. This not only made the class time more valuable, but also took the learning into the students' real lives.

I started using polls and Wiffitis in class; the students loved it and the other teachers wanted in. I wanted to "make it real" for my staff, so I took some of the researched-based teaching strategies I knew and loved from my favorite book, *Classroom Instruction That Works* (Marzano, Pickering, & Pollock, 2001) and enhanced them with cell phone technologies. With the students as our partners, we all learned new and exciting ways to enhance learning and motivate students by using cell phones. Interestingly, this acceptance also took the fight out of the issue. Together, my students and teachers developed acceptable use policies and we have had few issues since. Delta Opportunity School in Colorado became a leader in our district, often sharing our ideas with others. I knew I was really onto something when my English teacher came and got me, beaming from ear to ear. She wanted me to see the high level of engagement and intense concentration of her students as she did a lesson I had shared using cell phones. Seeing is believing, and she was sold.

After commenting in casual conversation to school officials, parents, and fellow teachers that I should write a book about teaching through texting, I began to do some research. I was excited to find that there were others like me throughout the world who were having success with cell phones in educational settings. Daily, more personal evidence for the value of texting happened right in front of my eyes. Having previously written four books, I was well aware of the commitment. I knew it was doable, but too time consuming and too technology based for me to do alone. During my research I had found Lisa Nielsen's Cell Phones in Education Group on Classroom 2.0. I read more about her, loved her blog, got up my nerve, and approached her about the book. She said yes and we began our journey, writing collaboratively using Google docs and texting each other, never knowing if we would ever meet in person. It didn't matter; we have the same basic beliefs and both want to do what is best for students.

At first, we were faced with some expected concerns from fellow educators who still felt that cell phones were a distraction and that not all students could benefit. It is a fact that not all students have phones. However, from my experience in a poverty-ridden high school texting is a lifeline. Currently, of my high school students, I can only think of two who do not have text-enabled phones, and they share phones with family and friends.

Because educators should always strive to do what is best for students, because educators should truly care for students, and because educators have a duty to prepare students not only for the future but also for the world in which they live, we must be able to relate to them in their world now. Teaching students appropriate uses, cell phone manners, and ways to learn with something they love makes sense. Educators who continue to fight something that students value are missing the boat. I wanted to write this book so educators everywhere can be encouraged to use such a powerful device to benefit students!

LISA NIELSEN

As we entered the twenty-first century, while there was much talk about bridging the digital divide, cell phones were not a consideration in addressing the problem. Instead, the decision to ban cell phones was gaining popularity. At the time there were policy makers who saw cell phones as nothing more than a distraction and tool for academic dishonesty but parents viewed these devices as a lifeline to their children. The "no cell phones" rule was strictly enforced with some cities even enlisting the police department to conduct random sweeps, complete with metal detectors to confiscate technology from kids, many of whom were reduced to tears. There were educators on both sides of the issue. Some were relieved by the policy but others not only trusted their students to behave responsibly, but also understood that cell phones could serve as powerful learning tools. My friend and thought leader Marc Prensky (2004) was outspoken on the issue, explaining in his presentations and writing, "What Can You Learn from a Cell Phone?—Almost Anything!" (www.marcprensky.com/writing/Prensky-What_Can_You_Learn_From_a_Cell_Phone-FINAL.pdf).

In his blog, Weblogg-ed, my friend and mentor Will Richardson shares some important lessons students learned as a result of the ban: "First, the cell phone ban teaches students they don't deserve to be empowered with technology the same way adults are. Second, the tools that adults use all the time in their everyday lives to communicate are not relevant to their own communication needs. Third, they can't be trusted (or taught, for that matter) to use phones appropriately in school" (Richardson, 2007).

I joined Richardson, Prensky, and other educators, parents, students, and even policy makers in being keenly aware that cell phones are an important part of the way kids communicate and learn. We know that if we don't model and allow students to demonstrate the appropriate use of these technologies for accessing information, for communicating in safe, ethical, and effective ways, then we have no right to be surprised when our worst fears come true.

I was frustrated by the ban, and like the students and their parents, I felt powerless. However, although students couldn't be empowered to use their technology in schools, what first inspired me to take notice of cell phones as learning tools was the day that I spent at the Google Teacher Academy. It was there that I learned about Google SMS, a tool I could use to harness anytime or anywhere without a computer and without the Internet. All that was required was the ability to text from my phone. Exciting! I could find definitions of words, translations of sentences, currency and measurement conversion, calculator functions, weather, and much more, all with just a basic cell phone.

Next up was when I attended Alan November's Building Learning Communities conference. I met with other innovative educators after the first conference day and we spent an hour or two experimenting with ChaCha. Just text 242242 on your phone and ask anything at all. Wow! I thought. With just a cell phone anyone could find out about anything they wanted to know. I saw this as a powerful tool for both teachers and students, many of whom had access to cell phones but not the Internet at home. It was then that I really recognized the power of cell phones as a tool that could help bridge the digital divide for students.

I began integrating the use of cell phones into my work with colleagues. I showed them how they could use things such as Google SMS and ChaCha and I also began using polling tools such as Poll Everywhere, TextTheMob, and Wiffiti. Unfortunately, my excitement was not shared by everyone. A supervisor discovered I was harnessing the power of cell phones in my work and mandated that I refrain from using the banned student devices with teachers. In 2008 it became a news story. The headline in the *New York Sun* read "Despite School Cell Phone Ban, Course Sees Them as Aid" (www.nysun.com/new-york/despite-school-cell-phone-ban-course-sees-them-as/76504/). I was told I could teach the class but that no one could use their cell phones! An expert at thinking outside the ban, I didn't let that stop me. I used the Google SMS virtual phone (www.google.com/mobile/products/sms.html) and showed teachers how to use tools like ChaCha and polling from their computers. Then I explained all of this could be done with just cell phones as well. Teachers were empowered with ways to access knowledge and information through either a phone or a laptop. They could use this knowledge for themselves and they could also model this for their students who may not have Internet at home but might have access to cell phones.

Interestingly, at the same time I was told I couldn't use phones when working with educators, cell phones were being given to students as incentives for achievement in school.

As a result of my blog, I was brought in to consult with education administrators on how cell phones can be embraced as instructional tools. Finally, students were empowered to use the devices in their pockets for learning outside of school. Progress!

In 2009 it seemed we had taken another step back when I was informed my employer was discontinuing texting services for administrators. This hindered our ability to build on what we had started. Not only were students not entrusted to use technology appropriately but educational leaders were also suspect. The lines of communication and strategies I had incorporated into my work were swept away in an instant. Many were frustrated, yet instead of accepting the ban, I shared the ways we were using texting for educational purposes. I wrote an article explaining how cells could be used to enhance the work of educational leaders (these ideas are covered later in this book) that was shared in my blog and in Gotham Schools, a local source for education information. Good news! After sharing ways educational leaders were using texting to work more effectively, our texting ability was reinstated for those who indicated they were using cell phones for such purposes.

Today I embed the use of cell phones into the work I do with students and teachers together in an environment of respect, trust, and learning in a "no ban zone." I have seen firsthand the excitement, creativity, and learning that occur when teachers and students are trusted and empowered to use the tools they choose. I'm not alone. Educators across the world (many of whom you'll hear about in this book) are harnessing the power of student-owned devices such as cell phones for learning with great success.

It is because I believe we should empower school leaders, teachers, students, and their families to use the best tools they have available to them for learning that my answer to Willyn when she approached me was an easy one. I agreed to coauthor this book because it is my hope that we will inspire others to not only think outside the ban but also to work to break the bans that are unnecessarily and unfairly holding our twenty-first-century children in the world of their teacher's, leaders, and policy maker's pasts.

ACKNOWLEDGMENTS

We would like to thank Marc Prensky for being one of the first to point out that we can learn "anything" right from the devices in our pockets; Will Richardson for driving home the damage we cause children when we don't empower students in school to use the tools they use in the real world; Robert Marzano, Debra Pickering, and Jane Pollock for their work in helping us know and do what works in the classroom and inviting us to their technology advisory team; Google Docs for providing the platform we needed to collaborate with ease; Rita Rozenkranz for representing us with integrity; Kate Bradford for her excellent advice during the revision process; our friends and families for sharing us with "the book"; students everywhere for leading the way in learning and communicating effectively with cell phones; and our cell phones for allowing us to write and text anywhere and anytime.

This book wouldn't be nearly as meaningful without the pioneering work of many innovative educators who are committed to ensuring that student learning is engaging, real, and empowers students to use the tools they love. It is because of them we are able to share the smart and successful ideas and experiences of educators everywhere. The authors would like to recognize the following individuals for being an important part of this work.

Name	Title	Organization	City	State	Blog or Website	Twitter Name
Jeff Branzburg	Instructional technology consultant		Rhinebeck	New York	http://branzburg.blogspot.com	@branzburg
Tamara Cox	Librarian	Palmetto Middle School	Williamston	South Carolina	www.e-literatelibrarian.blogspot.com	@coxtl
George Engel	Teacher	Clarkstown High School South	Clarkstown	New York	http://blogs.cellularlearning.org	@gbengel
Dolores Gende	Director of instructional technology	Parish Episcopal School	Dallas	Texas	http://dgende.net	@dgende
Rob Griffith	Social studies teacher	Hinsdale Central School	Randolph	New York	http://myedunotions.blogspot.com/	@rgriffithjr
Delaine Hudson	Director of Alternative Ed	Delta Opportunity School	Delta	Colorado	www.deltaschools.com	
Gwyneth A. Jones	Librarian	Murray Hill Middle School	Laurel	Maryland	www.thedaringlibrarian.com/	@gwynethjones
Tracy Karas	Library media specialist	Marta Valle High School	New York	New York	http://library.martavalle.org	@martavlibrary
Ben Keefer	Director of extended studies	Colorado Mesa University	Grand Junction	Colorado	www.mesastate.edu	

Name	Role	Organization	City	State	Website	Twitter
Robert Marzano	Cofounder and CEO of Marzano Research Laboratory, educational researcher, and author	Marzano Research Laboratory	Englewood	Colorado	www.marzanoresearch.com	@MarzanoResearch
Scott Newcomb	Educator	St. Marys City Schools	St. Marys	Ohio	www.smriders.net/Mobile_Learning/	@SNewco
Deborah Pickering	Educational consultant, author	Marzano Research Laboratory	Englewood	Colorado	www.marzanoresearch.com	
Jane Pollock	Educational consultant, author	Improve Student Learning	Centennial	Colorado	www.www.improvestudentlearning.com	
Will Richardson	Parent, author, speaker, education blogger	Powerful Learning Practice	Flemington	New Jersey	www.weblogg-ed.com	@willrich45
Eric Sheninger	Principal	New Milford High School	New Milford	New Jersey	http://erichsheninger.com	@NMHS_Principal
Jason Suter	Environmental and biology teacher	Hanover Public School District	Hanover	Pennsylvania	http://suter.hanoverpublic.org	@jksuter
Sandy Vickrey	Math/art teacher	Delta Opportunity School	Delta	Colorado	www.deltaschools.com	

Introduction

> *The world we have created is a product of our thinking. It cannot be changed without changing our thinking.*
> —Albert Einstein

We live in a world that is increasingly mobile. In order to reach our students and their parents and to build our own personal learning networks with like-minded educators, we need to mobilize. Imagine having students respond quickly to a reflection-type question from the day's lecture while checking their texts during a water break at basketball practice. Imagine having a mother learning through a text about the vocabulary test or project in her son's biology class tomorrow so she can review with him as they drive to karate lessons. Today's phones can alert students to study; serve as a smart vehicle to take notes; provide instant, on-demand answers and research; and even provide a great way to record and capture student oral reports or responses to polls and quizzes. The family dinner table is fading, the homework hour is constantly challenged, and we are out and about (with our phones) more than ever. As any parent knows, at increasingly younger ages children tend to pay more attention to cell phones than anything else. In this book we show educators and parents how to harness the power of cell phones for learning.

Readers will discover how to engage learners in fun, free, safe, and easy ways using nothing more than a basic, text-enabled cell phone.

In recent years, many educators across the country have found themselves frustrated by cell phones in their classrooms. Even for those of us who tend to embrace new technologies and use them to enhance the educational experiences of our students, cell phones have been a problem. However, with acceptance, we can turn cell phone distraction into educational opportunity. With understanding, we can turn discipline into a chance to enter into our students' worlds. With proper training and support, we can turn our frustration with cell phones into a means of better communication. Better relationships, meaningful educational experiences, and a more cooperative environment will be the result of realizing that cell phones are here to stay and that text messaging is the primary means of communication used by our current and future students.

Students love their phones, they are highly motivated to use them (constantly), and they always have them right there with them (if they're allowed). What a strong basis for an educational tool: empower students to use tools they already own as a means for better education! The Disney Mobile Cell and Tell survey of more than 1,500 ten- to seventeen-year-old cell phone users found that teens and tweens like their cell phones perhaps more than other luxuries in their lives.

If they had to choose between their phone or something else:

- One-third would give up listening to the radio, playing video games or going to the mall.
- Nearly one-fourth would give up their MP3 players.
- One in five would give up TV. (Disney Corporation, 2007)

Rather than walking into class and watching students jump and hide their phones under the table, or smoothly conceal them under their leg or in their pocket, we can embrace the fact that students have phones and enjoy our time together, using tools that modern technology has provided to help us communicate, learn, and interact. Building relationships and focusing on learning is always preferable to fighting battles and focusing on discipline.

WHAT STUDENTS NEED

The choice to focus on a basic-text enabled phone is an important one. As a device that has quickly become among the most ubiquitous of interactive digital devices in American households, the cell phone is part of the solution to bridging the digital divide. The intent of this book is to provide all learners, regardless of socioeconomic status, access to innovative ways of learning. Although smart phones (those with increased computerlike functionality, including the ability to run applications [apps] and connect to the Internet) such as BlackBerries, Androids, iPhones, and the like are gaining popularity, this book has ideas and strategies that can be used with all learners, with any phone that has texting and voice capabilities. Focusing on the most basic and available functions of the phones most students already have provides readers with numerous ideas to enrich learning in powerful ways without requiring a data plan or Internet access.

Some critics have raised concern regarding availability of cell phones for all students. This argument doesn't hold because schools make a habit of using many different types of technology even if every student doesn't have access to it every day. We work hard just to get some computers in the classroom, and in many classrooms there are not even enough textbooks to go around. With cell phones, not all students need to use the same device. It is estimated that currently 94 percent of U.S. households have cell phone access (Marist Poll, 2010). For kids who don't already have cell phones or access to them, they can share or use devices provided by schools such as netbooks, desktops, laptops, iPod touches, and so on, which provide similar functionally. Another option is for schools and districts to reach out to local cell phone providers who might be interested in providing devices to students in need at no cost or low cost with a bulk purchase.

WHAT TEACHERS NEED

Our assumption is that teachers reading this book will have access in their school to an Internet-enabled laptop and projector. The ideas, strategies, and lessons do not require students to have access to the Internet or a laptop; however, the teacher does need these tools to be effective.

Teachers will also need to be resourceful when using this book. Although the book is chock-full of ideas and services that are mostly free, in our fast-paced twenty-first-century world, technologies frequently change. Today's greatest tool is tomorrow's faded memory. What's free today may charge a fee tomorrow. We have made every effort to provide accurate resources and web addresses at the time of this book's publication; however, if the one we suggest is no longer available, not available where you are, or now charges a fee, a simple Google search for what it is you are trying to do will likely turn up an alternative. We also encourage you to tap into your personal learning network (PLN). Those you meet face-to-face or online who are also interested in this work are a tremendous resource that can help you with whatever it is you need. We discovered and featured many of the tools shared in this book through the power of social media. We have established a "Cell Phones in Education" group on Classroom 2.0, a "Teaching Generation Text" on Facebook, and we have learned with our followers on Twitter.

WHAT OUR SECRETARY OF EDUCATION BELIEVES

It starts from the top, and when the U.S. secretary of education promotes cell phones in the classroom, you know people are listening. Secretary of Education Arne Duncan on the PBS Frontline's *Digital Nation* (2009) project said that cell phones offer a new way to expand learning beyond the regular school day. As he noted, "Students may lose a lot of other things, but they don't lose their phones. They have those phones 24/7." He went on to ask, "Why shouldn't we be thinking about how we can help teach students using mobile phones?"

FROM BANNING TO EMBRACING

Students are ready for teachers and leaders to begin embracing the use of cell phones for learning; however, inviting student-owned devices into schools can be difficult. Unfortunately, most schools today still treat the phone as a disruptive force that must be managed and is often excluded from the school and the classroom (Lenhart, Ling, Campbell, & Purcell, 2010). At the same time an unfortunate change in policies of some cities and states are popping up making digital communication off limits between students and teachers (Marrero, 2010). There is no evidence that says because teachers communicate digitally that they are going to morph from the caring, responsible people they have always been into child predators. Regardless, misguided educational leaders and policy makers are focusing on the mode of communication, which has no intent, rather than behavior. As a result educational professionals in some schools are being restricted from making decisions about the tools they can use to most effectively communicate with students.

Despite the unfounded fear around communicating digitally, teachers and leaders empowered to think outside the ban and embrace the use of technology have been pleasantly rewarded. More and more schools across the country are rewriting policy and providing professional development in order to harness the power of cell phones for learning. In schools such as New Canaan High School in Connecticut, where students are welcome to bring their own technology, classroom teachers are empowered to let students use their own devices or not. Technology integration specialist Cathy Swan explains, "We've been doing this for a couple of years and have had zero problems since we started." In this book you'll hear from several teachers who work in schools that have allowed the teachers to embrace student-owned devices for learning. As a result, not only are students empowered to use their own technology for learning, but they are also more engaged and appreciate the trust and respect afforded by their teachers.

If your school has a policy banning cell phone use in classrooms, please refer to the Appendix for a wealth of information on how to break the ban.

Safety, Privacy, and Policy

When considering privacy and safety issues with cell phones, you will want to ensure you are in compliance with school and district policies. Parent permission, clearly explained safety guidelines, and solid boundaries are always good practices in education with or without the use of technology. You should also always keep privacy concerns in mind when deciding whether or not to use student names (with permission) on anything posted online or if it would make more sense to use aliases. Throughout the book there are safety notes for specific tools. Chapter Two offers a workshop for staff, parents, and students on boundaries, privacy, and safety entitled "Success with Cells for the Texting School Community." Parent-student agreements and acceptable use policies are featured in Chapter Four.

Texting Is the Communication Method of Choice

Among all teens, their frequency of use of texting has now overtaken the frequency of every other common form of interaction with their friends (Lenhart, Ling, Campbell, & Purcell, 2010). Fully 72 percent of all teens (88 percent of teen cell phone users) are text messengers. That is a sharp rise from the 51 percent of teens who were texters in 2006 (QWASI Research, 2009–2010). And according to the latest research from the Kaiser Family Foundation (2010), "[i]n a typical day, 46 percent of 8- to 18-year-olds report sending text messages on a cell phone. Those who do text estimate that they send an average of 118 messages in a typical day. On average, 7th–12th graders report spending about an hour and a half (1:35) engaged in sending and receiving texts" (p. 18). With thousands of texts being sent and received monthly, often hundreds per day, we must acknowledge this as a vital part of the lives of those we are teaching.

THE RESEARCH BASE

Using cell phone technologies to enhance education is a new innovation and as such evidence to support its effectiveness is just beginning to emerge as pioneering teachers are embracing this technology. What we show in this book is how existing research-based instructional strategies for increasing student achievement can be supported and enhanced using cell phones. The most well-known, comprehensive, and reputable source for research-based strategies is *Classroom Instruction That Works* by Marzano, Pickering, and Pollock (2001) and now the 2nd edition (Dean, Hubbell, Pitler, & Stone, 2012). As Debra Pickering (2010), one of the authors, stated in a description for one of her workshops, ". . . the potential for these devices [cell phones] to significantly influence student learning will only be realized if we use them to increase and enhance—not replace—research-based instructional and assessment strategies."

WHY THIS BOOK IS IMPORTANT FOR OUR STUDENTS' FUTURES

Employers are looking for employees who can use technology effectively. As we move into the future, the days of nine to five inside a cubicle are quickly disappearing as professions are becoming increasingly more mobile. Our students must be competent in many forms of digital technologies to be competitive in the professional job market of the future. According to the Partnership for twenty-first Century Skills (2009), whose mission is to "[s]erve as a catalyst to position twenty-first century skills at the center of US K–12 education by building collaborative partnerships among education, business, community and government leaders," students must do the following:

Apply Technology Effectively

- Use technology as a tool to research, organize, evaluate, and communicate information.
- Use digital technologies (computers, PDAs, media players, GPS, and so on), communication and networking tools, and social networks appropriately to access, manage, integrate, evaluate, and create information to successfully function in a knowledge economy.
- Apply a fundamental understanding of the ethical and legal issues surrounding the access and use of information technologies. (pp. 5–6)

Communicate Clearly

- Articulate thoughts and ideas effectively using oral, written, and nonverbal communication skills in a variety of forms and contexts.
- Listen effectively to decipher meaning, including knowledge, values, attitudes, and intentions.
- Use communication for a range of purposes (for example, to inform, instruct, motivate, and persuade).
- Utilize multiple media and technologies and know how to judge their effectiveness a priori as well as assess their impact.
- Communicate effectively in diverse environments (including multi-lingual). (p. 4)

Schools districts can address many of these skills through the cell phones students already possess.

HOW THIS BOOK IS ORGANIZED

This book is designed to provide hands-on ideas, activities, lessons, and strategies that you can use whenever and wherever you are comfortable. It begins by providing ideas for ways teachers can incorporate cell phones into their own practices. We believe that using technology to enrich the work you do is the best place for any educator to begin. Chapter One will guide teachers in smart ways to get started using cell phones themselves and in fun ways to connect with others and to engage learners. Chapter Two is aimed at teachers who are ready to begin using cell phones with their students. We acknowledge this is difficult and even banned in some districts. The ideas in this chapter can be used in the classroom or outside of school. We recommend that educators begin using cell phones with their students as an extension of learning outside the classroom to give teachers, students, and their families familiarity and experience with using these devices as learning tools. In Chapter Three we discuss how to adapt the research-based instructional strategies suggested in *Classroom Instruction That Works,* Second Edition (Dean, Hubbell, Pitler, & Stone, 2012) for cell phone use to enrich instruction and engage learners. Although readers of this book likely embrace the idea of incorporating cell phones into learning, we know that there are permission slips, letters to parents, acceptable use agreements, talking points for policy changes, and more that must be addressed. Chapter Four (and the Appendix) provide this material. In Chapter Five, we give ideas for incorporating cell phones into your instruction with a unit planning guide and standards-aligned lessons. In Chapter Six we address ways that administrators, guidance counselors, librarians, parents, and others in the school community can support the texting teachers and learners. And in Chapter Seven we look at how to use *Teaching Generation Text* for professional development.

BEGIN HARNESSING THE POWER OF CELLS IN EDUCATION TODAY— A FIVE-STEP PLAN

Whether or not cell phones are banned in your school there are steps you can take, even if your students don't all have them and even if you haven't done anything in advance to prepare introducing them into your class. All teachers can begin today by following the first four steps in this plan. Schools that embrace the use of cell phones can move on to step five.

Please note: The tools and ideas mentioned in this chapter are more fully described in Chapters One and Two and are explained in the table at the end of this chapter.

Step One: Use Your Cell Phone for Professional Purposes

Remember, just because some schools and districts ban students from using cell phones, this does not apply to teachers. Begin harnessing the power of your own cell phone today as an instructional tool.

Three Ideas for Using Cell Phones for Professional Purposes

- Use Poll Everywhere to conduct staff surveys that would be useful and interesting to share with students and the school community.
- Use Twitter and have the updates feed into your class or school blog, website, or wiki to reinforce the home-school connection and build class and school pride.
- Set up Google Voice to serve as your personal secretary to transcribe your messages and enable you to easily share the content with others.

Step Two: Model Appropriate Cell Phone Use for Learning

Once you're comfortable using your cell phone as an instructional tool, you can begin modeling best practice and instructional use of cell phones to your students. Let them see ways they might consider using their phones to support instruction.

It should go without saying that when modeling appropriate use of cell phones you do not let your phone ring or make any type of noise or otherwise use the phone in any way not related to instruction while in class. With that as a given, here are three ideas.

Three Ideas for Modeling Appropriate Use of Cell Phones for Learning

- Show your students how you use your cell phone to support your work, for example, using basic features such as the alarm clock, calendar, calculator, stopwatch, and note taking.
- Demonstrate how you can use your phone to gain information instantly using Google SMS or ChaCha.
- Use your cell phone as a camera to capture notes from the board, student work, and events and load them to Flickr so they can be embedded in your class or school website, wiki, or blog. If you plan to share student likenesses or work, ensure that you have student permissions. If you do not, refrain from using the child's last name or establish privacy settings in your online spaces.

Step Three: Strengthen the Home-School Connection with Cell Phones

Cell phones provide a terrific means for connecting with student's parents, family, and guardians. Begin using phones to develop and strengthen those relationships. This provides a foundation and helps develop understanding around the benefits and value of cell phone use in general and later for use with students. The first thing you want to do is get the phone numbers of your students' parents, guardians, and family members. There are always those families who are difficult to reach. There may be occasions when there is not a phone or it is out of minutes. However, even families who move frequently, are homeless, and/or don't have a landline often have a cell phone as their contact option. Once you have the numbers, there are many ways to use cells to support the home-school connection.

Three Ideas for Using Cells to Strengthen the Home-School Connection

- Use group texting through your phone provider or through a special service to send out reminders to parents.
- Show parents, families, or guardians their thoughts and opinions matter. Poll them or request an open response using a tool such as Poll Everywhere.
- Text home to celebrate student success or reach out via text if there is an area of concern. This can be done quickly with minimal disruption to either party.

After you've used your cell phones to strengthen the home-school connection, you might want to consider holding a workshop showing parents how they can use cell phones as an educational tool to support student learning. If you do, invite some students to help you plan and deliver the workshop.

Step Four: Have Students Use Their Cell Phones for Homework

Before using cell phones with students in your classroom, begin giving them the option to use cell phones to complete their homework. This gives the teacher the opportunity to allow students to use cell phones for learning without classroom management concerns. This also gives students experience in using cell phones for learning. As you will discover in the upcoming chapters, there are many cases in which students can do the same work on a cell that they can on a laptop or with pencil and paper, so if they have easier access to one over the other at different times they can choose what works best for them. Especially in families with limited technology resources, providing options such as these helps break down the digital divide. Suddenly the amount of technology available to a student for learning has increased dramatically.

Three Ideas for Enabling Students to Use Cell Phones for Homework

- Use ChaCha to connect your students to a free network of thousands of guides who can help them when they get stuck and have no one around to help.

- Test prior knowledge of a unit your class is about to study and use Wiffiti to have students share one thing they know about the subject.

- Have students do their oral reports using Google Voice. If they don't like how they sound the first time, they don't have to send the message. They can rerecord until they have something that makes them happy.

Step Five: Have Students Collaborate on How Cell Phones Might Be Used in the Classroom for Learning

Once you, your students, and their parents, guardians, and families have become comfortable using cell phones as instructional tools, you can begin discussing how cell phones can be used in the classroom and other educational opportunities with your students. The first thing you'll want to do, even if your district or school has a specific policy, is discuss acceptable use with students. Using tools like Wiffiti or Poll Everywhere may be a smart way to capture student ideas on acceptable use. You can have them contribute outside of school and once all students agree to the ideas shared they can sign a contract with a link to the resource containing the policies to which they developed and agreed. In many cases you'll find student rules and consequences are more stringent than those outlined in the school or district policy but it's written in language everyone can understand. If and when cell phones are allowed in the classroom, the results can be posted on the classroom wall or school website as well.

You may also take this a step further and ask students to participate in designing their learning. You might be surprised at the ideas they come up with if you lay out student learning goals.

Three Ideas for Empowering Students in the Use of Cell Phones for Learning

- You're going on a field trip. Ask students to determine how they might use cell phones to meet the learning goals of the trip using tools most phones have. They may decide to tweet for a scavenger hunt, send reflections to Wiffiti, or capture pictures with Flickr.

- You're about to learn about a new country or explore your own neighborhood. Ask students for ideas to meet learning goals using their cells. Maybe they can use ChaCha or Google SMS to collect data about the area.

- You have asked students to share how hard work affected someone influential in their lives. How would cell phones help with this assignment? Perhaps they could use a Voki character (an avatar with vocal capabilities) with a phone to record their voice. Perhaps they could set up a Google Voice account to capture responses.

A SENSIBLE APPROACH

The five-step plan provides a progression that enables educators to sensibly use technology for learning in a way that will make sense for students, their families, and themselves. Once classroom teachers are comfortable using the devices they can begin modeling their use for their students. As students see their teacher(s) using cells as an instructional tool it begins to make sense to view them as a learning tool, especially when they know their teachers use them to connect with those who care for them. At this point it's a natural progression to provide cell phones as an option for learning away from school. Those teachers who are fortunate enough to be empowered to make instructional decisions for their classrooms are now ready to start partnering with students to meet learning objectives with the tools they love. Students who help their teacher develop rules and consequences will be motivated and engaged, and schools will have a plethora of resources available to their students at no extra cost. Everyone wins!

If you are anxious to start exploring the resources shared in this chapter, the following table provides a short description and the URL or number for each. For detailed instructions on how to use these resources and more, keep reading.

Resources Discussed in This Chapter		
Resources (listed alphabetically)	**Description**	**URL and Number**
ChaCha	Text a question to ChaCha and it is answered by a live person along with his or her source. The no-fee version has advertising.	Text: 242242
Classroom 2.0 Group: Cell Phones in Education	Classroom 2.0 is one of the largest learning networks for educators. This group provides a space to connect those who are using cell phones for learning.	www.classroom20.com/ group/ CellPhonesinEducation
Facebook Group: Teaching Generation Text	A place where "friends" can gather on Facebook to share ideas and resources about using cell phones for learning	www.facebook .com/home.php?sk= group_122053457874137
Flickr	A photo-sharing website where cell phone pictures can be e-mailed	www.flickr.com
Google SMS	A service that allows you to text Google to discover information such as translations, currency conversions, weather, and directions	Text: 466453
Google Voice	Google's free phone service that records and transcribes calls, which then can be shared digitally	www.google.com/voice
Group texting	The ability to send texts simultaneously to multiple people through a service provider	Check with your phone service provider or do a search for "free group texting"
Poll Everywhere	A service to collect responses and polling data	www.polleverywhere.com/

Resources (listed alphabetically)	Description	URL and Number
Twitter	A service that enables you to connect and converse with others about shared topics of interest	http://twitter.com/InnovativeEdu http://twitter.com/WillynWebb
Voki	A talking avatar that can be recorded from your phone	www.Voki.com
Wiffiti	A service that publishes messages digitally to screens	http://wiffiti.com/

The Texting Teacher

If children can't learn the way we teach, maybe we should teach the way they learn.
Ignacio "Nacho" Estrada, ventriloquist, motivator, and educational consultant

Innovative educators are becoming increasingly reliant on texting as a form of communication. Texting can be more appropriate than the following:

- Phone calls (no need to disturb a class or colleague)
- E-mails (teachers don't always have time)
- Face-to-face visits (teachers almost never have time)
- Letters (by the time it passes through all proper channels and gets to the recipient, it is often irrelevant)

This chapter provides ideas for how educators can use texting in particular and cell phones in general as powerful and effective professional and educational tools. Each application includes a how-to-get-started section, a step-by-step guide that makes these great ideas easy, even for those educators who are hesitant when it comes to technology.

TEXTING AS AN EFFICIENT AND EFFECTIVE COMMUNICATION TOOL

Texting has become an effective communication tool for educators because it is nondisruptive, time-saving, and efficient. Few schools were ever able to succeed in installing landline phones in classrooms. Instead they use a disruptive announcement system that detracts from learning to communicate with students and staff even though the message usually only pertains to a small portion of the school population . . . or in some cases just one person, for example, "John Smith, please come to the main office" or the embarrassing type of announcement, "Mr. Williams, your students are waiting outside your door. Did you forget your class?" This instructional intrusion is no longer necessary because texting enables educators to communicate short, efficient messages to one another without robbing students of instructional time. It also enables educators to communicate with one another when necessary outside the school day with less interruption of their personal time. Because it's quick and unobtrusive, educators can text at times when it would be inappropriate or inconvenient to talk on the phone.

Here are some ways you may want to use your cell phone for communication.

Communication Efforts with Staff

Texting is a great way for staff to communicate with one another at school and much less disruptive than the old-fashioned public address system or having students leave class to deliver a note to another teacher or principal. Texting can give an administrator or school dean a heads-up about a discipline issue. It can be an efficient way to inform a school technician about a computer issue. A teacher can text another colleague who may have forgotten about a common planning meeting or give a colleague a heads-up about a student who is having a rough day.

Communication Efforts with Parents

Remember handwritten notes sent home by the teacher? Remember sending handwritten progress notes (of course only some of which made it into the right hands)? In today's world of increased class size, increased diversity among student populations, and more pressure to perform on standardized tests, the time required to build communication has often been jeopardized. Text messaging allows quick, personal notes to parents that can be typed in almost anywhere at anytime. Preventing problems and recognizing progress puts educators in the position to be more proactive and strengthens the home-school connection. Table 1.1 shows some examples of texts that support this connection.

```
┌─────────────────────────────────────────────────────┐
│                    Table 1.1                        │
│              Example of Quick Texts                 │
│  ─────────────────────────────────────────────────  │
│  To staff          meeting 2day at 3.               │
│                    Todd seems angry.                │
│                    Angie out sick for a week.       │
│                                                     │
│  To parents        Sara did gr8 in spelling.        │
│                    Tim finished reading his book!   │
│                    Octavio stayed on task 2day.     │
│  ─────────────────────────────────────────────────  │
└─────────────────────────────────────────────────────┘
```

HOW TO GET STARTED

If you've never texted before, there are many websites with video tutorials on the subject. At www.commonsensemedia.org/tech-tip-how-text-message, for example, you can read about the basic steps and watch a clip. If you have additional questions, your phone's handbook or your mobile phone company are good places to start. Or better yet, get a student to show you! You may also want to get on board by learning some text lingo such as BRB (be right back), OMG (oh my gosh), LOL (laugh out loud), and TTYL (talk to you later). See Chapter Two for a list of common text abbreviations.

ENHANCING THE HOME-SCHOOL CONNECTION

Educators are always looking for ways to strengthen communication with parents. There is tremendous value in good communication and supportive relationships with our students' families. Living in the busy world of today, twenty-first-century methods for communicating with parents are a must. The following cell phone tools are available for educators to use in building a strong home-school connection

GROUP TEXTING

School announcements, study tips, test dates, reminders, or even review and study questions need to be communicated to all parents. Parents are busy people. Reaching them with notes costs money and has doubtful effectiveness. Reaching them by phone takes a lot of time. Reaching them by e-mail can be helpful but is not necessarily reliable. However, reaching them by text message has had amazing results. According to the *New York Times*, "Mobile text messaging, the same 160-character dispatches first popularized by nimble-fingered teenagers, may be the closest thing in the information-overloaded digital marketing world to a guaranteed read. . . . It's also the one form of communication that many people are tethered to 24/7. Which helps explain why, at a time when in-boxes fill with hundreds of never-opened e-mail messages from direct marketers, 97 percent of all SMS marketing messages are opened (83 percent within one hour), according to the latest cell-carrier research" (Cohen, 2009).

How to Get Started

- Collect the numbers of the members you want in your cell phone group(s). Get their permission and ask them to watch for the welcome invitation so they can respond positively and become members of the group.

- Do a search for a free web-based group-texting service available in your area, such as WeTxt (see the how-to in Chapter Two), which was available for free at the writing of this book. Follow their set-up directions and enter the group's numbers as well as a group name that will make them easily identifiable.

- Send a welcome or invitation to the group.

- Once members have responded, you can send group texts.

- Different services have different options for responses (such as to whole group, only to sender, and so on) and you will want to set those according to how you want responses.

- Some services offer settings for times when you do not want to receive text responses.

- Most services show a written record of the text messages sent and received.

- All group texting managing, sending, and so on can be done on your phone as well.

Ideas for Educators Using Group Texting

- Notify parents about important events, question of the day, celebrations, exciting accomplishments. (If you have a multilingual student body you may want to group parents by language.)

- Let parents in on cool projects, assignment due dates, guest speakers, and field trips.

- Support study and test prep by texting a review question or study tip of the day.

Notification Services

Although most schools initially get notification systems for emergency situations, they often end up using them for everything else. Some schools use services such as SchoolMessenger to communicate through multiple modes such as text, voice, MMS (multimedia messaging services), e-mail, and so on.

In addition to the basic emergency notifications, some schools are using notification services in a way that can revolutionize parent involvement. Services such as TeleParent have Situational Student Messaging, which gives parents a daily student profile that includes information such as tardiness to class, participation, homework, and conduct. This moves the mundane conversation that usually goes something like, Dad: "How was your day?" Child: "Fine" to something more like, Dad: "I see you are working on a self-portrait in art class and that you are having some difficulty with your science project. Can you share more about this?" which can lead to a more robust conversation.

WIFFITI FOR PARENT FEEDBACK

Maybe you want to know what parents are experts in and would like to share with your class. Have parents send it into the Wiffiti board. Wiffiti (http://wiffiti.com/) is a billboard of texted responses that can be displayed in real time from anyone who wants to project the site. Ask parents to sign with their first name followed by their child's first name, for example, Maria Jose. Instantly parents have an opportunity to celebrate what they can contribute and other parents know the interests of their children's classmates.

How to Get Started with Wiffiti

- Sign in by clicking "log in with Facebook" or setting up an account with a username, e-mail address, and password. (Students don't need to sign in. They just text their answer to the Wiffiti code you share with them.)
- Once signed in select "make a screen" (http://wiffiti.com/screens/make).
- Give your screen a title and select "publish."
- You will be given a URL and special code that users can text to contribute to your screen.

CELL PHONES AS ORGANIZATIONAL TOOLS

Following is a quick breakdown of organizational tools available on most basic cell phones.

Calendar

Carrying around many devices gets cumbersome. At the beginning of the year, survey parents and students to see if they're interested in receiving electronic updates and create a distribution list of those who do. Place deadlines in your phone's calendar, select "invite attendee" and send it to the distribution list. This way without having to do any additional work, these calendar invites will show up on the phones of your students and their parent's phone and online calendar.

Stopwatch and Alarm

Being prepared is a first step in organization. Using your cell phone right at the start of your day, a wake-up alarm or previously scheduled wake-up text can be set to help you get going in the morning. At school, the stopwatch and timer features on most phones can come in handy for timing a speech or presentation, running an experiment in science class, and so on.

Calculator

Most cell phones have a basic calculator and some even come with a graphing calculator (or there's an app to download for that). No more keeping track of where you left your calculator or who borrowed it. With a cell phone, calculations are always at your (and your students', if they are allowed) fingertips wherever you are.

Note Taking

Cell phones are great for taking notes when you are away from the computer or when pen and paper would be in the way. Note-taking capabilities are identified by different names on different phones, such as "notepad" or "memo." You can find a note-taking function by looking through the menu or checking with the provider. When a note is taken, it is automatically saved. Notes can usually be organized by date or by title. Going into the note-taking function will bring up the saved notes, which can be read much like a text message is read. Notes are with you at anywhere and anytime. This makes reviewing notes as comfortable as reading text messages from friends, family, or colleagues. Additionally, notes can be easily searched and shared. Taking pictures also facilitates being able to refer back later. Note taking and reviewing can happen anywhere and anytime you have your phone.

GOOGLE VOICE

Google Voice is a terrific tool for busy educators for a number of reasons. First, it gives you one phone number that you can choose to have ring on any phone you'd like. You will never again need to carry multiple phones or swap phones. Another feature that the busy teacher will love is that it gives every teacher a personal secretary as all voice mails are transcribed. How fabulous is that?! You'll never need to transcribe a message or sort through many voice mails to get to the one you were trying to listen to. Just read or click on the message you want to hear and skip over the rest. Another way Google Voice is like a built-in teacher secretary is that it asks callers to announce themselves. No more being concerned about unknown numbers. You'll always know who is on the phone before you pick it up or you can choose to just send the call to voice mail. You can also screen your calls by letting them go to voice mail and using a ListenIn feature while messages are being left. If you decide to take the call, you can connect to the call by pressing "*." You can also record your conversation and listen to it later. The ability to record a conversation or voice mail provides educators with a simple and easy way to capture audio for podcasts or conversations with experts that students can listen to at any time. All conversations and voice-mail recordings are saved as audio files that can be used with the speaker's (or speaker's guardian in the case of students) written permission, for example, sent via e-mail, published on a website or blog, or saved on a wiki.

How to Get Started

- *Request an invitation.* Visit https://services.google.com/fb/forms/googlevoiceinvite to sign up for Google Voice.
- *Accept the invitation.* Be on the lookout for an invitation from Google Voice to your e-mail. You'll accept your invite there.
- *Watch the video.* While you're waiting for your invite, learn more about how Google Voice works by visiting their video channel www.youtube.com/googlevoice.
- *Choose your number.* Next you will be able to select a phone number that will be yours forever. Choose wisely. You'll need to select an area code. Many of the most popular area codes aren't available (for instance 212 and 646) but there seem to be some codes

for every city (for instance, I was able to get 347 for New York City). Your number can also spell out a word.

- *Select which phones ring.* You can determine which of your phones ring when this number is called. Think in advance if you want your cell, work, or home phone to ring when calls come in.

- *Import your contacts.* Next you'll want to ensure all your contacts are in your new Google Voice account. This is surprisingly easy to do. This post explains: "How to Export Your Outlook Contacts to a CSV File" (http://email.about.com/od/outlooktips/qt/Export_Outlook_Contacts_to_CSV.htm). It only takes about five to ten minutes to do.

- *Test it out.* Get someone to try it out with you. Have the friend call you and leave a voice mail. You'll see how it comes in as a text. Have the friend call you again and listen in as he or she leaves a voice mail. Have the friend call you once again and record your conversation.

- *Share your number.* Once you've tested the service and are comfortable, it's time to share your number. Update your number on all communication systems at work, your e-mail signature, websites, letterhead, and so on.

Ideas for Educators Using Google Voice

- Record yourself. To set up minitutorials about topics, just leave yourself a Google voice mail and you can include it in any online space.

- Provide voice recordings for student assessment. Leave messages for students about their work by recording your voice then sending it to them using the tool that works for you, for example, e-mailing it to the student, posting the link in your content management system, and so on.

- Easily share messages with your school administrator. Rather than explaining to your principal details about a message a concerned parent left, Google Voice lets you forward the audio message and transcript via e-mail. Nothing is lost in translation.

- Google Voice enables you to place an interactive icon, called a widget, where you can place your number on any online space that you can share with others. There's no need to give out your phone number. They simply click the widget, enter their number, and are connected either to your phone or voice mail, depending on how you set up your preferences.

- Google Voice lets parents leave you a voice mail anytime without interrupting your lesson. You can record messages that are unique to any parent's phone number and have calls go straight to voice mail without the phone ringing if they call while you are teaching a lesson.

AUDIENCE RESPONSE SYSTEMS

An audience response service, such as Poll Everywhere (www.polleverywhere.com/) or TextTheMob (http://textthemob.com/) can provide educators with simple methods to share their voice and ideas and get feedback on any topic right from their phones. With audience response services everyone's voice can be heard by texting a vote to the number provided. No extra equipment or software is needed and responses are captured within seconds. Another nice feature is that it doesn't matter which cell phones people use. Responses are instantly combined.

How to Get Started

- Register with a polling site like Poll Everywhere or TextTheMob using your e-mail and password and activate via your e-mail.
- For multiple choice polls:
  - On Poll Everywhere select "create poll" then select "multiple choice."
  - On TextTheMob select "create poll."
- For an open response poll:
  - On Poll Everywhere select "free text."
  - On TextTheMob select "create message board."
- Type your question and answer choices in the text box.
- Select "save new poll."
- You will be taken to a screen that shows your poll question and results along with how to respond via text.
- Participants will text the number of the selected service and reply with either their free response or a code that corresponds to the answer selected.
- Once the answer is submitted the results are instantly displayed on your phone.
- Responses can also be embedded into your selected online space, for example, a website, blog, or wiki.

Ideas for Educators Using Audience Response Systems

- It's cold outside and there is going to be an indoor lunch. Survey the teachers about which movie their class wants to watch.

- Celebrate student birthdays. Each week (or month) teachers can text in students who are celebrating their birthdays so they can be recognized by their peers. This feeds into one stream with a "happy birthday" message that can be displayed on digital monitors in classrooms and the building entrance on the selected day of the week or month.

- Let parents have a say and show them their thoughts and opinions matter. Here are examples of audience-response questions you may ask:

  - Open and free response question:

    What service learning projects would you like to see offered?

  - Polling question:

    Which of the following services would benefit your family?

    - Study time after school

    - Family reading nights

    - Backpack of weekend food for your child

    - On-site health screenings

    - Open media center before and after school

TWITTER

Twitter (www.twitter.com) is a great tool for schools to share interesting and relevant information with the student body, staff, parents, and family. There is no software to download and even with just one teacher cell phone per class, contributions can be made and modeled anywhere, anytime. Twitter has become such a popular tool because it asks one question, "What's happening?" Answers must be under 140 characters in length and can be sent via mobile texting, instant message, or the web. Similar to texting, the beauty of Twitter is that its core technology is a device-agnostic system (operates across different systems) that lets the masses participate.

How to Get Started

- To use Twitter from your phone go to www.twitter.com and set up an account. (*Note:* You may want to set up a personal account as well as one for your class.)

- Principals may want to set up a school account and give teachers access to send in tweets.

- You can tweet from your phone by entering your number at twitter.com/devices and entering Twitter into your phone with this number: 40404. Don't worry that it is only five digits. Just send a text to it and it will show up in your twitterfeed.

- Next you'll need to select a short tag (an approximately six-letters-or-less searchable word or acronym) and then have your audience's tweets include that tag. (For example, one of the more famous tags on Twitter was IranElection (http://twitter.com/#search?q=iranelection). Schools can use an acronym. For example, Barack Obama High School might be BOHS. In New York City schools all have a district, borough, and location (DBN) identifier, for example, 06M001, that can be used.

- Users can contribute by simply texting on their phone and ensuring the text includes the tag.

- You can capture the tag-specific tweets in any number of forms. The easiest is to do a simple Twitter search for the tag by typing it into the search box on the right side of the main Twitter page.

- For more information watch the *Twitter in Plain English* video tutorial at www.commoncraft.com/Twitter.

- You are now set up to start tweeting your way into the microblogging community.

Ideas for Educators Using Twitter

- If school staff are attending a conference or professional development activity they can tweet reflections, favorite quotes, or reactions to what they're learning. For example, one of the authors recently worked with a group of educators at a conference in which they set up Twitter accounts that were used passively to follow the goings on of the conference using the conference tag for the first two days. By day three most school leaders were also contributing tweets that included instant reflections of what they planned to bring back to their schools using a special tag for the group. The group tag provided all leaders with access to see what their colleagues were thinking and doing, allowing them to further connect and collaborate.

- School staff can tweet interesting announcements, updates, and activities at any time into the school account. This can be fed right into a school website providing the school community, parents, and more with an ongoing stream of updates about

school happenings. See how two schools do this at www.martavalle.org and www
.kurthahnschool.org. Here are examples of some of the school tweets:

Tweets About School Happenings or Recommendations

- Family literacy guide to strength your child's reading: http://schools.nyc.gov/
Academics/LibraryServices/FamilyLiteracyGuideTranslations
- Parent-teacher conferences are on Wed., Dec. 16, at 4:30 p.m. Parents: Please log onto
ARIS Parent Link https://arisparentlink.org
- Need quality information fast? Give netTrekker a try! http://school.nettrekker.com
- Apply for school meals online at ACCESS NYC

Principal Tweets Celebrating Student Success

- Aaron is working hard on a poem that is sure to inspire a lot of people. Ask him
about it.
- Evan contributed a really insightful comment toward a discussion of stereotyping in
advertising during his explore week class.
- Ann and Ms. Stick's class are getting ready to read A Raisin in the Sun.
- Just like she said she would, Robyn earned her spot on the honor roll!

Share News and Information About Your Class, Library, or Lab

For a great example of how this is done, follow Tracy Karas of Marta Valle High School
in New York City at http://twitter.com/MartaVLibrary. Here are some sample tweets
from Ms. Karas's library:

- Great news!!! Marta Valle has a Discovery Education United Streaming subscription!
The content is amazing! See me for the school passcode.
- Obama calls for math, science push: www.informationweek.com/news/government/
policy/showArticle.jhtml?articleID=221900739&queryText=education
- The best books of 2009 from School Library Journal www.schoollibraryjournal.com/
article/CA6708210.html
- Free writing resources! A great reference when you need to write almost anything!
http://owl.english.purdue.edu

PHONECASTING

Many teachers feel their busy schedules don't allow for the complexities of the equipment and set-up necessary for podcasting. But it needn't be that way. Even the busiest of teachers can get started quickly and easily with just their cell phone. Because of its ease and simplicity, phonecasting has become a popular tool in the bag of tricks used by innovative educators. Although the specific companies that provide such services are often coming and going, a Google search should point you to some popular options for services such as ipadio.com or BlogTalkRadio.com.

How to Get Started

Here are the instructions for the ipadio service:

- Go to http://ipadio.com and sign up for a free account with your username, e-mail, and password. Use your country code in the number. For example, the United States code is 011 44, which should be placed before your number.
- Once you register you will be assigned a pin number that shows up on your account information page that you can use when calling into the iPadio number.
- Once you call in and enter your pin you can record a message that will post instantly to your ipadio account. This is live and can be listened to right on the ipadio website.
- You can also have your "phlogs" (or phone blogs) posted directly to most blogs.

Ideas for Educators Using Phonecasting

- You can create daily messages on your class blog. Phonecasts can be posted directly to your class blog. This is similar to posting a daily message on a class website. This is what sixth-grade language arts and social studies teacher Josh Stumpenhorst does for his class in Naperville, Illinois. He uses phonecasts as a way to communicate to parents and students about what he is doing in his classroom. This window into his classroom provides students, their families, and other interested school community members with up-to-date information about what is being done in class.
- Phonecasts can energize students when they have a substitute. When high school technology integrator Lydia Leimbach can't be at her school in Farmingdale, Maine, she creates a phonecast to let students know what they need to do in class. In the assignments section of her class web page, she simply publishes a phonecast for each subject area that day letting students know what they're expected to do with further directions embedded right on the page.

- Phonecasts discretely provide accommodations for students with special needs. In some cases, students with special needs have accommodations such as extended time or having parts of the test read to them. In the past this has caused some disruption of the class, either requiring the student to be removed from the class and a school staff member removed from regular responsibilities to read to the student or in some cases the teacher and student sit in the back of the class as the teacher tries to read quietly to the student. Not only is this disruptive to the class and to the teacher's schedule, but it can also be embarrassing to the students. In her classes certified K–12 special education teacher Meg Wilson in Connecticut has used podcasting to change the game. Staff are no longer required to be removed from their duties and students are no longer singled out. Instead, Meg reads the student passage and creates a podcast for the student using her cell phone. During the test any student with this accommodation is given unobtrusive ear buds and a mobile device to listen to the passage. In today's digital age, testing companies should be required to provide such accommodations, but until then, we have teachers like Meg.

GOOGLE SMS

Educators have access to an endless amount of information at their fingertips by texting 466453 (spells the word *Google*). Once you have Google in your contact list you have untapped an unlimited treasure trove of knowledge and information.

How to Get Started

- Go to www.google.com/mobile/default/sms.html to see an explanation and demonstration of how to search using Google SMS. The explanation describes how to use specific query language to find things such as definitions, weather, directions, and much more.
- Text message your search query to 466453 (*Google* on most devices) and Google will text message back results. For example, text "weather boston" to get current weather in that city or "1 us pint in liters" to get that measurement conversion.

Ideas for Educators Using Google SMS

- If you don't know the definition of a particular word, text *Google* with the query "define" and type in the word. You'll get the definition and the source moments later.

- Need to quickly calculate how far 100 kilometers is in miles? Type in "100 kilometers in miles" and you'll get your answer.
- Use Google SMS's translate feature to send text messages to families who speak different languages.

CELL PHONE CAMERAS

Although this book focuses on using the basic features of texting, most teachers do have cell phones with photo capability so in this chapter we also introduce a few ideas for integrating images into instruction. It is very simple for teachers to send pictures from their phones to their e-mail or an online space such as a school or class website, blog, or wiki. The pictures never need to be developed so there is no cost for printing and no time involved in getting them processed. If you're not sure how to use your phone's camera, ask your students! There are several free websites such as Picassa or Flickr that can be used to compile your pictures.

Safety note: Consider setting up a class account to keep your personal and school-related photos separate. Determine your school policy about photos of students and their work. If your school supports celebrating student work and likenesses publicly, make sure you have permission slips. If your school policy prohibits you from sharing student work or likenesses publicly, you'll either want to set your album settings to private or you'll want to ensure that student aliases or first names only are used on their work so as not to reveal their identity.

How to Get Started

Depending on the model of the phone, these steps may vary slightly.

- Use the built-in camera to take a picture.
- Choose send "as email" or "as MMS" to create a picture message. Write the text you want to add and the e-mail or number of the recipient. Choose "OK."

Ideas for Educators Using Cell Phone Cameras

The following ideas are from Jeff VanDrimmelen's "8 Ways to Use Camera Phones in Education" (http://edutechie.com/2007/06/8-ways-to-use-camera-phones-in-education/):

- Whiteboard/Blackboard archive

  - Do you ever get done with a class and look at the board with regret because you have to erase everything you or your class just created? Snap a quick picture and archive that for future use. You could even post it on a class discussion board, wiki, blog, webpage, or even just e-mail it to your class for review.

- Handheld scanner

  - Remember those old spy movies when the secret agents captured documents with a tiny secret minicamera? Now we all have one. Believe it or not, photographing documents works.

  - I don't recommend stealing information, but for random paper information, notes . . . you can snap a picture to capture the data.

- Reminder list

  - Sometimes you see something that jogs your memory. Take a picture of that thing as a reminder of what you need to do.

- Learn students' names and faces

  - One of the biggest struggles we have as teachers is learning the names and faces of the constant rotation of students coming through our classes. Take some time at the beginning of the year to photograph the students or even better yet have them take pictures of each other and e-mail to you if they have that capability.

- Security/liability device

  - I hesitate adding this one in here but we all know crazy things can happen in the classroom. Sometimes you may need to take a picture of something happening or something that happened to protect yourself and your students.

- Assignments

  - Depending on the subject you teach, it may be appropriate to send the students out one day to take pictures of nature, people, or other things. Try to think of ways to use the phone. Just using the phone in an assignment will help students be more excited about it. Remember, there's nothing wrong with using technology as a motivator. It works great with these digital natives.

- Instant blogging
  - This is one of my favorite options. If you are a blogger or have a class blog or website you can set up an e-mail address that you can post directly to that blog. You can give that address out to students or use it yourself. Granted, you need an Internet-connected phone for this, but I had to add it in. It is so awesome to be out in the middle of nowhere posting to a blog, archiving.
- Memories
  - We all know we get attached to those we teach and often we don't want to forget them. Take some pictures throughout the year and print them out at the end of the year for a scrapbook or collage. Five, ten, twenty years from now those pictures will bring up dear memories.):

USING FLICKR TO COLLECT IMAGES CAPTURED ON CELL PHONES

Although using a cell to capture photos is quick, easy, and efficient, frequently the pictures are just stuck on the phone. Flickr provides a free and organized way to share pictures taken on your cell phone. With Flickr you get an e-mail address where you (or anyone you share the e-mail with) can send your pictures. Flickr makes it very easy to sort and group pictures using tags or drag and drop features. You can get a link or code to embed any picture or group of pictures into any online space. When e-mailing, your subject line becomes the picture caption and the message or body becomes the description. Creating a slide show with Flickr saves you several hours over alternate methods, such as sending individual e-mails to yourself, downloading every picture, then creating a PowerPoint in which you would upload each picture and copy and paste the titles and captions.

How to Get Started

- Go to http.www.flickr.com.
- Set up an account on Flickr to be used with school-related projects.
- Flickr gives you an e-mail address to which you (and others) can send pictures.
- Tell Flickr what tag should be associated with pictures sent to that e-mail by going to www.flickr.com/account/uploadbyemail. As you are working in different units you will update and change your tag. For example, if you were studying poetry with grade 8 in class 403 your tag could be poetry8403. If you were studying fiction it could be

fiction8403. Using a tag allows you to instantly generate a slide show with photo titles and captions. No work required. Your tag will enable you to create a slide show with the pictures students submit that can be shared with a link to the URL as well as a code that can be embedded into any online space.

- When sending pictures to your Flickr account make sure you use a subject (photo title) and message (photo caption).

Ideas for Educators Using Flickr

- Create a slide show of all your blackboard lessons or instructional charts and tag them by unit of study for students and families to refer to at any time.

- Take pictures of things you see during field trips. You can take the photos or pass your phone around to your students to indicate subject (title) and message (caption). Afterward your photos instantly become a slide show memory of the trip, which can be referenced by students and shared with the school community.

- Make a Facebook-type entry of your students. You can take photos of your students or pass your phone around to take student portraits that you e-mail to your Flickr account with their first name in the subject and something they want to share about themselves in the message. What a great way for you to get to know your students and for them to get to know each other.

- Take a picture of the day. Assign a student each day responsible for selecting a picture of the day to capture. Have the student write the subject (title, caption) and message (description). What a great scrapbook for the year for students, for a home-school connection tool, and for photos to share with administration.

STARTING WITH THE DEVICE IN YOUR OWN POCKET

Integrating texting into teaching isn't hard. Once you open your mind to the possibilities of how text messaging and cell phone technologies can enhance your teaching it becomes such an exciting process, especially because you start by using the device you already know, own, and that resides in your own pocket or pocketbook. When doing so, educators are not only helping themselves, they are also providing students with a great example of how these tools can be used for more than just socializing. By using all or just some of the ideas discussed in this chapter you'll be on your way to using and modeling effective, educational, and appropriate uses of cell phones. This lays a nice foundation and provides a comfortable starting point for teachers and schools who want to begin incorporating these devices into the work their students do. In order to make things as convenient as possible the next section features a quick guide with all the uses featured in this chapter. It can be taken with you on the go, to your computer, or simply serve as a cheat sheet. As you have gotten your feet wet with the applications in this chapter, your motivation will surely increase. Now you are ready to really spice things up as a texting teacher with the wealth of ideas you'll discover in Chapter Two, where you will learn how to engage your students with texting.

TEXTING TEACHER RESOURCES QUICK GUIDE

Table 1.2 provides a quick guide to the ideas and resources mentioned in this chapter and will help get you on the road to incorporating cell phones into instruction.

Table 1.2
Texting Teacher Resources Quick Guide

Topic	Resource	URL
How to get started	Common Sense Media	www.commonsensemedia.org/tech-tip-how-text-message
Group texting	WeTxt or GroupMe	www.wetxt.com or www.groupme.com
Notification services	Home notification services	http://schoolmessenger.com www.teleparent.net
Wiffiti for parent feedback	Wiffiti	http://wiffiti.com
One number, online voice mail, transcribed messages, and more	Google Voice	www.google.com/voice
Audience response systems	Poll Everywhere or TextTheMob	www.polleverywhere.com http://textthemob.com
Tweeting	Twitter	www.twitter.com
Phonecasting	ipadio	http://ipadio.com
Text message search queries	Google SMS	www.google.com/mobile/default/sms.html Text: 466453
Collect images captured on cell phones	Flickr	www.flickr.com

chapter TWO

The Texting Learner

Over the past forty years, technology has changed so rapidly that by now kids are blasé about its wonders. The unimaginable for us has become their norm.
Michael Osit, author of *Generation Text: Raising Well-Adjusted Kids in an Age of Instant Everything*

Today's teachers are lucky! Most of their students already own or have access to cell phones, so getting technology in the hands of students is less of an issue than in the past. More and more teachers have harnessed the power of technology in general and cell phones in particular for themselves, and many are eager to do so with their students; however, for some there are barriers to overcome. For instance not every student has a phone but don't let that stop you. We don't say we can't use computers, calculators, or even textbooks because not every student has one. There are opportunities for students to learn in pairs, groups, or to share a device. Writing a technology grant is another option or perhaps a teacher, parent, mentor, or student can approach local businesses or community members who may be willing to donate a device or add a student to their plan. Unfortunately, in some schools and districts, even when access isn't an issue other barriers may exist. Students may be banned from using personally owned digital devices at school or there may be restrictions placed on teachers and students communicating electronically. (See the Appendix for information on how to break the ban.) Even when these issues don't exist, there are some teachers who have embraced using technology for themselves and see the value of using it for learning, but who are still unsure of how to do so effectively in a classroom full of students.

Whether you are burdened by barriers or empowered to educate in ways you find most effective, a terrific starting point is incorporating cell phone use into homework. This enables students to develop expertise in using their cell phones for learning and it also sets the stage for developing an acceptable use policy. Following are free or inexpensive ways educators can begin to use basic (no Internet required) text-enabled cell phones to engage learners, enrich instruction, and communicate effectively with students. Each of these ideas can be used during class when a teacher has the right conditions for that option to occur or as a part of homework activities if policies or conditions are not suitable for using cell phones in the classroom.

STUDENT AND TEACHER TEXTING

Effective teacher-student communication all comes down to comfort, preference, and school or district policies. Ideally educators are working in schools and districts that trust them as professionals and empower staff to make decisions that best suit their communication style. When that's the case, educators who are comfortable communicating digitally have strengthened the student-teacher bond using various forms of electronic communication from Facebook to e-mail to texting. These are educators who believe it is the behavior and message, not the medium, that dictates what is appropriate. Science Leadership Academy principal Chris Lehmann puts it this way, "I'm available to support and communicate with my students using whatever means or medium they choose."

Unfortunately, in some schools and districts, educators have had their right to communicate in the way that best suits the needs of their students and themselves taken away. As we move more deeply into the digital age there are some policy makers who have mandated the ways in which and the tools with which educators and students can connect. In districts that ban teachers from communicating with students using digital methods, straight texting will not be an option, but just as there is much more to do with laptops beyond e-mail and Facebook, there are also many more ways to harness the power of cell phones beyond simple texting. In this section we will address ideas that can be incorporated by teachers who are able to use texting with students. The remainder of this chapter will address other ways teachers and students can use cell phones for learning.

CONCERNS ABOUT TEACHER-STUDENT TEXTING

Although some teachers love the idea of integrating the tools students know and love into learning, some may be hesitant when it comes to communicating with students via text. One reason could be concern over the volume of messages that may come through. Another concern could be the fact that texting provides a social context that might not be best suited for communicating with students. This is not much different than a teacher's preference when it comes to communicating with students via telephone or other means outside of class. Many students and teachers find such communication beneficial and those who do not, communicate in ways they prefer. Ultimately, educators must determine what works best for them and their students within the parameters of their school policies.

GETTING STARTED WITH TEXTING

When texting with students, you want to ensure you can speak the same language. This list will get you started with some of the more common texting abbreviations and the chart in the next section will tell you just what those funny faces (aka *emoticons*) kids use actually mean.

Popular Texting Abbreviations

asap	as soon as possible
b4	before
BF	boyfriend
brb	be right back
btw	by the way
cos	because
cya	see ya
fyi	for your information

GF	girlfriend
gtg	got to go
idk	I don't know
jk	just kidding
kk	okay
l8r	later
lol	laugh out loud
omg	oh my gosh
oxox	hugs and kisses
pos	parent over shoulder
rofl	roll on floor laughing
sup	what's up
thx	thanks
tml	text me later
ttyl	talk to ya later
w/	with
zzzz	sleeping or bored

If you come across a text you don't understand, try using an online service that translates SMS lingo to regular phrases or regular phrases to text lingo. Use a service such as Lingo2Word (www.lingo2word.com/index.php) and ur stdnts wl thnk ur QL n no tym (*translation:* Your students will think you are cool in no time).

EMOTICONS FOR ENHANCING EXPRESSION

Some critics of text messaging feel it is ineffective communication because it is void of emotion, lacking the message enhancements that tone of voice and nonverbal expression provide. Maybe those critics never received a love note. Yes, text messages are short, quick, and full of abbreviations. However, the back-and-forth nature of texting more closely resembles conversation than a note or letter. To help convey emotions even more clearly, a whole new vocabulary of communicating feelings and emotions has developed for use with texting called *emoticons*. Emoticons are symbols used to represent feelings.

Many cell phones now come equipped with some emoticons. You may want to search around on your phone or ask your students to show you what they have on their phones. Table 2.1 presents a quick guide to common emoticons.

Table 2.1
Emoticons Guide

Emoticon	Emotion	Emoticon	Emotion	Emoticon	Emotion
X-(	Angry	:->	Grin	)-:	Left-handed sad face
</3	Broken heart	=) or :-)	Happy	(-:	Left-handed smiley face
O.o or :-S	Confused	<3	Heart or love	=/	Mad
B-)	Cool	{ }	Hug	^_^	Overjoyed
:_(or :'(	Crying	:-I	Indifferent	:-/	Perplexed
-	Dazed	X-p	Joking	=(or :-(or :(	Sad
		=D	Laughing out loud	:-P	Sticking tongue out

These are some of the more common emoticons, but if there is something you don't know or if there is something you want to express but don't know how, there are plenty of websites that offer emoticon glossaries. Sharpened.net provides a useful glossary at www.sharpened.net/glossary/emoticons.php.

Once you have the basic lingo and emoticon smilies under your belt you'll be ready to consider some ideas for using texting to strengthen the teacher-student relationship.

IDEAS FOR COMMUNICATION WITH STUDENTS

How often do you want to just check in with a student but do not have the time for a real conversation? How often do you think of a fact you left out of a lecture or another point that your should have made in a class discussion? Do you ever wish you could remind students to study for the test the night before? Then a text conversation is perfect. *Test 2moro, Did u get the homework? Vocab due fri, any questions?* Facts, figures, formulas are easily made text friendly as well. Reminders of tests, study tips, and praises are all quickly texted. You and your students are busy people and want to ensure time is used efficiently. Texting aids with this tremendously. When you do not want to bother a student with a phone call, a text is less intrusive of students' time and out-of-class activities. Although you'll want to ensure texting is used sparingly, students are very good at knowing when it makes the most sense to respond. This is a skill they have developed from lots of practice and experience.

IDEAS FOR HAVING STUDENTS COMMUNICATE WITH YOU

It is wonderful for students to be able to check in, update, say or ask things they wouldn't feel comfortable revealing in person or even in a phone call. Texts such as *i got a job, homework hard 2nit, wat time r those conferences 2moro?* are helpful for building relationships, knowing your students, and being an effective teacher. Timing is so important and, as we all know, our students live in the moment. Texting provides a means for students to communicate with teachers within their time frame. If you choose to allow texts with students, a discussion about personal boundaries will be in order before sharing your number. The following workshop about boundaries, privacy, and safety can be conducted with students, parents, and staff ensuring everyone is on the same page about how to appropriately use cell phones in education.

BOUNDARIES, PRIVACY, AND SAFETY WORKSHOP

Table 2.2 provides a proactive and informative workshop that can be presented to various groups depending on scheduling needs and getting a facilitator, who could be an administrator, school counselor, teacher, parent group leader, or student. The objectives of the workshop are to create unity among all cell phone users (adults and students alike), a comfort level with cell phones and text messaging, and provide tools for ensuring proper use. It can be delivered in approximately sixty minutes. (*Note:* All names have been changed to protect the privacy of people mentioned.)

SUPPORTING STUDENTS

We all have students who need a little extra support. For example, one of my (Willyn Webb) students sent this text: *could u txt me 2moro morning so i can go to school, my alarm clock doesnt work on my phone.* This illustrates how students depend on their phones. Simply caring, listening, problem solving (suggesting to the student another wake-up option), or reflecting can happen in a timely, efficient manner through texting. Of course, when the occasions call for it, make arrangements to follow up with a conversation.

Instead of worrying about students in particularly challenging circumstances or with troubled states of mind on weekends and evenings, you can do a quick check by texting

Table 2.2
Success with Cells for the Texting School Community Workshop Agenda

Time	Activity	Facilitator Notes
00:00	**Welcome and Introduction** • We rely on our phones for many uses, communication, camera, calculator, and more. We can all relate to some part of this commercial. The point made is that we *all* use our phones extensively. • Show a short video that illustrates the amount of texting done by adults. Suggestion: "Really: Windows Phone 7 Official Commercial TV Ad" (www.youtube.com/watch?v=EHlN21ebeak) • With purposeful boundaries and proper example we can better monitor and guide students in their use, enjoy closer relationships with our children, and gain valuable educational support.	When showing the video ask participants to count how many of the examples they saw are ones that they have engaged in. Ask them to share the number either by a show of hands or using a polling service such as Poll Everywhere.
00:05	**Boundaries** *No cussing was a text boundary I had to set with a student we'll call Allison in the early days of my progression with using cell phones with students. Allison had been absent from school that day and my secretary had sent her our customary text, "We miss you at school. R u ok?" We had not gotten a response during the school day. However, in the evening I received a text from Allison asking if she could talk to me in the morning and asking if I knew if they took a test in language arts. This was all good and something I encouraged student to do. The problem occurred because I was reading to my youngest daughter at the time. My children are used to a quick text response to a student occasionally in the evening. It is rarely very disruptive but this time was inappropriate because Allison's signature was "fucktheworld." My daughter saw the signature and asked me about it. I had to explain that Allison had made a bad choice and should not have used that ugly word in the first place, but especially not to a teacher. She probably sent the homework question without thinking about the previously established signature. However, I do not want my children exposed to that type of behavior so I learned from this and now include it in the discussion portion of the lesson on boundaries. Being thoughtful of others and considering how your language portrays you are great life skills to teach, and texting provides a platform to make those points.*	Share this story from Willyn Webb or one of your own to begin the boundary conversation.

(continued)

Table 2.2 (*continued*)

Time	Activity	Facilitator Notes
00:10	**Boundaries** Poll your audience and ask questions about each of the following areas: **Signature lines.** Would a signature with a curse word be okay? • Think of everyone whom you could text, not just your friends, when choosing a signature line. **Forwards—texts intended for multiple people.** Would it be okay to send a forward that is saying you are grateful for all of the supportive people in your life and just wanted to let them know? • Some forwards want you to send to *x* number of people, so think who will be reading it before selecting multiple contacts to send it to. **Time of day.** Would it be okay to text the teacher at 11:00 PM? • Set appropriate times together. **Nature of content.** Would it be okay to text the school counselor that you just had sex and are freaking out? • Follow confidentiality rules and exceptions. • Rule of thumb, don't text something to the school counselor (or anyone else) that you don't want to talk about later. **Giving out your number.** Would it be okay to give your number to someone you just met at the mall? • Make choices about whom to begin communicating with. • Discuss how you can block senders if you were wrong about someone you thought you could trust. **Unknown calls or messages.** Is it okay to respond to messages from unknown senders? • Be aware of stranger danger. • Do not communicate with someone you do not know. • Never meet up with someone you do not know. • Inform a trusted adult if someone you don't know asks to meet you.	Set up your poll on a site such as Poll Everywhere www.polleverywhere.com to enable participants to respond anonymously with "yes," "no," "sometimes," or "not sure." Create a chart with each step listed on the left side and the headings: "boundaries," "establishing good practices," and "making good choices." Capture participant responses on this chart that can be shared later with participants. Middle school counselors especially could create minilessons on each of these areas and practice making good choices with the students using role-play scenarios.

Table 2.2 (*continued*)

Time	Activity	Facilitator Notes
00:25	**Privacy** *Doug was a very intelligent, hard-working student. He was a sweet boy and a gifted writer. I always was impressed with his way with words and amazingly visual descriptions. There did not seem to be a violent bone in his body. So I was more than shocked when the police showed up at school to arrest him for something he had said in a text message. It turned out that Doug had a girlfriend at another high school and some boys had been bothering her. Doug texted one of the boys a physically threatening message. I'm sure Doug never intended to do anything, but because the threat was there, in writing, he was sent to a detention facility.*	Share this story from Willyn Webb or one of your own to begin the privacy conversation.
00:30	**Privacy** Poll questions: • Is a text message that you have erased gone forever? • Is it safer to text something when you are too embarrassed or shy to say it? • If you block your number, are you safe from being caught? • Is sending great pictures of yourself to someone you like, your significant other, or friends okay? **Texting Guidelines** • Text messaging provides an extra layer of privacy and can seem less embarrassing or risky. However, remember, text messages are permanent and easy to share with others. • Parents should establish practices for being in tune with the contacts and texting of their children while also setting good examples themselves. • Students should remember that anything they text can be retrieved and even used in a prosecution. • Don't write or share (via pictures or video) anything you wouldn't feel comfortable having others know about publicly.	Continue the poll so the audience has an opportunity for anonymous response with "yes," "no," "sometimes," or "not sure." Share the texting guidelines and ask participants if they have any stories to illustrate the guidelines. Real examples from you and the participants make it more impressionable.

(continued)

Table 2.2 (*continued*)

Time	Activity	Facilitator Notes

- If someone sends you something inappropriate, address the person as you would in face-to-face encounters. Don't attack the person but instead focus on what it is that is an issue for you. For example instead of saying, "You're a jerk for sending me that picture," consider saying, "Getting pictures like the one you sent me makes me feel uncomfortable. I value our friendship and hope you'll respect my request not to send me communication like this in the future." If you are uncomfortable doing this, speak with an adult you can trust such as a parent, teacher, or guidance counselor.
- If messages are of a bullying or sexual tone you should save the message. You and the trusted adult you are confiding in may consider contacting the police.

Photos and Videos

- Before taking or sharing pictures or videos, you should get the consent of the subject(s). Ensure they know your intentions if you are sharing. Once it's shared digitally it is public for the world to see. Make sure you are conveying an image you stand behind and are proud of.
- Never show anything to others in a texted picture that you would be too embarrassed to show them in real life.

00:40 **Safety**

At the time Joyce was the only girl in her third-grade group with a phone. Joyce's phone was being "borrowed" by friends at a birthday party. They texted a girl who was not at the party, sending some rude messages. The girl's mother went to the party and yelled at Joyce. She also called me at home. I went to the party and got the phone from the other girls. In the end, there were many hurt feelings, relationships were affected, and trust was broken among the girls.

Share this story from Willyn Webb or one of your own to begin the safety conversation.

Table 2.2 (*continued*)

Time	Activity	Facilitator Notes
00:45	**Safety** • We have addressed good practice, good choices, and safety tips throughout this program. • What safety tips do you recommend when using cell phones?	Have participants text into Wiffiti safety tips for cell phones. Set up your free Wiffiti page at http://wiffiti.com.
00:55	**Questions, Comments, Discussion**	
00:60	**Adjourn**	

a simple, *how r u?* When the answer is, *okay*, you'll be able to go about life without worry. If the answer is not so positive, text a follow-up to show you care. End with a statement about being available at school the next day to talk some more. In a few minutes you can connect with a student needing support without interrupting family or personal time as much as with a phone call. Once students realize you are a "texter," they often appreciate that you care enough to communicate with them in the way they prefer.

SUPPORTING STUDENTS WITH SPECIAL NEEDS

Cell phones open a new world of tools that can be accessed and used for accommodations required to serve students with special needs. Simple voice mail messages, Google Voice, texting, WeTxt notes, pictures, picture messages to create Flickr shows, and any other tool depending on the phone are ways to assist students orally, visually, auditorily, and physically without any negative stigma. For example, a student had a physical disability that made him unable to write legibly or speak clearly. However, he could use one hand to text rapidly. He taught his teachers that he could answer review questions on his phone and send them to their e-mails faster than trying to type on a keyboard or using a pen. Students love their phones. They are an acceptable, even cool, device offering a variety of input and output capabilities. Another student could not write and was tied to a room with a computer that had a microphone until we set up Google Voice and Voki for him to speak his assignments into his phone from anywhere. Students are already familiar with cell phone functions and how to use them. This is an adaptive aid with little or no cost to the school that can be used not only for school but also outside of school and into the world of work. In fact, it is with special needs students that many teachers have been able to bring in cell phone tools and show success, which has had a ripple effect into regular education classrooms.

GROUP TEXTING

All of your students and families can be supported through the ease of one text message, broadcast to all through group texting. Group texting can increase your communication with very little effort by using your phone's capabilities or a free service such as WeTxt. Smith (2006) noted the following:

When I started experimenting with text messaging, I would text this student or that student, usually one or two at a time. Once I got all my seniors' numbers, though, I decided to try a broadcast. During my class, second period, I talked with the seniors about a variety of topics, so I thought I would follow up on one topic in a text message to all of them. During third period, I thought of some points I wanted to make, so I gave them a blast. Now, I regularly "ping" our students with updates on schedules, assignment reminders, even wake-up calls, and they answer with questions of their own. They even send me messages regularly to let me know that they are up to.

Students should also be instructed in the use of group texting to support their learning through text study groups, to ease communication for group projects, and as an aid for cooperative learning both during class and after.

You can use group texting with your service provider or you can use a free group texting service such as WeTxt, GroupMe, to send text messages. A texting service often provides more features enabling you to set up groups according to class periods or other ways you may differentiate your class such as by native language. The group text feature can be used to assess students on a particular project, to tie lessons together, to encourage students to make connections, or simply to get kids engaged in content outside of class. If requested, the same text can go out to the parents, building the home-school connection. The text can be as simple as texting the main idea of tomorrow's lecture for them to think about. When students are going to be absent, if they have set up their teachers as a text group, one text saying they will be absent and a request for make-up work can be sent to all. The one-time set-up is quick and easy.

Busy teachers may decide to designate a reporter to send group texts. This could be a paraprofessional, student teacher, or teacher's aide. You can invite new members when you get new students and remove members when a student moves or changes classes. It can all be done with a few simple text commands from your phone or on the website. Students can have group project groups and change them as assignments, classes, and projects are finished or assigned.

How to Get Started with WeTxt

You can have multiple groups for individual classes, cooperative learning groups, clubs, teams, and so on. Setting up times when texts cannot be received is good way to set healthy boundaries and prevent unnecessary disruptions to family activities, sports, or sleeping. Students can also register on the WeTxt site to create their own groups and notebooks (see following section). WeTxt provides an online record of all texts sent, which provides proof of ethical and responsible texting communication and evidence of learning through texting.

- Register your number on the WeTxt website (www.wetxt.com/) and create a quick profile.

- Create a group by naming it, selecting a profile (the one you just created), and choosing one of three types, "reply-to-all," "reply-to-me," or "one-way message blast."

- The group manager window will then show you all of your groups and you can begin adding numbers. Add numbers in contact manager so once they are in, you can create subgroups with a different name, such as a class or project; then you can include certain students in each group.

- You will get a text from WeTxt congratulating you on creating your group. You simply respond to their text to send a text to your whole group. Save the link in your phone contacts under the name you created for quick use.

- You have an in-box to view messages similar to an e-mail. They are sorted by group, just like a grade book of classes.

- You can set it up to send and receive through text or computer or both. It is nice to have a computer record of all texts sent and received. It is very user friendly and you can customize to fit your needs further from there. You can set "don't deliver before . . ." and "don't deliver after . . ." times so that you will never get a text when it would be disruptive to you or your students.

Ideas for Projects Using Group Texting

- For an English class, group texting can be used to create a group story. Right after school, text all of your students a story starter. From the replies, the teacher selects a line and texts it to the group so they can add to it and so on. This way, each student in the group "adds" to the story and it is then texted to the next person on the list. The story should go around to each member of the group three times. The next day the group members have a "story" they wrote collectively. Have students analyze the story for plot, theme, character development, and so on.

- For a math class, assign student groups or use student-created groups and give each group a math story problem to solve together using texts.

- In science class, have students in a group collectively create a science project on a subject you assign using texting to communicate their ideas and findings, then come to class and report their results together.

- In a social studies class, a group of students can interview different adults with questions about a historical event and then compare and combine their top answers through texting. Video and picture messages can be included with the answers into one report about the event.

Online Notebooks with WeTxt

Most cell phones have a notepad tool but when you want to be able to print notes, organize notes, and keep a running record on your computer, WeTxt offers a free way for you and your students to text in notes from anywhere and at anytime. For example, you can create notebook sections for field trips, homework projects, research topics, outside readings, and so on and have the notes all organized, printable, and saved. Students might be at a friend's house, on the bus to a game, or some other place without paper and pencil when a thought, a piece of evidence, or a memory comes up that needs to be recorded for something they are doing in class. They can just text it then and use it later.

How to Get Started with WeTxt Notebook

- Once registered on WeTxt (see the previous section), it's easy to start creating notebooks. Students will set up notebooks on the www.wetxt.com website.

- The online notebook is a pull down from the top menu Services. Select "send notebook address" from that pull-down menu. A text will immediately go to your phone or the students' phones if they are creating their own notebooks.

- When the address for the notebook text comes to the phone, open it, select "options," select "extract address" (to send notes to the notebook), select "save," say "ok" to add new contact, type in the contact name you want for your notebook, and say "ok." (Phones vary in the steps to extracting an address and adding it to your contacts. Check with your provider.)

- Another option in the Notebook window is "create notebook section" on the WeTxt site. You may type in a section name and click on "create notebook section." For example, students could have a notebook for each class, saved by the subject or class name in their phone, or a notebook for a project or one for personal reminders. The teacher could set up a notebook section and share the text to address with students, thus creating a collaborative collection of notes for a project or research topic. Once the notebook section has been added, a text will be sent to the phone associated with the account and the same process to add it to contacts (with the notebook section name used as the contact name) is followed as in the last step. Notes can be sent and organized at the same time just by sending them to the appropriate contact name of the online notebook associated with the class, subject, project, and so on.

GOOGLE VOICE

Google Voice is an option for those who are interested in embracing the power and simplicity of using a phone to communicate with students but who would appreciate an option that did not result in having students leave messages and texts directly to their phone. Google Voice enables educators to capture voice and text messages from students without providing them with their direct phone number. This can be done in a few ways. One way is to provide the student with your Google Voice number, a universal number that will ring on whichever device you choose. When placing a call, callers must state their name for the call to go through so you'll never be surprised by an unknown number. Or you can let Google Voice answer the call and use the ListenIn feature to hear the message. You can also choose not to listen to the voice mail at all and it will be converted to text. The voice mail and text transcription will be saved in your voice mail archive. This allows you to read the text of the message or listen to the message at your leisure. The same holds true for text messages. All messages are captured and archived. You can respond from your phone or computer.

There is also another option. Google Voice will give you a widget to place on your web page, wiki, blog, and so on. This widget can be clicked on and callers can enter their name and phone number, at which time they will get a call on their phone with the entered name indicated. Then they can speak their assignment, which is captured as audio. When they are done, they simply hang up and their message is delivered to the teacher's in-box without the phone ever ringing.

Even in schools that might have trepidations about using digital communication, because Google Voice keeps a log of the calls, messages, and texts, this is in essence one of the safest ways students and adults can communicate. From an instructional standpoint, Google Voice is powerful because it can become a repository for oral reports, assignments, or sound bytes. What's more, the teacher can attach notes to each clip in their in-box, share the reports and notes with students, or post them publicly or privately as the assignment and school policy dictate. See Chapter One for instructions on getting started with Google Voice.

Ideas for Using Google Voice with Students

- Use Google Voice to support running records and reading level assessment. You can record students reading passages using just a phone and headset and Google Voice. You'll have the actual voice recording to accompany the passage along with a transcript of the message on which to capture notes. Rather than talk to a parent or show students how they have progressed across a year, let them go back and listen for themselves.

- Google Voice is an effective tool for auditory learners that could be used as an alternative to written assignments. Students who are emerging writers or are not fluent in English writing could be given a choice to submit their work via a Google Voice recording or perhaps even a song. This enables all students to contribute work in the style best aligned to their abilities and strengths.

- English language learners could use Google Voice to record a reading passage or simply a dialogue or conversation. When they see the transcribed message they'll see how well their voice is translated into English. This can be particularly helpful for students who are reluctant to speak up in class because they are afraid of making mistakes. They can do this work from the comfort of their own home without fear or embarrassment.

MAKE IT REAL WITH PICTURES

When students' cell phones have cameras, a new world is opened. Students can take pictures of homework projects, research material, field work, activities, and so on for their own use or to share with others. Pictures can also be used to take the classroom home. Sometimes students sit down to do homework and cannot remember what was written on the board or on classroom charts. Cell phones can remedy that situation. Encourage students to take pictures of material shared on the board, on class charts, in handouts, or just to make sure the material does not get lost and stays handy. The pictures can be moved from phone and onto a site for studying using a free Internet-based service such as Flickr (see Chapter One). There photos can be organized by date, subject, topic, or tag. In classrooms where students aren't allowed to have cells the teacher can take requested photos and send them to the photo site or distribute to the class through a group text.

Ideas for Using Pictures with Students

- Students can use their cell phone cameras to take pictures of activities such as the steps of a science project or the process to complete an art project or a performance and then create a slide show using those pictures on a site such as Flickr.
- Capture field trip photos and send them all to a common photo-sharing site to instantly create a field trip memory slide show. If student names and likenesses are used, ensure there are permission slips or that those photos are kept private.
- Students and their families can take pictures of their travel experiences or vacations to share with the class.
- Student craft projects, role-play activities, and make-up work can be done at home and be captured and presented through photos taken on the phone. The picture provides support or evidence for the learning that happened at home. These photos can be texted to the teacher, e-mailed to the teacher, and published to a class photo site or on a student photo site, depending on the project.

AUDIENCE RESPONSE SYSTEMS

Most educators are familiar with audience response systems (ARS) aka clickers. Common brands are eInstruction, Sentio, TurningPoint, and ActiVote. Those who use the systems know they run about $2,500 to $4,000 (depending on various options selected) for a class set and that they allow educators to track student learning, engage an entire class as they collect real-time responses from students, and quickly assess understanding and achievement. Although these are valuable instructional outcomes, clickers are costly and the distribution, collection, and maintenance of devices is rather cumbersome. In many cases, using an ARS requires training to figure out how to upload the software, input questions, maneuver from one question to the next, and share answers. Additionally these systems don't tend to keep up with the latest in technology. At the time of the writing of this book, most devices still had an old-style, phone-like keypad without a letter on each button, which makes submitting a response quite tedious. The clickers just don't look like the technology students use in real life. Classroom clickers also only allow for place-based participation, meaning all respondents need to be in the same location.

Fortunately for teachers who incorporate cell phones into instruction there are services like Poll Everywhere and TextTheMob, which serve not only as student response systems, but also provide educators with a terrific alternative to the direct-to-phone text. Instead all texts can be collected in one place. These services provide students with a simple method to share their ideas right from their phones. Teachers can set up various free text polls to gather information from students and keep the responses private or make them public. Educators can view individual student answers in their web browser or download them as a spreadsheet. They can then import answers into course management systems such as Blackboard WebCT or Moodle. Student identity can be established with a simple device registration process in which students enter their user name and the link to all future answers is established. See Chapter One for instructions on getting started with Poll Everywhere or TextTheMob.

Ideas for Using a Classroom Response System with Students

- Set up a homework help poll for a particular assignment or unit of study. Students can simply text in the questions when they have them. This could set the stage beautifully for the next day's lesson enabling the teacher to differentiate instruction based on student need.

- Have students respond to a discussion topic. The teacher shares the topic and students text in their answers to be viewed publicly or privately by the teacher.

- Of course, what these services do better than the rest is polls. Need to do a quick check for understanding? Poll your students. Want them to vote on a favorite character in a book? Poll your students. Collecting data on a science experiment? Poll your students. Student response services provide educators with the ability to know what all their students are thinking at anytime and works great as a pre- and postassessment quizzing tool.

CHACHA

Imagine having an expert to turn to at any time for information, advice, and guidance . . . for free! That's ChaCha, an amazing service that will become invaluable to students. As their website says, "ChaCha is like having a smart friend you can call or text for answers on your cell phone anytime for free!" (http://answers.chacha.com/about-chacha/).

ChaCha, which works on any cell phone, enables students to ask any question and receive an answer from a live person with the source cited in just a few minutes. You'll want to discuss with students the importance of confirming that their information is accurate, just as they'd do with any search. Also as with all search engine providers, ChaCha is funded by advertising. Tech-savvy students live in an age when advertisements surround them on screens, newspapers, billboards, and so on. Whether using laptops, televisions, or cell phones, it is a good idea to support students in being savvy consumers.

How to Get Started with ChaCha

- Enter 242242 (or ChaCha) into your phone or call 1-800-2ChaCha (800-224-2242) from your mobile phone.
- Text or call with your question to ChaCha.
- You will receive an answer in minutes that also cites the source and informs you who your guide is answering the question.
- You may want to ask your question more than once as different guides may use different sources and you'll receive different answers.

Ideas for Using ChaCha with Students

- Have all your students ask ChaCha questions about a topic being studied in class. Have them share their answers in whatever way you'd like, for example, on a discussion board about the topic, on sticky notes in the class, as tweets, and so on. Then have students try to guess what the question was for each answer. This is a fun and engaging way to review a unit. If students are in schools where cell phones are banned, this can be done outside of school. Just have students bring their answers with them to school on paper or submit them digitally.
- ChaCha is a great homework help aide. There are often times when students don't have someone around to help them with their homework. ChaCha solves this problem by connecting students to a free network of about 25,000 ChaCha guides. Although many households still do not have Internet access, most have at least one cell phone. ChaCha is an alternative resource for students who do not have access to the Internet at home.

Of course students should also be encouraged to create a personal learning and support network by "texting an expert" whom they know when they need information or assistance. Students can text parents, grandparents, friends, past teachers, and so on to discuss coursework, homework, and projects or simply access information and insight.

GOOGLE SMS

Google SMS is powerful! Even for students with a text-only plan, Google SMS provides students with much of the vast amount of knowledge and information formerly available to only those with the Internet. All they have to do is enter the number 466453, which spells the word *Google* on their phones. This is the code that unlocks the key to a world of knowledge for students who will now be able to use their phones to translate languages, convert currency, calculate, define words, find out what's going on in other parts of the world, and much, much more. If you have access to a laptop and projector, you can show students the features of Google SMS using a virtual phone that Google has set up online at www.google.com/mobile/default/sms.html. And if you haven't tried it yourself already, see Chapter One for instructions on how to get started with Google SMS.

Ideas for Using Google SMS with Students

- Have students create a guide to their local area. You may want to model this first by creating a guide to the immediate area around your school, then let students use this model to create a guide to another neighborhood such as their own block or that of a family member. Possible tools include "web snippets," "currency," "local," "translation," and "weather."

- Recommend that ELL and foreign language students use the "translate" tool when they come on a word they don't know.

- Recommend that students use the "define" or "web snippets" tools to look up a word or concept they don't know when reading.

TWITTER

Twitter provides a terrific way for teachers to get an unlimited stream of feedback from students over a period of time on any subject. But before you have students set up Twitter accounts, you should know that some schools may have policies against following your students on Twitter. That's okay. With tags, you don't need to follow your students and searches will only turn up tweets related to the topic you are exploring with your students. (See Chapter One for information about setting up your own Twitter account and using tags to identify your school.)

Ideas for Using Twitter with Students

- At Marta Valle High School they held an innovation fair to celebrate the innovative work teachers are doing with their students. Some students were selected as fair reporters. These students interviewed attendees with the question, "Please tell me in 140 characters or less what has impressed you most about what you've seen at our innovation fair." Students tweeted the responses using their school tag. The Twitter feed could be seen on monitors throughout the school using http://twitterfall.com and on their school website using an RSS (really simple syndication) feed. This provided a unique way to capture their school celebration publicly and offered recognition of the work students were doing in an exciting way that they could share with their parents.

- Have students tweet to capture reflections during field trips. (Even if you're in a school where cell phones are banned, you may still be able to have students bring them on field trips. If that is not allowed, they might be able to use the chaperones' devices.) Rather than have students take notes on paper as they walk around, have them tweet their reflections. You can set up a tag for your tweets if the place you are visiting doesn't already have one. Give parents the feed and they'll instantly know what their child did at school today and can have robust conversations about it. When students are back at home or school a review of the tweets could lead to powerful conversation or could serve as a launch for further study. For example, pick the most interesting tweet or set of tweets and create something to share with others about the topic. This could be a podcast, video, blog post, and so on. These digital creations can all be posted in one place as a reflection collection and even shared on the website of the school and place visited.

- Have students do a daily or weekly tweet. Will Richardson (2009) shares some great possibilities that could be used in a daily tweet: What did you teach others? What unanswered questions are you struggling with? How did you change the world in some small (or big) way? What's something your teachers learned today? What did you share with the world? Not only is this a great way for teachers to have a sense of what is going on with their students, but it also provides students with a way to connect with each other and their parents.

- Give your students a voice in their own education by having them respond to class lectures using Twitter. Texas educator Dr. Monica Rankin has had a tremendous amount of success with this and noted how much more engaged students were during lessons and how they were able to make meaning in new ways. Watch a video on how this worked at http://tinyurl.com/TwitterinEdVideo.

TEXTNOVEL

Few students are given the opportunity to write for a real audience. Sadly, the A+ only has an audience of one (the teacher) or some (teacher + classmates + maybe family), and the

B- is not given much chance to improve. Textnovel can change that. Textnovel is a social network for authors and readers of serial fiction and allows users to write and read fiction with their cell phones or computers, e-mail, online tools, and MMS text message. This is a multimedia message, the same you would use to send a photo. Some carriers require a data plan to send this kind of message. Make sure to check if there are charges for sending data—there might be.

Textnovel runs contests for fiction writers, allowing them to demonstrate the market potential of their work through its unique serial publication and voting format. You have to be thirteen to enter their contests. The novels are rated (G, PG, PG-13, and R). Illustrations can also be uploaded. There are many settings to customize the experience and make it fit for your students.

Safety note: You should have parent permission for student use of this site and it is recommended only for older high school students. As with many web-based sites, teachers and parents should ensure they feel students can be trusted to use the site appropriately because there is some R-rated material that can be accessed much like content that can be accessed through YouTube or via an image search. Educators and parents will need to decide if they feel comfortable entrusting students with control for appropriate use and discuss what is acceptable and what consequences are in advance of using sites such as this. Empowering students under the supervision of a caring adult often results in favorable outcomes.

How to Get Started with Textnovel

- Go to the Textnovel home page (www.Textnovel.com) and sign up. Include your cell phone number.
- Wait for the confirmation e-mail and click on the link.
- You are set up to log in and begin.
- Familiarize yourself with all of the settings and choose the ones you want for your students prior to walking them through the set-up to create their own accounts
- When the students create their novel make sure they set it to a G rating and that they create a pen name.
  - You will want to be aware of your school policy around supporting students with an authentic and purposeful digital footprint. If students have permission for their work to be authentic and celebrated, they will likely want to use their real names. If the school has a policy against students using their real name or the student or

parent has not agreed to using their real name, an appropriate pen name can be selected.

- To start or add sections to the story, enter the e-mail address add@textnovel.com to your cell phone contacts. Type your story text into the body of the text message. The subject of the text message should be of the following format: storycode:chapter number. So for example if the story code is 12 and the chapter number is 2, then the subject should be 12:2.

Ideas for Using Textnovel with Students

- Encourage exploration of various styles and authors.
- Challenge students to create a novel of their own.
- Create a book group using one of the Textnovel novels. To get story updates by text or e-mail, readers subscribe to the story then follow the link in the text or e-mail from your cell phone to the story update. This works best with browser-enabled cell phones, but for students without such phones, a group member can copy and paste the story as text to classmates in need individually or as a group text.

WIFFITI

Wiffiti (http://wiffiti.com) allows students to submit an anonymous text message to an online bulletin board. The board can be used to display student responses to a question or just be a place to express ideas on a particular topic. Wiffiti publishes real-time messages to live screens anywhere on any screen. The teacher simply makes a screen with the question or topic posted. Students text in their answers to the code that corresponds to the screen and the responses instantly appear usually on the teacher's laptop connected to a projector, but depending on the assignment, the Wiffiti board may be embedded onto a teacher's website or blog corresponding to a particular topic or unit of study. Capturing all students' ideas in an instant can serve as a tremendously powerful educational tool. Before starting, have students share their ideas regarding appropriate use and consequences.

How to Get Started

Connect to Wiffiti with Facebook or simply go to http://wiffiti.com, select "make a screen," and enter your polling question. You will receive a special @Wif code to send to parents asking them to share by texting to Wiffiti. If you chose to set up an account it is free and all of your screens will be saved to your account.

Ideas for Using Wiffiti with Students

- Have students share how they think a story might end.
- Have students share what they'd like to know about a particular topic.
- Have students share what they already know about a topic.
- At the conclusion of a unit, have students share what they have learned as a summary activity.

PHONECASTING

Innovative educators know that using the tools students love is a sure-fire way to engage twenty-first-century learners but podcasting, purchasing, and using all the fancy equipment and software with students can be a turn off. That's why phonecasting is so great. Phonecasting provides the ability to easily create and capture an audio broadcast from your phone that can be published and shared anywhere. Ipadio is currently one such option for recording audio from a phone. (See Chapter One for instructions on setting up an ipadio account.) You can either create one account for the whole class or students can have their own accounts.

Ideas for Using Phonecasting with Students

- Have students interview leaders. Paul Bogush, a social studies teacher at a middle school in Connecticut, started a group with his students called "Lunchtime Leaders," in which students interview leaders on their opinions about what students should do to be prepared for the future. It started in fall 2008 when he and his students decided to interview all the candidates who were running for mayor in their city. When they were done they decided to keep the project going and found more people to interview. They are called the Lunchtime Leaders because they interview the guests during their lunch period, which means that they have to start and finish within twenty minutes.
- Although Paul and his students do most of their interviews using Skype and fancy equipment, students can start their own project easily using phonecasting. A service such as ipadio makes this easy to do as long as your phone has conference or three-way calling

ability. Just have the interviewee on the line, then dial ipadio for your phonecast. The simplicity of phonecasting is traded with a reduction in quality but this is fine for most projects in general and in particular for teachers and students new to this work. You can listen to the Lunchtime Leaders podcasts at http://lunchtimeleaders.podbean.com.

- Use phone casting to get to know your students. At the start of the year, reach out to parents and students and ask them to make an "All About Me" phonecast. These can be placed on an "All About Our Class" page of the teacher's website, wiki, or other online space. The teacher will likely want to guide the parents and students with suggestions for what they may consider including in the phonecast, such as "What are you most proud of?" "What do you generally do on weekends?" "What are you passionate about and how are you pursuing that passion?" "What do you stand for?" "What can or have you done to make the world a better place?"

- Let students create a weekly phonecast featuring their school. This not only helps build the home-school connection, but it also provides students with the opportunity to showcase great things that are happening at the school. Phonecasts could include student of the week, teacher of the week, project of the week, event of the week . . . you get the picture. What a great way to not only celebrate the school community and build school pride, but also to highlight the people, events, and projects that rarely are featured. If the school has a newspaper, this can serve as a great companion.

- Publish student ideas about important topics. Students love video and audio but we don't always want to show their faces for safety reasons. Phonecasts are perfect for this and the use of cell phone increases engagement. Lydia Leimbach used phonecasting with her secondary students in Farmingdale, Maine, as part of a cyberbullying project. After a quick Poll Everywhere survey she found if given the choice, students preferred hearing or watching information on this topic so Lydia used phonecasting to get their message out. She limited their time, encouraging them to be concise and also making sure each sentence was information laden. From there the phonecasts could be both embedded on the class cyberbullying page as well as the student's own web page.

- Help struggling writers create drafts. Have struggling writers create phonecasts with ipadio by telling their story right into a cell phone. Not only will they be able to hear their story back but ipadio does voice-to-text conversion. Remind the students to speak loudly and clearly, then dial ipadio and input your personal ID number. After the students record their stories, ipadio does the rest by converting their spoken words into written ones. From there, the story can be copied and pasted into a word processing document for final revisions and editing.

VOKI

Voki is a terrific way to enable your students to share a message using an animated avatar that talks with the student's own voice recorded right from a phone. Students design their avatar's appearance, add their voice, and can pop it into any Web 2.0 compatible site (wikis, blogs, Facebook, websites). The avatars then move and speak based on what they say into their phone. Vokis are a great way to enable students to publish their work safely because the avatars are nameless. However, you should still remind your students that they shouldn't share their name or other personal information in their Voki messages.

How to Get Started with Voki

- Register at www.voki.com and enter your e-mail address and password.
- Select "create."
- Select a character.
- Select the look, clothing, and accessories for your character.
- Add your own voice by calling the number Voki provides or have Voki call your number by entering it.
- Choose a background from the Voki library or upload your own.
- Click "publish" to e-mail to a friend or get a code to take your Voki avatar anywhere.

Ideas for Using Voki with Students

- Jim McDermott, an educational technology administrator in New York City, suggests using Voki in the review and proofing stages of the writing process, which is often skipped over. The Voki avatar can increase interest in this phase, give students another lens through which they can review their writing, sharpen their speaking and listening skills, and add another creative outlet for displaying their work in their digital portfolios.
- John Natuzzi, a technology coach in New York's Chinatown, noticed that many students, including special education, ELL, and even regular education students were uncomfortable reading their work aloud to the class. Thanks to Voki, these students

were able to present their work through the use of an online customizable avatar. The finished Vokis were embedded in both the school's and student's online space.

- Technology innovation expert Allison Sciandra from Staten Island, New York, shares that some of the technology liaisons she works with help their teachers use Voki to support the comprehension of ELL students who need to hear the patterns of the spoken word to help with fluency. The students and teachers loved using Voki and found it to be a great tool to practice speaking and improve understanding and fluency in English.

TEXT MESSAGES FOR PRELESSON, POSTLESSON, AND HANDS-ON LESSON ENHANCEMENTS AND ASSESSMENTS

We began this chapter with some basic ideas for using texting with your students. In this section, we build on those ideas and combine student texts with some of the tools you were introduced to in this chapter, such as polling and free-text response. Text messaging may aid student motivation and save time when used in conjunction with what you are already doing that works. Once your thinking is completely open to using cell phones as part of your teaching, you will quickly see how they make some of our best practices more doable in the amount of time we have. In fact, cell phones will increase the amount of time you have to teach students in class by allowing formative assessments and postlesson enhancements and assessments to happen outside of class. For example, instead of starting your class period with a question, problem, or thought of the day written on the board for students to respond to, you can have already completed this beneficial practice before class with a group text. Instead of making copies of homework worksheets, chapter reviews, or take-home problems, just blast a few text questions each day that students can answer by text. Depending on the assignment, the answers can be compiled in places like Poll Everywhere, Wiffiti, in a Voki, on Google Voice, or just locally on the student's phone for reference later and discussion in class. A quick review of the answers and you'll know who needs remediation and who is ready to move forward.

This is usually easier said than done in diverse classrooms that are often short on time with a lot to cover. Using text messaging makes it possible. Tables 2.3 and 2.4 provide activities intended to act as a springboard for your own thinking about how text messaging can create those effective lesson sandwiches. These ideas are nothing new and are often assigned during class as homework; however, giving them in a text earlier or later in the day makes it more fun, more timely, and more relevant.

Table 2.3
Prelesson Activities

Best Teaching Practice	Example Text Message
Formative assessments	*What do u know about frogs?* *Explain friction.*
Key vocabulary word preview	*2day we will learn: legislative, executive, judicial*
Concepts inventory	*What do u know about the Battle of Bunker Hill?* *When u get to class list all u know about cells.*
Complete the phrase	*The ending of the book should be . . .* *Freedom is . . .* *A development in our community was . . .*
Writing prompts	*There needs to be a law to . . .* *Describe your favorite character.* *Start poetically thinking about the rain.*
Question	*What supports our bodies?* *Who has the power to veto?* *What is a preposition?*
Inquiry	*Form a question regarding socialism.* *Ask something about the parts of the human eye.*
Schema activation	*What do u know about trees?* *Have u ever skipped a rock?*
Reflect	*Did learning about behaviorism make sense to u?* *How has it happened in ur life?*

HANDS-ON ACTIVITIES

Haury and Rillero (1994) state that hands-on learning benefits "include increased learning; increased motivation to learn; increased enjoyment of learning; increased skill proficiency, including communication skills; increased independent thinking and decision making based on direct evidence and experiences; and increased perception and creativity." The following example text messages show some ways teachers can engage students in hands-on learning outside of the classroom through the use of cell phone technologies:

Table 2.4
Postlesson Activities

Best Teaching Practice	Example Text Message
Assessment and checking for understanding	*List the main ideas of chapter 5.* *Solve for x: 2x + 5 = 28* *Define refraction.*
Evaluate	*What was the most important part?* *Do u feel Piaget made a difference?* *How will this help u?*
Connect	*Have you ever been scared?* *What part of this war affected ur life today?* *Do u ever pollute?*
Metacognition	*What were u thinking in 2days experiment?* *What did u think about Romeos choice?* *Ask me a question.* *Frogs, what ru thinking?*
Reflect	*What did u learn 2day?* *Should Gulliver stay?* *Name the most impt part.* *Define a word u learned 2day.* *Does the environment matter?*
Question	*What do hydrogen and oxygen make?* *What is pi?* *Why did it end that way?* *How should the experiment come out?* *Why did we fight?*
Review	*Tell me about George Washington.* *Name the parts of the heart.* *Imagine u in the story, what ru doing?*
Summarize	*Give me 3 words to describe today's lesson.* *Write a poem about today's topic.* *Bring in a paragraph summary.*
Feedback	*Did the lab help?* *What could we write about now?* *How was the powerpoint?* *Is there a website that would help?*

Find an example of a simple element, text in the name, or take a pic.

Find or make a simple compound, text in the name, or take a pic.

Have someone video u doing 10 jumping jacks or take a pic.

Use fractions to cook. What were they? Take a pic of the recipe.

Interview an adult about a recent dream, summarize it in a text.

Look at the sky, name the cloud types in your notepad.

Write a thank you note via text message.

Read ur shampoo label. Text in the main ingredients.

Measure ur doorway and text two friends. Are theirs the same or different?

Ask someone about todays news.

Watch sports and list the numbers used.

Text a classmate a review question from chpt 2.

Ask three classmates what a participle is.

Plan a trip to Alaska for March 15–30. Text back ur itinerary.

Put all of the deadlines in our syllabus into your phone calendar.

USING THE BILLION PLUS DEVICES STUDENTS AND TEACHERS ALREADY OWN TO ENHANCE INSTRUCTION

Marc Prensky, the thought leader credited for coining the term *digital natives,* advises that it's time we begin thinking of our cell phones as computers—even more powerful in some ways than their bigger cousins (Prensky, 2004). He brings to light the fact that today's high-end cell phones have the computing power of a mid-1990s PC (while consuming only one one-hundredth of the energy) and shares that even the simplest, voice-only phones have more complex and powerful chips than the 1969 on-board computer that landed a spaceship on the moon! Our students deserve nothing less than for their teachers to embrace the power of this technology and support them in becoming learners who can soar to new heights.

TEXTING LEARNER RESOURCES QUICK GUIDE

Table 2.5 provides a quick guide to the sites mentioned in this chapter that will help get you on the road to begin incorporating cell phones into learning.

Table 2.5
Learner Resources Quick Guide

Topic	Resource	URL
Texting abbreviations	Lingo2Word	www.lingo2word.com/index.php
Emoticons guide	Sharpened.net	www.sharpened.net/glossary/emoticons.php
Group texting	WeTxt	www.wetxt.com
Online notes via text	WeTxt Notebook	www.wetxt.com to start and www.wetxt.com/index.cgi?nav=service&srv=notebook once you are logged in
Capture and archive voice and text messages. Translate voice to text.	Google Voice	www.google.com/voice
Audience response systems	Poll Everywhere TextTheMob	www.polleverywhere.com http://textthemob.com
Questions and answers powered by people	ChaCha	www.chacha.com Text: 242242
Google text message search query	Google SMS	www.google.com/mobile/default/sms.html
Connect with others about what's happening	Twitter	www.twitter.com Text: 646646
A cell phone novel social network website for authors and readers of serial fiction	Text Novel	www.textnovel.com
Publish real-time messages from digital bulletin boards from your computer	Wiffiti	http://wiffiti.com
Phonecasting (podcasting from your phone)	ipadio	http://ipadio.com
Talking digital avatar	Voki	www.voki.com

Supporting Research-Based Instructional Strategies Using Cell Phones

> *The nine categories of instructional strategies are "best bets" for developing twenty-first-century learners.*
> Ceri Dean, Elizabeth Hubbell, Howard Pitler, and Bj Stone, authors of the second edition of *Classroom Instruction That Works* (2012)

As you read in Chapters One and Two, there are a variety of free and easy ways to enrich instruction and engage learners using basic cell phones. However, because the idea of using a cell phone as a learning tool rather than a social tool is so new, teachers often need justification to support incorporating such tools into the classroom. Showing how cell phones can be used to enrich instruction, engage learners using research-based instructional strategies, and enhance the classroom practices you already are using can convince administration, parents, and guardians that incorporating cell phones into instruction makes sense. The original *Classroom Instruction That Works* (Marzano, Pickering, & Pollock, 2001) outlines nine instructional strategies that most likely will improve student achievement across all content areas and across all grade levels. The second edition of *Classroom Instruction That Works* (Dean, Hubbell, Pitler, & Stone, 2012) confirms the value of the nine research-based strategies and provides an overview of teaching and learning in the twenty-first century. Educators interested in deepening their understanding of using research-based strategies to increase student achievement will find these strategies of great value.

In this chapter we suggest lessons using the resources introduced in previous chapters and show ways how cell phone technologies might support and enhance each of the research-based strategies identified in *Classroom Instruction That Works*. For more detailed discussion, the actual research base, and step-by-step instruction on the strategies, please refer to the second edition of *Classroom Instruction that Works* (Dean, Hubbell, Pitler, & Stone, 2012).

You will also see ways to enrich your personal, effective strategies. In schools where cell phones are banned, these activities can be done as part of student's homework. Schools that empower teachers to allow students to use their own technology can do these activities inside or outside of the classroom. Whether employed inside or outside of school, these strategies can be used as a review, a springboard, or both. Using cell phones to support these effective teaching strategies will provide an engaging learning experience for students. The strategies are as follows:

Creating an Environment for Learning

- Setting objectives and providing feedback
- Reinforcing effort and providing recognition
- Cooperative learning

Helping Students Develop Understanding

- Cues, questions, and advance organizers
- Nonlinguistic representations
- Summarizing and note taking
- Homework and practice

Helping Students Extend and Apply Knowledge

- Identifying similarities and differences
- Generating and testing hypotheses

USING CELL PHONES FOR SETTING OBJECTIVES AND PROVIDING FEEDBACK

Dean, Hubbell, Pitler, and Stone (2012) state that "when teachers identify and communicate clear learning objectives, they send the message that there is a focus for the learning activities to come. This reassures students that there is a reason for learning and provides teachers with a focal point for planning instruction." Students gain a direction for study and knowledge about how they learn, which are effective instructional tools. "Providing feedback specific to learning objectives helps students improve their performance and solidify their understanding." Here are some ways that setting objectives and providing feedback can be enriched with the use of cell phones.

Classroom Practice in Setting Objectives

According to Dean, Hubbell, Pitler, and Stone (2012), learning objectives should be specific, but not restrictive, communicated to students and parents, and connected to present and future learning. Additionally, they feel that students should be encouraged to set personal learning objectives. Teachers provide general targets or lesson objectives and the students personalize them according to their interests, skills, and desires. The following lesson outlines how allowing students the privacy of setting personal goals (within the context of the overall lesson goals) on their cell phones, helped by the anonymity of the Wiffiti page, is a way that cell phones can enhance the goal-setting process and make lessons more motivating, personal, and meaningful for students.

Subject
Science

Topic
The human body

Preparation

After setting up a Wiffiti account (see Chapter Two) make a screen that reads "I want to know . . ." and a screen that reads "I want to know more about . . ." Share the code to text with the students.

Lesson Overview

Provide general targets for students: learn the major organs of the body, learn how they work, learn how they work together as a system. You may want to tell the students the major organs. Ask students to personalize your learning targets by setting personal goals for the unit. All students develop their personal learning goals for which you provide the sentence starters: "I want to know . . . and "I want to know more about . . ."

To do this, ask the students to text their personal learning goals to the Wiffiti bulletin board you have created for the class. This instantly enables you and the class to see the type of personal learning goals students have. The value for students is (1) they may learn from their classmates new ideas to incorporate or ideas to modify and (2) they may want to partner up with other students who share similar learning goals. The value for you is that you can instantly get a big-picture view of your class's learning goals and also instantly see goals that may need modification.

Near the close of the unit you can set up a second Wiffiti board where students can share what they learned in relation to their learning goals. Students with similar goals should be encouraged to partner to share their answers. Not only is this beneficial in recognizing the learning of the class, but it also serves as a fantastic review of the unit and can provide a great discussion prior to the end-of-unit assessment.

How Technology Enriches This Lesson

- Posting learning goals to a Wiffiti board shares learning goals across the class and also is a great resource to share with parents and guardians at the start of a unit.

- Sharing learning outcomes on a Wiffiti board provides a great way to help the students review what they learned as a class in the unit and also is a terrific resource to share with parents and guardians at the end of a unit so they are filled in on their child's learning.

- There are no papers to collect and you can see all student goals and learning at a glance.

- The students can easily learn from one another. Learning is no longer contained only within each student.

Classroom Practice in Providing Feedback

Students expect to get feedback on their work. Although in traditional classrooms this has typically come from the teacher, feedback from peers is also beneficial provided there has been a discussion of what constitutes good feedback. "Providing students with feedback that is corrective, timely, and focused on criteria, and involving them in the feedback process creates a classroom environment that fosters and supports learning (Dean, Hubbell, Pitler, & Stone, 2012). The following lesson outline models how cell phones can be used when employing this strategy.

CELL PHONE TOOL: VOKI

Subject
Social studies

Topic
Women's studies, civics, public speaking

Preparation
Set up a class Voki account (see Chapter Two) using your class e-mail that all students can access. Give students the class account user name and password. Have students work in pairs or groups. One student in each group will need time with an Internet-enabled laptop at some time during the lesson (at school or home) to select and design the group's Voki. Another student will be responsible for writing the speech, and another for recording the speech to Voki using a cell phone. The student with laptop access will set up a time for the Voki to record the student giving the speech by clicking on the phone icon and entering the classmate's phone number. If this occurs after school students with access to a laptop will need to schedule a time with their classmates. The

teacher will also need to have or develop a persuasive speech rubric to use with the class for assessment.

Lesson Overview

This lesson focuses on famous historical women and uses Vokis to engage students. Students will work in groups and select one figure they've studied as a part of women's history. Students will discuss how the selected historical figure might have run for class president if she were a student in their school. Students will discuss current issues in their school and class and think about how the facts they know about their selected figure would have influenced her campaign and what her class president speech might include. Students will create a Voki and use their cell phones to record their voice.

Vokis provide a perfect tool for feedback because they are designed so that others can comment. In this lesson students, guided by the persuasive speech rubric, will be asked to provide feedback on their own group's Voki (self-reflection), as well as feedback on the Vokis of others groups (peer review). Ultimately the teacher will also provide feedback on each group's Voki. Students will have an opportunity to rerecord their Voki based on the feedback they received. All Vokis will be placed on the page of an online space of your choosing, such as a website, blog, wiki, or learning management system.

When all students have completed their projects, students will have the opportunity to listen to additional candidates and can comment on additional Vokis. On election day, students will use the secret ballot method to vote for their top candidate, though no group may vote for themselves.

How Technology Enriches This Lesson

- Using a Voki provides a ready-to-go mechanism for students to provide reflective feedback on themselves and to gather review from their peers. What's nice about this is it can be done anytime, anywhere the students are ready to call Voki and enter the passcode associated with their Voki or comment.

- Using a Voki provides a one-stop option for teachers to listen to all students' ideas, reflections, and peer review in one place.

- Voki enables interested parties to access the information anytime, anywhere, and respond. Inviting relevant stakeholders to the site and encouraging them to comment will provide a meaningful experience for students.

- The Voki page provides a strong home-school communication. It provides parents with a peek into what is going on in the classroom as well as what their students and others are doing. On completion of the project, student's work can be shared and parents can be given guidelines and encouraged to comment.

USING CELL PHONES TO REINFORCE EFFORT AND PROVIDE RECOGNITION

Reinforcing effort and providing recognition are instructional techniques that address students' attitudes, beliefs, and motivation. When teachers reinforce effort, they are teaching students that there is a connection between trying and succeeding. By recognizing their efforts and acknowledging when they reach goals, teachers support students to continue, complete, and learn (Dean, Hubbell, Pitler, & Stone, 2012). Here are some ways that reinforcing effort and providing recognition can be enriched with cell phones.

Classroom Practice in Reinforcing Effort: Teaching About Effort

You can share stories of famous people who succeeded through effort or ask students to think about and share their own stories of succeeding after trying something repeatedly. Such examples and personal stories are an effective way to help students understand the importance of effort. The following lesson outline models how cell phones can be used when employing this strategy.

CELL PHONE TOOL: VOKI

Subject
Language arts

Topic
Memoir

Preparation

Set up a Voki account (see Chapter Two). Input the student's number into the Voki account so that students can use their phones to record their Vokis. If this is being done outside of school, you will need to let students know approximately what time to expect the call.

Lesson Overview

In this lesson students will use Voki to record their voice via telephone to share a short personal story about a time when they or someone they know accomplished something important because they didn't give up. These will all be embedded on the class website, blog, or wiki. Each story will be titled and students will be asked to provide a Voki comment on the stories of others that touched them.

How Technology Enriches This Lesson

- Technology enriches this lesson over traditional methods because it puts the entire class's inspirational stories in one convenient place. Students will have the opportunity to learn a little more about one another as a result.

- Vokis provide the option to comment on other students' work, which can help to elicit conversation that does not generally happen when students hand assignments in to a teacher, even when those assignments get posted in the classroom or on a bulletin board.

- Creating an "effort" page for a class provides the teacher and school with material that can be shared and celebrated with parents and the community. It is also can be used on parent-teacher night when waiting parents can look at this work from the class. During parent conferences, this story can serve as a nice common ground for the teacher and parent.

- Using a Voki to capture a verbal story can be an effective option for English language learners and students with special needs. It allows them to convey a story as they would naturally speak and they can record the story as often as they want if they don't get it right the first time. Additionally, they can do the recording privately so those who are shy don't have to be concerned with speaking in front of others.

Classroom Practice in Keeping Track of Effort and Achievement

It is powerful to help students make the connection between effort and achievement. "Once students are clear about what it means to expend effort, teachers can ask them to track their effort in relation to their achievement" (Dean, Hubbell, Pitler, & Stone, 2012). This can be done by using an effort and achievement rubric that ranks each on a scale of 4 (excellent) to 1 (unacceptable). The following lesson outline models how cell phones can be used when employing this strategy.

CELL PHONE TOOL: STUDENT RESPONSE SERVICE— POLLING QUESTION

Subject
Any subject

Topic
Any topic

Preparation
Set up an account in a polling service and create a poll for each student or for the class as indicated in the following. Share the polling response number to which students should text their responses. Student responses are instantly visible on the teacher's poll.

Lesson Overview
Cell phones can be powerful tools to support students in seeing the relationship between effort and achievement during a project or within a particular unit of study at school using a poll as shown in the following rubric. Another option is to create the rubric with students, perhaps even in text lingo.

How Did You Work?
Scale: 4 = excellent; 3 = good; 2 = needs improvement; 1 = unacceptable

A: Effort	B: Achievement
4 I worked until done, pushed harder when it got hard, and thought the challenge would help me learn better.	4 I accomplished and learned more than I needed to.

A: Effort	B: Achievement
3 I worked until I was done even when it was hard or I wasn't sure of the answer at first.	3 I learned what I was supposed to. It helped me to learn better.
2 I tried, but stopped when it got hard or I couldn't find the answer or what to do next.	2 I got some of it, but not all.
1 I really didn't try.	1 I did not get it.

This could be set up in two ways depending on your preference. One way is that you can have an effort rubric and achievement rubric for the entire class on one page. This could foster some competition and enable students to see the effect on effort and achievement not only in themselves, but also in others. The other option is to set up a page for each student that enables students to see just the correlation between their own effort and achievement across the year. By setting this up as a poll, you and the student can see an instant graphic representation.

How Technology Enriches This Lesson

- Using a polling tool with SMS (short message service) texting technology provides a fast and easy anytime, anywhere method for students to instantly log results.

- A digital poll provides an instant graphic representation that may make it easier for viewers to see the correlation between effort and achievement.

- Placing the results from the class in an online forum can create a sense of accountability to increase effort. (*Note:* The pages can be kept as visible as the teachers wishes, such as only to students, to students and parents, or it can be public.)

Classroom Practice in Providing Recognition

Providing recognition enhances achievement and stimulates motivation. Recognition that "promotes a mastery-goal orientation, provides praise that is specific and aligned with expected performances and behaviors, and uses concrete symbols" is most effective (Dean, Hubbell, Pitler, & Stone, 2012). It is better to acknowledge learning and achieving goals than to compare students. Thus, students know what they need to do to succeed. The following lesson outline models how cell phones can be used when employing this strategy.

CELL PHONE TOOL: WIFFITI

Subject
English language arts

Topic
Standardized test preparation

Preparation
After setting up a Wiffiti account (see Chapter Two) make a screen with a name aligned with your lesson. Share the code to text with your students.

Lesson Overview
Once you have set specific and measurable goals for your students, you can use a Wiffiti digital bulletin board to capture personal and concrete recognition of your students. For example, if your school was measuring progress on ELA (English language arts) test scores, you could set up a bulletin board and name it something like "Watch Us Soar on the ELA Test," then write a Wiffiti update celebrating the students making progress on practice tests and indicate the strategy they use to succeed. For example you may post something like, "Angel is having success with the FUN (*find, underline, number*) method to better understand his reading passages!" You can set the account up so only you contribute or you can invite students and parents and guardians to contribute.

How Technology Enriches This Lesson

- Using a resource such as Wiffiti provides a forum for students to be recognized and celebrated in a way that can be shared with the school community and beyond.

- This lesson can empower various stakeholders (teachers, leaders, parents, guardians, students) to recognize the accomplishments of students.

USING CELL PHONES FOR COOPERATIVE LEARNING

Cooperative learning groups prepare students for the workplace and support content learning. As one of the most theoretically grounded instructional strategies, cooperative learning "helps teachers lay the foundations for students' success in a world that depends on collaboration and cooperation" (Dean, Hubbell, Pitler, & Stone, 2012). The recommendations for classroom practice using cooperative learning provided by Dean, Hubbell, Pitler, and Stone (2012) are to "include the elements of positive interdependence and individual accountability, keep group size to three, four, or five, and use cooperative learning consistently and systematically." In classes where not all students have phones, grouping is a researched-based, effective practice to use that makes cell phone technologies available for all.

Classroom Practice: Informal Groups

Varying the types of groups will keep students engaged. One of Johnson and Johnson's (2009) group type is informal, such as pair-share or turn-to-your-neighbor, which are short, lasting only a few minutes or a class period. In a classroom where cell phones are used, these types of groups could be formed quickly at the end of class with the assignment to "text your partner the three main points from today's lesson" or "text a one-sentence reflection on the meaning of each poem read today" or "text your neighbor a math problem that will need to be solved by today's formula" or "text a vocabulary question to your partner; bring in each other's responses." Encouraging informal groups to continue communication is a matter of simply having students exchange numbers when they are paired. The following lesson outline models how cell phones can be used when employing this strategy.

CELL PHONE TOOL: TEXT MESSAGING, WIFFITI

Subject
English language arts

Topic
Common and proper nouns—capitalization

Preparation
Have classroom procedures and parent permissions in place that include the exchange of cell phone numbers by students. Set up a Wiffiti page entitled "Common and Proper Nouns" and share the code with the class. This assignment can be done as homework and the Wiffiti viewed in class with a laptop and projector.

Lesson Overview
After a lesson on the difference between common and proper nouns, pair up students. Give each pair the task of working on the assignment through texting. Student one texts student two a common noun. Student two texts back a proper noun (name) form of the common noun, making sure it is capitalized. (Students should be sure the common noun has a proper noun form.)

For example,

school can become *Lincoln Elementary School*

state can become *Wisconsin*

day can become *Tuesday*

girl can becomes *Melissa*

After two nouns they switch roles and student two texts common nouns to student one to be made into proper nouns. The pair can then text their lists to a Wiffiti board to be shared with the class.

How Technology Enriches This Lesson

- Because students enjoy and are used to texting, using cell phones facilitates informal group communication. Students who may not be comfortable talking to each other face-to-face or even calling each other on the phone in the evening will be able to complete the group task through texting.

- Through the ease of sending their lists to the Wiffiti board the entire class will benefit from seeing the many examples of common and proper nouns.

Classroom Practice: Formal Groups

When setting up formal groups, "ensure the students have enough time to thoroughly complete an academic assignment; therefore, they may last for several days or even weeks" (Dean, Hubbell, Pitler, & Stone, 2012). In formal groups, each member often has a specific role or job to complete. The following lesson outline models how cell phones can be used when employing this strategy.

CELL PHONE TOOL: GROUP TEXTING, STUDENT RESPONSE SERVICE—OPEN RESPONSE AND POLLING QUESTION

Subject
American history

Topic
Civil War generals

Preparation
Arrange students into groups giving each group member one of the following jobs: researcher(s), presenter(s), and technical advisor. Use a group texting service such as WeTxt for group communications. Set up each group as "reply-to-me" with the technical advisor as the manager. Set up an open response poll at www.polleverywhere.com for each of the groups. An open response poll allows students to share facts, thoughts, and answers rather than just vote as in the standard poll. Give the Poll Everywhere code to the group technical advisor. The open response poll will be the platform for the information about the

general assigned to each group. A voting poll with all of the generals' names will be set up for voting at the end of the lesson.

Lesson Overview

Each group will be assigned a Civil War general. The groups' task is to serve as the publicity team for their general. Their goal is to sell the class on their general. Their job is to do such an effective PR campaign via Poll Everywhere that their general is voted by the class as the "most important Civil War general."

The following describe the group roles and jobs:

- Researcher(s) find information on the Civil War general and text facts to the group.
- Presenter(s) write up the facts into selling points and text them to the open response poll for presentation to the class.
- Technical advisor shares codes, fields questions, and manages communications.

The researchers will find facts about the general and text them to the presenter(s). The presenters will collaborate on creating selling points to be added to their PR board (the open response poll). After the open response boards are complete and viewed by the entire class, the most important general poll can be done. The class can text in the code of the general of their choice. Students are assessed based on the research, presentation, and cooperative communication from the groups, not on which general wins in the poll. The communication of the members of the group can be viewed by the teacher in the WeTxt site.

How Technology Enriches This Lesson

- As the groups carry out their research, summarize, determine what to share on their open response board, and communicate about the merits of their general they will be learning group skills and content as well as the twenty-first-century skill of using technology to enhance their presentation.
- Open response boards are easily shared with the entire class and summarize the important information in a way that is fun to read.

- Each group learns about all of the generals as they are displayed on the open response board.

- The job of publicist and use of technology enhancements create a real-life feel to the project.

- Polling for a "winner" creates friendly competition to enhance motivation for learning and presenting content information.

Classroom Practice: Base Groups

Base groups are long-term groups set up to give support throughout the entire semester or year (Dean, Hubbell, Pitler, & Stone, 2012). Formally creating groups using WeTxt will facilitate the continuing efforts of the groups. The following lesson outline models how cell phones can be used when employing this strategy.

CELL PHONE TOOL: WETXT GROUPS, WETXT NOTEBOOK, GOOGLE SMS

Subject
English language arts

Topic
Spelling and vocabulary

Preparation
Have students form groups of about four to work in and choose a name. Set up WeTxt groups according to the names chosen. By selecting "reply-to-all" all group members can be reached with the ease of one text message. The members will experience each of the "jobs" (explained following) throughout the semester. A class-generated spelling and vocabulary list will be sent to each groups' WeTxt notebook number and compiled throughout the semester.

Lesson Overview
The jobs in the spelling groups are editor, researcher, and sentence writer. The first job, editor, is one all members perform. Within class, during the group time

(once per week), have the students trade writing and edit for spelling errors. The papers should go around the group two times to catch as many errors as possible. A central list of misspelled words is compiled by the group, then divided equally. The remainder of the groups' tasks will be completed outside of class using cell phone technologies. The members have one of two jobs: researcher or sentence writer. With "reply-to-all" the entire group will have input on the spelling of the word, the definition of the word, and the sentence chosen to represent that meaning.

- The researchers find the correct spelling and definition for their words. This can be done using a dictionary, a computer, a human resource, or a cell phone source such as Google SMS or ChaCha.
- The researchers then text the correct spelling and definitions to the sentence writers and to the WeTxt notebook number for their group.
- The sentence writers write a sentence using the word and text it back to the researchers. When the sentences are agreed on, the sentence writers text it to the WeTxt notebook.

The list is saved on the WeTxt website. The teacher views the notebook pages of each group and uses them to select a spelling and vocabulary list for that week. The next day the compiled list of group-generated words and sentences is shared with the class.

How Technology Enriches This Lesson

- By texting the information back and forth, students can communicate outside of class. Class time for group work is minimized and the benefits of group communication are maximized.
- Cell phone sources for word definitions can be used by busy students outside of class.
- The WeTxt notebook provides a running record of the groups' work.

Students most likely have more practice with group texting than any other strategy in this chapter. However, free conference calling is another benefit of having students use their phones. Most individuals in the business world today are familiar with the benefits of a conference call. When used in conjunction with learning objectives, conference calling is a wonderful means to encourage groups to work cooperatively. Students without phones could use landlines. Without additional planning for group work, educators can simply remind students of this feature and encourage them to use their phones in this way for group communication. This will model for them the benefits of conference calling and prepare them for their future.

USING CELL PHONES FOR CUES, QUESTIONS, AND ADVANCE ORGANIZERS

The research-supported idea of activating prior knowledge focuses on the use of cues, questions, and advance organizers. Cues, questions, and advance organizers are beneficial for showing the importance of material to be learned, motivate, spark interest, and build on curiosity (Dean, Hubbell, Pitler, & Stone, 2012). Cues give students a "heads up" about what they are going to learn. Questions encourage students to think about what they already know about what they are going to learn. These help students make connections. "Advance organizers are stories pictures, and other introductory materials that set the stage for learning" (Dean, Hubbell, Pitler, & Stone, 2012). With cell phones, teachers can text well-thought-out, higher level questions, explicit cues, and analytic questions to groups of students, individual students, or entire classes prior to the lesson, during the lesson, or after sufficient wait time after the lesson. Students can text responses back to the teacher, which can be captured in one place using a tool such as Wiffiti.

As with cues or questions, a description of new content can be sent to students through group texting in advance. When you want to describe the new content to which students are going to be exposed, you can text the main ideas prior to class. For example, you may want to text the new vocabulary in the upcoming science unit, short descriptions of what the class activity will be about, or the plot summary of the literature that will be read and studied in class.

Classroom Practice: Cues and Questions

Cues involve hints about what students are about to experience. Questions perform the same function of activating prior knowledge and getting students thinking about the information to come. Four recommendations for their use are to "focus on what is important, use explicit cues, use inferential questions, and use analytic questions" (Dean, Hubbell, Pitler, & Stone, 2012). The following lesson outline models how cell phones can be used when employing this strategy.

CELL PHONE TOOL: GROUP TEXTING AND OPEN RESPONSE

Subject
Speech

Topic
Persuasive techniques

Preparation
Set up the class in a group text service with your local provider or online alternative. Set up a Wiffiti account and select "make a screen" where you will enter the question or topic. Share the Wiffiti number, the response code, and the question with the class face-to-face or as a part of your text message to them. The responses will go to the Wiffiti page, which can be displayed with a laptop projector in class.

Lesson Overview
When a cue would be a benefit to the lesson, you can text it to the entire class with one message sent to the class name (as saved in your contacts list) the day before a lesson. All of the students will be able to start thinking about the topic, activating their prior knowledge. They will be ready to go when class begins.

An example is something like *2day we will watch a video on persuasive speech techniques, some of it u already know, some will b new.* Through the use of a texted question, you can activate prior knowledge and share it with the class prior to watching the film with a group texted question, *What do u know about how to be persuasive?* Include the Wiffiti number and response code in your text. Students can then text their response to a Wiffiti page. The entire class will be able to respond and benefit from the responses of others.

How Technology Enriches This Lesson

- Within a few seconds, the time it takes to send one text, all students will have the opportunity to get cued into what they are about to experience, process questions relating to the material being learned, and make inferences, analyze, and even critique the information presented to them.

- Even students who are absent will get the cue and begin the process.

- All students are allowed to answer.

- Wait time is built in.

- Class experience is expanded outside of class time.

- Questions and cues can be used prior to or immediately following the lessons in a timely manner.

Classroom Practice: Narrative Advance Organizers

Telling stories before a lesson that address the essential ideas of the lesson can make the lesson more personal and help students connect the learning with prior knowledge (Dean, Hubbell, Pitler, & Stone, 2012). The following lesson outline models how cell phones can be used when employing this strategy

CELL PHONE TOOL: GOOGLE VOICE

Subject
Science

Topic
Natural disasters

Preparation
Set up a Google Voice account as described in Chapter One and share your Google Voice number with your students.

Lesson Overview
In this lesson students will use Google Voice to record a narrative advance organizer in preparation for a science unit on natural disasters. Ask students to

share a story about an experience they or a family member had during a natural disaster. The student, friend, or family member can be the one to call in the story to the teacher's Google Voice number. Give the students clear directions on how to capture the story. For example, ask "What was the disaster?" "What was your location?" "Where specifically were you?" "What did you see, hear, smell?" "How did you feel?" and so on. The students should be asked to keep the stories short: no more than a minute. When the class comes back together they can listen to their classmate's stories noticing the particulars of each type of disaster. As they do this they should compile a list of questions and facts they want to check as they learn about natural disasters. Students will learn about this topic in science and also learn a lot more about each other, making this personal and relevant.

How Technology Enriches This Lesson

- Google Voice provides a simple way to capture all students' voices without taking class time to record or upload audio.

- You and the students don't need to worry about finding special recording equipment. All they need is a phone.

- Even absent students can share their stories.

Classroom Practice: Skimming

Students will benefit from skimming, or scanning, material before reading it, which can create a picture of what will be read and organizing it, providing a conceptual framework for building new learning (Dean, Hubbell, Pitler, & Stone, 2012). The short, 160-character, nature of text messaging makes it a great tool to use when skimming material, maps, charts, and so on. Students can add a note in their notepad section, text it into their WeTxt notebook, text it into their e-mails, or text to each other. Becoming familiar with new information by skimming can be aided by encouraging or even instructing students on how to use their cell phones when skimming new information. The following lesson outline models how cell phones can be used when employing this strategy.

CELL PHONE TOOL: CELL PHONE NOTEPAD, MEMO, WETXT NOTEBOOK, FLICKR

Subject
Social studies

Topic
Trading fort field trip

Preparation
Guide students in finding the notepad or memo tool found in most basic cell phones or set up students in WeTxt and provide the number for their online notebook as described in Chapter Two. Review students use of their cell phone cameras and safety, boundary, and privacy policies as needed. Create an e-mail in Flickr for the project as described in Chapter One.

Lesson Overview
For homework, prior to a field trip to a trading fort museum, ask students to read a selection on trading at the fort. Instruct students to skim the selection and put a list of the items that were most often traded in their cell phone notepad or memo. This gives students a feel for what they will be seeing at the fort. When students visit the fort, ask them to refer to the lists in their cell phones and indicate all the items they found by placing the number of times they saw the item next to the item on their phone. Have students search for the items in groups with an adult in each group ensuring they are accurately recording the number of items. Selected students with camera phones can also take pictures of the items and send them to the teacher-created Flickr e-mail address. When they send the pictures, they should put the item name in the subject line and the historical relevance in the message, which will become the photo caption. This will automatically become a slide show that can be reviewed and revised in the class and shared with the school community, parents, and family.

How Technology Enriches This Lesson

- Cell phones enable students to take the skimmed information with them in a device they already carry at all times.

- Students can enjoy the field trip without having to juggle pencil and paper.

- Pictures can be taken by just a few students and automatically compiled into a slide show with Flickr that can be shared with students and their families. No work for the teacher.

USING CELL PHONES FOR NONLINGUISTIC REPRESENTATIONS

The research-based strategy of nonlinguistic representations focuses on imagery as a means to how information is stored in memory. Dean, Hubbell, Pitler, and Stone (2012) discuss five nonlinguistic representation strategies, "creating graphic organizers, making physical models/manipulatives, generating mental pictures, drawing pictures/illustrations and pictographs, and engaging in kinesthetic activity." These are best used when students elaborate on, or add to, their knowledge, which can result in deeper understanding and better recall. You might text students a quote or excerpt from a reading (in any subject) and have them text back what they see in their imagination when they read it. They can use their cell camera to take a picture of what the paragraph describes and send it back as a picture message (visual representation) or they might call and record a voice description (physical sensation of sound). Because most new cell phones come with a camera and are able to send picture messages, our focus in this section is on using the pictorial capabilities of the cell phone. Many cell phones even record video, which is also a wonderful nonlinguistic enhancement incorporating both pictorial and kinesthetic activity. Elaboration of knowledge through cell phone technologies, such as sound and pictures, may increase student achievement.

Classroom Practice: Using Pictures

Most cell phones are equipped with a simple camera. With appropriate-use guidelines in place, picture-taking options can be a fun and creative way to enhance homework assignments and ensure that certain students get it done. The following lesson outline models how cell phones can be used when employing this strategy.

CELL PHONE TOOL: CELL PHONE CAMERA, PICTURE MESSAGING, FLICKR

Subject
Science

Topic
The human skeletal system

Preparation

Set up a class Flickr account. Flickr gives you an e-mail address to which pictures can be sent. Tell Flickr what tag should be associated with pictures sent to that e-mail by going to www.flickr.com/account/uploadbyemail. In this case you could use the tag "bones." Your tag will enable you to create a slide show with the pictures students submit that can be shared with a link to the URL as well as a code that can be embedded into any online space.

Lesson Overview

After learning the main bones of the human skeletal system, assign each student one of the bones you have studied. Then have each student take a picture of that particular bone on themselves or a classmate. They should then e-mail it to the class's Flickr account with the name of the bone in the subject line and something they noticed about the bone in the message. The subject line becomes the title and the message becomes the caption. For example, a student might take a picture of the thumb with *metacarpal* in the subject line and in the body say, *My favorite bone for texting.* Because you've set up the Flickr account so e-mailed photos have the tag "bones," these photos will all feed into one slide show of the class's collective knowledge of bones with actual photos that they captured.

How Technology Enriches This Lesson

- Students use their cell phone cameras to apply and expand their use of the content material. They take it off the page and into their world.

- Rather than relying on students' artistic abilities, cell phone cameras allow all students to represent learning pictorially.

- More fun than labeling a worksheet, students are using their preferred mode of communication to illustrate their learning.

Classroom Practice with Kinesthetic Activity

Many students love to get up and move around, yet often have little opportunity in the classroom setting. Yet, when students' movement is associated with specific knowledge, a mental image of the knowledge is generated, which can be done through role-play, acting, or using their bodies to show concepts (Dean, Hubbell, Pitler, & Stone, 2012). The following lesson outline models how cell phones can be used during a kinesthetic activity that provides students with a fun option to incorporate movement into learning.

CELL PHONE TOOL: VIDEO

Subject
Reading

Topic
Fiction

Preparation
This can only be done with a camera that has video capability. Select video and record on the phone then e-mail the video to the class Flickr account as described in the preceding human bone picture activity. Once all the videos are sent in they can be tagged and placed in the order of the story to be watched as one consecutive slide show.

Lesson Overview
In this lesson students get to turn their stories into movies with the use of a cell phone video camera. Even the acting out and capturing of stories on basic, unedited video can increase the knowledge and understanding of reading. Divide a piece of fiction that students are reading into sections or chapters. Let students know they will be forming groups to act out assigned parts of the reading. After the students have completed their reading, assign each group a part of the reading to act out. Give students time to practice their scene.

When students are ready, videos from each scene can be recorded using the video capability on the cell phone. These videos can be e-mailed to the class Flickr account with the videos tagged with the corresponding story name. When sending the video, remind students to indicate the section of the book they are acting out in the subject line and identify their group in the body of the e-mail as these will become the caption and description of each video. Depending on the policy for your class, you will want to determine if the videos should be kept public or private. If videos are made public, students can share their videos with others who are reading the story in their school or elsewhere.

How Technology Enriches This Lesson

- By acting out what they read students really have to work through ensuring they understand the vocabulary and concepts in their reading. Capturing this on video motivates the students to get it right.

- Watching the video provides the teacher with a means to get inside the student's heads to see if they really understand the material.

- Most students love the opportunity to be stars and they love to watch themselves and their peers on video. This lesson provides a fun way to motivate students to have a deeper understanding of the book than with just reading alone.

Classroom Practice: Sound

According to Dean, Hubbell, Pitler, and Stone (2012), "Teachers can facilitate students' construction of mental pictures by providing details that enable students to incorporate sounds, smells, tastes, and visual details as part of the mental picture." Activities using Google Voice, conference calling, phonecasting, or voice messages support learners in a nonlinguistic manner focused on sound. The following lesson outline models how cell phones can be used when employing this strategy.

CELL PHONE TOOL: PHONECASTING

Subject
Literature

Topic
Nature poetry

Preparation
Create a phonecasting account with a service such as ipadio as described in Chapter Two. Have students call into the number assigned to your phonecasting account.

Lesson Overview

Ask students who are studying nature poetry to select one poem about nature by a famous poet, such as "Patience Taught by Nature" by Elizabeth Barrett Browning, "Nature—the Gentlest Mother Is" by Emily Dickinson, or "Daffodils" by William Wordsworth. Have the students go outside, preferably to a park, zoo, or open, natural area and read the poem aloud. The next step is to write their own poem about the place they are experiencing and record it using a phonecasting service such as ipadio. All the recordings will be captured on your phonecasting page, and you, other students, and even parents and family can listen to and comment on the student's audio poems.

How Technology Enriches This Lesson

- Technology empowers students to capture the moment in sound and embrace their sensory awareness of the place.

- Students are able to express themselves through words that can be shared with individuals or the world by simply sending the link to whomever they feel would be interested or embedding it in their own online space or digital portfolio.

- Phones enable students to easily capture audio and the teacher doesn't have to worry about finding tape recorders or other electronic devices.

- Because ipadio allows comments, the poems become the source of conversation online that can lead to vibrant in-class discussion.

Cell phone cameras, video messaging capabilities, and sound are an option for teachers who lack the time, space, artistic supplies, or classroom control to encourage nonlinguistic efforts. Using cell phones with this strategy provides a fun, motivating way to enhance lessons that will likely build on your use of the other strategies in this chapter.

USING CELL PHONES TO SUMMARIZE AND TAKE NOTES

Summarizing and note taking promote greater comprehension by asking students to analyze a subject and determine what is most important and to share that information in a new way that makes sense given the task at hand. Summarizing involves working information down to its most important points so that it can be learned, understood, and remembered, and note taking involves capturing main ideas to look back to later. "We include summarizing and note taking in the same category because they both require students to distill information into a parsimonious and synthesized form" (Dean, Hubbell, Pitler, & Stone, 2012). To do this students must be able to analyze information at a deep level.

The short, condensed nature of text messaging lends itself perfectly to summarizing and taking notes. On most cell phones, the length of a single text is limited to 160 to 300 characters. Text messaging as a form of communication requires a similar type of substituting, deleting, and keeping some information as note taking. Students already have this skill and educators only need to encourage them to transfer it by analyzing information at a deep level. Here are some ideas for strategies to summarize and show how taking notes can be enriched with cell phones.

Classroom Practice in Summarizing: The Rule-Based Strategy

It is beneficial to use a specific set of steps when learning a new process. The rule-based summarizing strategy provides "help on what to keep and what to omit when summarizing information" (Dean, Hubbell, Pitler, & Stone, 2012). The rules used to guide students are to remove anything not important to understanding, remove what is repeated, use one word to describe any lists, and find or write a topic sentence. The following lesson outline models how cell phones can be used when employing this strategy.

CELL PHONE TOOL: TWITTER

Subject
Social studies

Topic
Current events

Preparation
Have students set up Twitter accounts at home or on school computers. They will link them to their mobile devices by entering their phone numbers at https://twitter.com/devices. This enables students to tweet even when they don't have access to a computer.

Lesson Overview
When it comes to current events, Twitter has become the number one source to get the most up-to-date information about what's happening now. Find out

what topics are hot in class by taking a look at the trending topics when visiting www.twitter.com. Ask students to find out more about the current event from a recent news story using print or digital newspaper, video, or magazine sources. As students start to learn more about the event, let them know they can connect with other real people in real time using Twitter.

Ask the students to summarize to create a tweet that provides an engaging summary, reaction, or question about the current event using the correct tag from the trending topics. They will also use the tag designated for their school so the tags are searchable (for example, a school tag may be PS123). Model this activity for the class showing how the rule-based strategy can be implemented around a trending topic on Twitter. Ideally in the modeled lesson you will tweet a summary that leads to replies and retweets as part of an authentic global conversation. Remind students to record their sources for discussion later.

How Technology Enriches This Lesson

- Students gain an important twenty-first-century skill necessary for success in the world of social media, which is how to have a global conversation about current issues. Twitter instantly opens the door to others interested in common topic and enables thinkers and learners to connect.

- Summarizing in this way instantly provides students with an authentic purpose for summarizing.

Classroom Practice in Summarizing: Summary Frames

Summary frames are an effective summarizing strategy. With summary frames the teacher provides students with a series of questions designed to highlight critical elements for specific types of information. The six types of summary frames they identify are (1) the narrative frame, (2) the topic-restriction-illustration frame, (3) the definition frame, (4) the argumentation frame, (5) the problem/solution frame, and (6) the conversation frame (Dean, Hubbell, Pitler, & Stone, 2012). The following lesson outline models how cell phones can be used when employing this strategy.

CELL PHONE TOOL: GOOGLE VOICE

Subject
Language arts

Topic
Summarizing books

Preparation
Set up a Google Voice account at www.google.com/voice (see Chapter One). Share your Google Voice number with students so they can call in and record their messages.

Lesson Overview
In this lesson, you will work with students to develop summaries of their school library's fairy tale collection. Select a summary frame to use with the students to walk them through the process of summarizing their selected fairy tale. Begin by modeling this as a class activity to summarize a previously read book. While at school each student will pick a fairy tale to summarize using a summary frame. For homework all students will call the teacher's Google Voice number to record their book summary. *Note:* All summaries should follow a standard format such as name of book, summary, name of student (first name or alias only). These will be placed on a "Fairy Tales" page of the library area of the school's website. When visitors come to this page they'll see book covers with the Google Voice summary recording underneath. This will help other students in the school select books that might be of interest to them when visiting the library.

How Technology Enriches This Lesson

- Using Google Voice to capture student summaries provides students with a real reason for summarizing a book. The work they do will be added to the class website and shared with other students to help them make book choices. This is a skill that is not only useful for students in school, but it's also an activity that they can use for their home libraries. In fact kids in a neighborhood or apartment building may even work collaboratively to share summaries of each child's home library to encourage book trading and swapping.

- Capturing the audio of a summary enables students to hear their writing. Listening to your writing read back to you is helpful in checking if it is clear and makes sense.

Classroom Practice in Note Taking

Although note taking is commonly thought of as a school activity, the reality is that in life people take notes all the time. Perhaps you're having a conversation with someone and they mention a book you should read, perhaps you're enjoying a delicious meal with a friend and she shares the recipe, maybe you find yourself lucky enough to run into a pro athlete who plays a sport you are involved in and she gives you tips. These are all great times to take notes. Students can learn to harness the power of their cell phones when taking quick notes on field trips, while listening to a guest speaker at an assembly, or while doing research on a computer or in a book. It is simple, quick, and easy with the use of cell phone technologies. Dean, Hubbell, Pitler, and Stone (2012) conclude from research that "students need explicit instruction in note taking and that guided note taking appears more effective than unstructured note taking." They recommend giving students notes that were prepared by the teacher, teaching various forms of note taking, and giving students chances to change their notes and use them for review.

Although traditionally in school students are taught techniques for taking notes in class on paper, more and more students are using their cell phones for taking notes. Even basic cell phones these days have a note or memo feature. Using this to take notes provides a number of advantages over traditional paper and pen including (1) using the texting vernacular provides a ready-made short hand, (2) many students say they find it easier to write on their phones than on paper, (3) notes are searchable, and (4) notes can be shared. The following lesson outline models how cell phones can be used when employing this strategy.

CELL PHONE TOOL: MEMO PAD, NOTES, CAMERA

Subject
Science

Topic
Dinosaurs

Preparation

Most phones with texting capabilities have a note taking or memo feature. Ensure your students know where this exists on their phone. Identify students who have phones with photo capability and place one such student in each group.

Lesson Overview

More and more of today's students share that they prefer texting on the cell phone to typing or handwriting stating that the closeness of the keys to one another makes it a fast and easy way to create a message or capture an idea. Educators who (are allowed to) embrace this preference can support students by letting them take class notes on their phones. Students with more advanced cell phones may use the camera feature for taking pictures of longer pieces of information, facts, graphs, charts, and so on to which they can refer later. This also enables students to transfer this method of learning into other areas of their lives and at other times during their day.

Using the note taking and camera features on a phone during field trips can be very effective. The teacher doesn't have to worry about bringing along clipboards, pens, and paper for a whole class, and many students will prefer using cell phones. Most phones allow for texts to be forwarded in a number of formats, such as e-mail, group messages, texts, Facebook posts, and so on.

In this lesson, students work in groups to find the items indicated in a museum scavenger hunt. When forming groups, you should ensure that each group has at least two members with cell phones, ideally one with photo capabilities. As they find the items listed in the hunt, they should record their locations and take pictures if possible. At the end of the hunt, students can check in with their answers and see which group found the most items. As an extension of the activity you might ask students to use their notes and photos to make a learning collage of their experience at the museum.

How Technology Enriches This Lesson

- Creating good notes that are organized and usable is a challenge for many students. Taking notes on a cell phone helps alleviate this problem because the notes are searchable and in many cases even have a spell-check feature. All students have to do is go to their cell phone memo or notes application and start typing in the name of their notes. They should instantly pop up.

- The notes on a cell phone are available on demand, anytime, anywhere.

- On many cell phones, notes can be shared. This could be helpful for a student who is absent or for study groups who want to compare notes.

- Those students who tend to lose their notes rarely lose their phones. Phones are a perfect place to encourage students to pull out main ideas, define words, text in facts, save formulas, list web addresses, and so on.

- Using these types of notes are life skills that will help twenty-first-century students to keep up with the pace of technology.

USING CELL PHONES FOR HOMEWORK AND PRACTICE

Homework and practice are instructional techniques that give students the opportunity to deepen their understanding and skills relative to content that has already been presented to them, connect existing knowledge for an upcoming unit, and repeat or review skills outside of the classroom. Dean, Hubbell, Pitler, and Stone (2012) share mixed research on the effects of homework on student achievement, so they encourage teachers to think carefully about the design and use of homework and to monitor the effects of homework on students and modify accordingly. Here are some specific ways that homework and practice can be enriched with the use of cell phones.

Classroom Practice in Assigning Homework

Three recommendations for assigning homework are to create and share a district homework policy, make sure all homework assignments are designed to support academic learning, share that purpose with students and parents, and always provide feedback on all homework assigned (Dean, Hubbell, Pitler, & Stone, 2012). The following lesson outline models how cell phones can be used when employing this strategy.

CELL PHONE TOOL: GROUP TEXTING

Subject
Any subject

Topic
Any topic

Preparation

Contact your local service provider to determine options for group texting. You can also do a search for online services that provide group texting capabilities.

Lesson Overview

Parents and teachers can partner to ensure that students are doing homework more effectively using group texting. Group text your students and their parents daily or weekly with assignments including due date, assignment purpose, parental role, questions for students, and clarifying and summarizing questions for parents to discuss with students. Parents can then set a daily alarm to alert them to check in with their child. If you wish, parents can also support you in being an additional person to comment on the homework. This also serves the purpose of providing recognition for the students in doing their work.

How Technology Enriches This Lesson

- Using group texting enables you to write one message and instantly connect with many students or parents.

- A group text not only helps to strengthen the home-school connection, but also, unlike a note in the backpack, the message won't get lost. It is a great way in general to keep parents in the loop, in the know, and to keep lines of communication open.

- Having parents set a daily reminder time to check in with their child helps students stay on track.

Classroom Practice in Practicing Skills: Charting Accuracy and Speed

Practice is helpful for skill mastery. In order to best use practice, teachers should always identify the purpose of the practice activities and share that purpose with students and parents, create practice activities that are "short, focused, and distributed over time," and give feedback on all practice (Dean, Hubbell, Pitler, & Stone, 2012). The following lesson outline models how cell phones can be used when employing this strategy.

CELL PHONE TOOL: STUDENT RESPONSE SERVICE— POLLING QUESTION

Subject
Math

Topic
Multiplication tables

Preparation
Create an account and set up an open response poll using a service such as Poll Everywhere (see Chapter One). Share the polling response number to which students should text their responses.

Lesson Overview
A fun way to use cell phones to chart the speed and accuracy of a class of students is to use a student response service. A school that promotes the use of personally owned technology might encourage a grade-wide competition of student speed and accuracy in multiplication tables.

At the beginning of the unit each teacher encourages students to respond to a polling question about the speed and accuracy of completing their multiplication tables. Students are asked to text in their speed and accuracy using a polling question on a service such as Poll Everywhere, the caveat being that their parent or guardian needs to sign off on the students' response to provide accountability on the reliability of results. This serves the added benefit of encouraging the home-school connection and keeping families in the loop on their child's progress. Although all students and family members know their score, the results are not attached to student name, but each student contributes to the results of the class.

At predetermined intervals classes would chart their speed and accuracy and the data could be shared on a school web page with privacy predetermined (that is, just for school members, for students, for families, or open to the public). The class that had the biggest overall gain (by percentage) could win an award such as a certificate, free time, pizza party, or something of their choosing.

How Technology Enriches This Lesson

- The use of SMS student response to chart the speed and accuracy of a class provides a quick, simple, and visible (to selected audiences) way to instantly see progress.

- Using a polling service to chart speed and accuracy provides motivation for classes as a whole to improve on their work. If they don't try hard to achieve, they'll let down their class. If they do try hard, they help their class.

- The use of a student response service has the additional benefit of providing recognition for a class's hard work and growth over time.

USING CELL PHONES TO IDENTIFY SIMILARITIES AND DIFFERENCES

According to Dean, Hubbell, Pitler, and Stone (2012), these strategies help students move from current knowledge to new knowledge, concrete to abstract, and separate to connected ideas. Looking at the similar and dissimilar characteristics of a concept or idea enhances a student's understanding of and ability to use knowledge, thus make sense of the world. Marzano, Pickering, and Pollock (2001) stated four strategies for identifying similarities and differences, "comparing, classifying, creating metaphors, and creating analogies." These are defined and further explained by Dean, Hubbell, Pitler, and Stone (2012). The three recommendations made for classroom practice are "teach students a variety of ways to identify similarities and differences, guide students as they engage in this process, and/ or provide supporting cues. Here are some ideas about how identifying similarities and differences can be enriched with cell phones.

Classroom Practice in Comparing (Teaching Students Ways to Identify Similarities and Differences)

This provides focus for the type of conclusions students will reach. When teaching students the processes to identify similarities and differences, teachers should provide students with the steps and model the process (Dean, Hubbell, Pitler, & Stone, 2012). The following lesson outline models how cell phones can be used when employing this strategy.

CELL PHONE TOOL: STUDENT RESPONSE SERVICE— FREE RESPONSE

Subject
Social studies

Topic
Women in history

Preparation
Create an account and set up an open response poll using a service such as Poll Everywhere (see Chapter One). Share the polling response number to which students should text their responses.

Lesson Overview
Increase students' understanding of women's role in history with a study of women who have run for office, such as Shirley Chisholm, Geraldine Ferraro, and Hillary Clinton. Provide students with material that gives them a common platform of information about these historical figures. Ask students to take notice of the traits of each politician, looking at characteristics such as background, major responsibilities, and notable achievements. Create an open response poll for each of these women. Ask students to review their notes and submit a reflection about each politician to the corresponding poll.

Model this for students in class by texting a reflection to the corresponding politicians. When the students come together the next day, project responses for students to review and then have a conversation based on the reflections, comparing the traits of each of the women.

How Technology Enriches This Lesson

- Students can get to the thinking faster because class time is not spent on calling on select students to read their answers. All answers are already collected before class begins and class time can move to the making of meaning.

- All student voices are heard. This gives every student an opportunity to contribute and participate as every student's input is collected.

- Teachers can know in advance if students have grasped the key concepts and relevant points and adjust instruction accordingly before, not after, the lesson.

Classroom Practice in Comparing (Guiding Students as They Engage in the Process of Identifying Similarities and Differences)

With "structured tasks" teachers can guide students in identifying similarities and differences (Dean, Hubbell, Pitler, & Stone, 2012). The following lesson outline models how cell phones can be used when employing this strategy.

CELL PHONE TOOL: PHONE CASTING WITH IPADIO

Subject
Literacy

Topic
Elements of literature

Preparation
Create a phonecasting account with ipadio (see Chapter One). You will be provided with a number to share with students so they can call into the number and leave their phonecasts.

Lesson Overview
Students are engaged in a unit of study about the major elements of literature (for example, universal theme, point of view, and so on). Ask students to select two stories they've read in the selected genre and to compare them on the literary elements. Have the students describe what they learned about the stories' literary characteristics by calling into the phonecasting number that you have set up in a service such as ipadio. You can also leave a comment on recordings to provide students with feedback. Back at school, you can use a laptop and projector to share audio recordings. If students are able to access computers inside or outside of school encourage them to comment on their classmates' work.

How Technology Enriches This Lesson

- All student work is published so that it is shared with other students in the class. As a result, students can learn from each other.

- Phonecasting promotes conversation. Students can listen to their classmates recordings from any computer and provide thoughtful responses on the topics of interest to them.

Classroom Practice in Classifying

Another method of identifying similarities and differences is classifying. "In order to classify, students must be able to identify important characteristics and determine the ways in which they are similar and different" (Dean, Hubbell, Pitler, & Stone, 2012). This can be done by grouping, or classifying, according to similarities. The following lesson outline models how cell phones can be used when employing this strategy.

CELL PHONE TOOL: STUDENT RESPONSE SERVICE— POLLING QUESTION

Subject
Physical education

Topic
Knowledge of sports

Preparation
Set up an account in a polling service (see Chapter One) and create a poll for each sport of focus. Share the polling response number to which students should text their responses. Student responses are instantly visible on the teacher's poll.

Lesson Overview
Students watch the Olympics and are asked to classify various events into categories of those that require mainly strength, those that require mainly precision and accuracy, and those that require about an equal amount of each. In class students describe how they categorized events and defend why they put them in specific categories. Set up polls that list the Olympic sports that require focus and allow students to text one of the three answers: (1) strength, (2) agility, or (3) strength and agility. As students watch each sport and record their

answers, the poll is instantly tabulated graphically for class review. The charts can be embedded into a web page, wiki, or blog and are ready for class discussion.

How Technology Enriches This Lesson

- Student responses are not collected in isolation. They become part of the collective whole. Once students respond, they can see how their answer compared with the answers of others and the entire class response can be seen instantly on arrival to class.

- All graphs can be shared in the online space making an easy-to-understand visual representation of results.

- Discussions can be richer when a collective intelligence is shared rather than just one student's observation.

- Narratives, collaborative Google documents, or a recorded discussion of each item can be shared in the online space to give life to each poll.

USING CELL PHONES FOR GENERATING AND TESTING HYPOTHESES

Generating and testing hypotheses involves deduction, "using general rules to make a prediction about a future event or action," and induction, "drawing new conclusions (or inferences) based on knowledge students already have or information that is presented to them" (Dean, Hubbell, Pitler, & Stone, 2012). These are some of the most powerful and analytic of cognitive process and they can be used separately or together. Generating and testing hypotheses requires critical thinking. Two recommendations are to "engage students in a variety of structured tasks for generating and testing hypotheses and ask students to explain their hypotheses or predictions and their conclusions" (Dean, Hubbell, Pitler, & Stone, 2012). Here are some ways cell phones can be used to enrich instruction and engage learners involved in such tasks.

Classroom Practice in Clearly Explaining Hypotheses and Conclusions

Teachers should create lesson assignments that ensure students will be able to describe how they generated their hypotheses and explain what they learned through the testing of their hypotheses. This way students will focus on the important aspects of the process and thus their ability to apply it (Dean, Hubbell, Pitler, & Stone, 2012). Although traditional writing on paper and handing this in to the teacher is one way to accomplish this, students who have access to a phone have an additional option. The following lesson outline models how cell phones can be used when employing this strategy.

CELL PHONE TOOL: PHONECASTING, TWITTER, FACEBOOK

Subject
Social studies

Topic
World War II

Preparation
Create a phonecasting account with a service such as ipadio as described in Chapter One. Have students call into the number assigned to your phonecasting account.

Lesson Overview
After providing students with some foundational facts and issues about World War II, ask them to generate a variety of hypotheses, such as, "What might have been the best method for ending the war?" Rather than turning this assignment in on paper, students will be asked to work in groups and designate a reporter to call their hypotheses into the phonecasting number you have set up. You can then comment on this work, but what would be more powerful is harnessing the power of social media networks such as Twitter and Facebook. For example, you might be able to tap into your learning networks to see if some history teacher colleagues might agree to comment on your student's hypotheses. You could then share the phonecasts (which should be compiled on one page of a selected online space) with those interested and share with the class what the other history teachers had to say about their hypotheses, leading to a lively in-class discussion. Of course, these other history teachers might have students who want to comment as well.

How Technology Enriches This Lesson

- Using phonecasting takes student-generated hypotheses to the next level, resulting in students publishing their work to be shared with a relevant audience.

- Providing this as an option also will be helpful for some auditory learners who prefer delivering and consuming information in this format.

- The phonecasting format can also be a great project to share with parents and other school community members. Remember, based on your school policy, you may want to have a protocol in place for students to use aliases rather than their real names in their messages.

- Reaching out to experts in a PLN provides students with rich insights into topics of interest that they likely wouldn't have access to without an online platform.

Classroom Practice in Generating and Testing Hypotheses with Experimental Inquiry

Experimental inquiry is one of the six structured tasks used to guide students through generating and testing hypotheses. Experimental inquiry is used to "guide students in applying their understanding of important content using a general framework consisting of observation and description, applying theories to explain observation, generate a hypothesis to predict what would happen if you applied your theory, set up an experiment to test your theory, explain the results, and decide if your hypothesis is correct or if you need to conduct additional activities" (Dean, Hubbell, Pitler, & Stone, 2012). The following lesson outline models how cell phones can be used when employing this strategy.

CELL PHONE TOOL: FLICKR

Subject
Science

Topic
Plant growth

Preparation

Set up a Flickr account and e-mail as described in Chapter One with a "Lima Bean" tag set. Your students will e-mail their plant pictures with the element name in the title and the growth in the subject.

Lesson Overview

After providing students with foundational information about plants and growth, ask them to generate a variety of hypotheses about how different elements in soil might affect plant growth. Students will come up with various answers and determine a hypothesis such as, "if plant growth is related to what is in the soil, then changing what is in the soil will result in changes in the height of the plant." Provide all students with a plastic bag with their name on it containing a wet paper towel and a lima bean. By the end of the week the beans will have sprouted. Give students a handful of soil, a cup in which to plant their lima beans, and a popsicle stick for measuring. Tell students that the class lima bean will only be watered, but they can grow their lima bean with whatever one additional element they choose. Help them think of some possible extra elements, such as cola, coffee grinds, egg shells, salt, Miracle Grow, fertilizer, or baking soda. Have students write the selected element on their cup.

Have students bring home their lima bean plants and ask them to place them in an area that will get sunlight. Tell students to water the plants every other day so the soil is moist. Ideally, you should time this assignment to occur a few days prior to a school holiday, such as winter or spring break. On the last day of break students will be asked to use a cell phone with a camera to take a picture of their plant and send it to the account you have set up on Flickr. In the subject of the message, they will indicate what was in their soil and the height of the plant. In the body of the message, they will indicate if there were other things they noticed about their plant.

Lima beans are a great choice because they grow quickly. By the end of the week there will be growth for students to measure. When students return to school, they will look at the Flickr slide show of the photos. The teacher should create a bar graph on paper or in a spreadsheet listing the element for each plant and the growth of each plant. Track which elements had the greatest to least effect on plant growth. Project the Flickr slide show and add the findings to the photos.

How Technology Enriches This Lesson

- Using Flickr is a fun and easy way for students to collect data from their homes and instantly bring it together without much work.

- Not only can students see the results, but the slide show can also be shared with parents and guardians. A nice extension to this experiment is to partner with other classes within or outside of the school.

Classroom Practice in Generating and Testing Hypotheses Problem Solving

Problem solving is another structured task for generating and testing hypotheses. It incorporates decision making and invention. Dean, Hubbell, Pitler, and Stone (2012) define problem solving as "the process of overcoming limits or barriers that are in the way of reaching goals." The following lesson outline models how cell phones can be used when employing this strategy.

CELL PHONE TOOL: POLL EVERYWHERE OR TEXTTHEMOB

Subject
Life skills or advisory

Topic
Peer pressure

Preparation
Set up the scenarios you want to discuss using a polling site such as TextTheMob (see Chapter Two). Share the voting and response codes with the class.

Lesson Overview
Have students text example situations when they have experienced peer pressure to a free text poll. Using the situations shared by the students, discuss different scenarios. For example, with drinking pressure discuss a scenario in which students meet at the movie theater to watch a movie and a second scenario in which students go to a party at house where the parents are out of

town. Have students vote for each scenario indicating level of pressure they would feel—i.e., a lot of pressure, a little pressure, no pressure. After each scenario has been voted on, have students use a decision-making framework and text into a free text poll the reasons and knowledge related to the topic that resulted in their choice. Having the students explain "why" they made the choice to vote as they did encourages reflection and the use of a broad range of knowledge related to the topic.

How Technology Enriches This Lesson

- Using voting and free response through cell phones engages all students in the decision-making process and allows all students to share their responses and their reasoning. A discussion that involves all students participating is much preferred to a few students raising their hands and being called on individually.

CELL PHONE–SUPPORTED, RESEARCH-BASED STRATEGIES PROVIDE INSPIRING INSTRUCTIONAL IDEAS

Educators can't go wrong when they base their teaching strategies on the research of *Classroom Instruction That Works* (Dean, Hubbell, Pitler, & Stone, 2012). Using cell phone technologies is a fun, new, motivating method to support and enhance these practices. Continuing to build on these practices will ensure your teaching success. As cell phones continue to evolve, educators can continue to harness their power in support of solid teaching. We hope some of these ideas have inspired you to use the power of cell phones to enhance these research-based strategies for your grade level and content area.

chapter FOUR

The Six Building Blocks for Success with Cell Phones in Education

You don't have to be great to get started, but you have to get started to be great.
Les Brown, author and motivational speaker

In this chapter, we discover the six building blocks you need to put into place to develop a foundation for successful use of cell phones in the classroom. By securing school and parent permissions, teaching students about cell phone safety and cell phone etiquette, developing and teaching solid acceptable use and classroom management procedures, and by carefully planning activities and including students, you will have placed the essential building blocks for success using cell phones. The six building blocks are as follows:

1. Get your school's approval to use cell phones.

2. Secure parent and guardian and student agreements.

3. Teach students about cell phone safety and etiquette.

4. Develop an acceptable use policy.

5. Establish classroom management procedures.

6. Plan activities with students.

GET YOUR SCHOOL'S APPROVAL TO USE CELL PHONES

Although there are many things you can do with cell phones that don't require approval (just as you don't need approval for students to use a personal computer outside of school), ideally you want to move to an environment in which cell phones can be used for learning and strengthening connections as needed without restrictions. So, although we encourage you to start using cell phones in the classroom by incorporating the many ideas we shared in Chapters One through Three that do not require approval immediately (for example, when cell phones are used outside of school), we do hope you will work toward establishing an environment in which cell phones can be used both inside and outside of school for a variety of purposes.

The six-part plan in the Appendix provides you with a step-by-step guide to break the ban if there is one in place. If cell phones are currently banned in your district, you'll certainly want to use all or part of the six-part plan as you begin conversations and efforts toward policy change. If you are successful, all educators in your school or district will have the opportunity to harness the power of cell phones. If you are not working in a school or district that bans the use of cell phones or once you have broken the ban you will want a written statement from your school administrator or in your school policies guide that allows you to use cell phones with your students.

Once you have approval, the next five building blocks will help ensure you have just what you need in place for a smooth integration of cell phones into your teaching, learning, and connecting with students and parents.

SECURE PARENT AND GUARDIAN AND STUDENT AGREEMENTS

Before you use cell phones with students, you must secure agreement with them and their parents or guardians. By the time you ask for it, it is suggested that you have already begun home-school connection strategies so that cell phones pave the way for parents and guardians to see the devices as a useful tool for connecting in important ways.

The first step whenever cell phone numbers are exchanged is to sign an agreement. Ideally, you will be able to offer a workshop (see Chapter Two) or give a short presentation to parents at open house or registration and the agreement is signed then. Many times, however, agreements must be sent home. Writing an agreement that is easy to understand, fits your school and classroom needs, and addresses the following key areas is a must. These areas should be covered:

- Boundaries
    - Establish times of the day that you would be comfortable receiving text messages from students. Some cell phones also have controls limiting when messages can be received. There are also services such as WeTxt that allow you to establish times when you do not want to receive text messages. If this is the case, times of day may not need to be addressed.
    - Explain that there is no guarantee that a text message sent to you will be read, even during the available times. A dead phone battery, a lost phone, a phone left at home, and so on could prevent a text from being read immediately.
    - Explain that signature lines and forwards must be appropriate. Curse words and references to drinking, drugs, or sex are inappropriate.
- Privacy
    - Using an online texting service such as Google Voice, WeTxt, or GroupMe provides a record of sent and received messages. The same exceptions to confidentiality for all educators apply to text messages. Know your school district rules and state laws requiring the reporting of suspected child abuse, neglect, or harm to self or others. Always make students and parents aware of exceptions to confidentiality.
- Safety
    - For the most part being safe and appropriate online and in text messages is no different than being safe and appropriate in life. Ensure alignment with the state, district, and school guidelines for protecting student safety. Follow all educator ethical guidelines. Get approval of administrators prior to sending home agreements. Have their signature on your agreements as well. Ongoing work with students, parents, and administrators in reviewing, updating, and communicating safe practices is a must. Agreements should be reviewed annually.

The following are examples of agreements used by educators who are harnessing the power of cell phones with their students and parents. There is also a sample letter that can be used for nonteaching staff. You will want to develop a letter that fits the needs of your particular class and school. Be sure to have your administration approve the letter before sharing with parents and students.

CELL PHONE AGREEMENT USED BY SCIENCE TEACHER JASON SUTER

Dear Parents and Guardians:

We are looking forward to another great year of teaching science to your students. We would like to inform you that we are planning lessons that will incorporate the use of cell phones in the classroom. As you may know there is a lot of great information in print and on the Internet describing how cells can be used as an educational tool.

We realize not every student owns a cell phone or has cell phone plan that will allow them to participate with their own personal device. We also want to make it clear that we are in no way encouraging parents to provide a cell phone to students who do not already own one. The lessons in which cell phones will be permissible can be completed using a cell your student brings to class *or* we will provide classroom netbooks or cell phones for students to use that will enable all students to participate.

Most of the resources we will be using in class are applications that allow students to communicate using the Internet via text messaging. All of the applications are free but usual text messaging fees apply. We are aware that most students with cell phones have very large or unlimited text messaging plans. Please review cell phone plans with your children so they are clear on how much they can use their phone without accruing any cost to you. We cannot be held responsible if your student goes over his or her minutes or allotted text messages.

We are also always looking for ways to increase communication and keep you informed about what is taking place in your child's science class. Please visit our classroom websites to learn more. They can be found by clicking on the "teacher pages" link on the school website.

If you would like to learn more about using cell phones in the classroom click on the "cell phone" link under the ed-tech resources section of Mr. Suter's website. The information provided should be able to answer many of your questions or concerns.

Thank you,

GENERAL TECHNOLOGY USE AND PUBLISHING AGREEMENT USED BY SCIENCE TEACHER JASON SUTER

Dear Parents and Guardians:

This year we will be making use of the resources available on the Internet to complete assignments and keep you informed about what is happening in the classroom. I know you receive many forms to fill out at the beginning of each year. In effort to reduce the paperwork for you I have compiled a list of items of which I believe you should be aware as well as ones in which your permission is needed. Safety is a primary concern when having your children use the Internet for school work. More detailed information can be found on my websites about any of the topics listed below. I feel strongly that these items will help break down the physical classroom walls and provide the students with a very unusual educational experience. Please review the following items and grant your student the right to participate by signing and returning the bottom portion of this letter.

- *Don't turn it in . . . publish!* This is an idea taken from *The Innovative Educator*'s blog. In an effort to move away from the traditional audience of one (the teacher), we will be using various websites to publish student work. Often we will be using sites that can only be accessed by the members of HHS [Hanover High School] such as Moodle or Google Docs. However, there will be occasions when students will be posting their work to sites like YouTube, Edublogs, Glogsters, or even Twitter.

- *Cell phones for education.* There will be times when students will be permitted to use their personal cell phones for class projects. Typically classroom lessons take advantage of the cell phones text messaging capabilities, but there are other uses as well. Sites such as Poll Everywhere and Wiffiti allow students to communicate using the Internet via text messaging. Students have also used the picture- or video-taking capabilities of their phones in class. Last year my environmental class linked their phone to Twitter and created a live stream of what they were learning while on a field trip to the Chesapeake Bay.

- *Student pictures.* I have become very fond of documenting student activities in class with both pictures and video. It is very easy to make a few-minute video of various activities and place them on my website (via YouTube) for the students to share with their parents. Also, students in my environmental class sometime interview other students for documentaries that they make during the year. These projects might also contain pictures of students and be shared on my website. Once again, student information will not be associated with any pictures or video.

- *Classroom Facebook.* Last year I started a classroom Facebook page for my students. The classroom updates that I send out show up on my wall. Friends of this account will see class updates in their home feed. Current students and their parents are welcome to friend request this page. If you are already a Facebook user this is the perfect way to keep up-to-date with your student's science class. Parents please include your student's name in a message when friend requesting me. Also, please make sure to request my classroom account and not my personal Facebook page. You can find more information on my website.

Please sign below so that I know you have read this information and have given your permission for your student to participate in the topics described. For more detailed information visit my websites or feel free to call me at [your number] (this is my personal Google Voice number). I would be more than happy to discuss any of these items with you if you have further concerns. I am looking forward to a great year with your student!

Thank You,

_____

_____

_____

_____

_____

I have read the parent information and permission form for Mr. Suter's class and give permission for my student to participate in the described activities.

Student name _____

Parent or guardian name _____

Date _____

Signature _____

CELL PHONE AGREEMENT LETTER USED BY MATH TEACHER GEORGE ENGEL

Dear Parents and Guardians:

We have a new and exciting program that we are piloting in class this year. We are going to be using a hand-held computer that your child possesses at this moment: the cell phone. You child will be using his or her cell phone in a variety ways to foster learning.

The use of the cell phone in class for course work will not only meet district standards and objectives for mathematics and technology but also the National Educational Technology Standards for Students (developed by the International Society for Technology in Education) and the standards put forth by the National Council of Teachers of Mathematics.

In the short term, students will be using their cell phones to contribute to class discussions and to answer quiz questions. In the long term, your children will be using their cell phones to record images of work and even videos of work to develop a mathematics portfolio that represents their work and growth throughout the year. These video and images of work will be published online on class wikis. They will also be using materials captured on their cell phones to publish in a class blog where they will make weekly contributions.

I am working with [teacher name(s)], our principal, and our district's director of instructional technology to decide what resources best fit our needs. The district will be offering spaces for students to build wikis and post videos. Once your child has begun placing work online, I will notify you so you can view your child's work. When we begin posting your child's work online, we will notify you of the web address so you may view the work and make comments as well. Using cell phones as a learning resource is a privilege and students will be given instruction on how to use this resource appropriately. If they abuse this privilege, they will be given an alternate assignment that does not involve the Internet or their cell phone. Because we will be publishing their work online, we would like your permission for your child to participate. We would also ask that your child sign the agreement.

I understand that not every student in the class will have a texting plan or a data plan that will allow them to use their cell phone for all the activities planned. If this is the case, you child will be given an alternative assignment.

Please do not think that you need to change your phone plans for this class. Let me know if this is the case so I can prepare alternative work for them.

_____

_____

_____

I _____ agree to allow my child _____
_____ to participate in class by using his or her cell phone as a tool for learning. I agree to follow the rules for the appropriate use of the cell phone in class.

Parent or guardian signature _____

Student signature _____

If you have any questions or concerns please do not hesitate to contact me or our building principal. We think this is an amazing opportunity for students to learn how to use their cell phones as educational tools as well as learn about Internet safety and publishing online. We hope that you will participate as well by viewing and commenting on their published work.

SAMPLE BASIC CELL PHONE PERMISSION LETTER TEMPLATE

Dear Parents and Guardians:

We want to access the tools available through student-owned cell phones, teach the students how to use cell phones for learning, and practice appropriate manners with cell phones in all areas of life. Therefore, we are piloting a program in the use of cell phones for education. The use of the cell phone in class for course work and out of class for homework will better prepare students for their future and meet National Educational Technology Standards for Students (developed by the International Society for Technology in Education).

There are many educational uses for cell phones, for example, starting with the organizational uses built into the phones, learning research tools, creating assignments by voice or text, group texts of assignments dates, cues, questions, content, and requests for responses to various sites. After considering cell phone safety, cell phone etiquette, and the wealth of educational uses, the students themselves will be developing the "rules for tools" this week. We will share those with you.

Students will be given instruction on how to appropriately use cell phones as a learning resource. If they abuse this privilege, they will be given an alternate assignment that does not involve their cell phone. We understand that not every student in the class has a texting plan that will allow them to use their cell phone for all the activities planned. Please do not think that you need to change your phone plan for this class. There will be no additional cost for you. If this is the case or if a phone is lost or broken, we will create sharing options, use alternative tools, get a sponsor, alter the assignment, and so on.

By signing this form you recognize that we are not responsible for lost or stolen phones. You also understand that inappropriate use will result in the loss of the privilege. If you have any questions or concerns please do not hesitate to contact me or our building principal. [add your contact information]

_____
_____
_____
_____

For Parents:
I agree to allow my child to participate in class assignments and activities by using his or her cell phone as directed by the teacher for learning purposes.
Parent or guardian signature _____

For Students:
I agree to follow the rules for the appropriate use of the cell phone in class assignments and activities.
Student signature_____

CELL PHONE AGREEMENT FOR NONTEACHING SCHOOL PERSONNEL

(Note that this is a sample agreement only. You will want to create your own based on your individual school and state policies.)

- We can exchange cell phone numbers for the purpose of sending and receiving text or voice messages. The content of the messages must be applicable to the school adult–student relationship.
- Messages can be sent and received from [indicate time if applicable].
- There is no guarantee that messages will be read in a timely manner.
- All messages are subject to the exceptions to confidentiality in regard to your safety. I have a duty to protect and will share messages that indicate possible harm to self or others, abuse or neglect, or in any way indicate an unsafe situation.
- Inappropriate messages will be cause for disciplinary action.
- Numbers may not be shared with others unless permission to share is requested and is given by the owner of the number.
- It is the responsibility of the cell phone owner to monitor all cell phone costs and pay all applicable charges.

_____

_____

By sharing my number and by taking [school staff's] number, I agree to follow these rules.

_____   _____
Student name/number   Date

By sharing my number and taking [student's] number, I agree to follow these rules.

_____   _____
School staff/number   Date

By allowing my son or daughter and myself to communicate with the school staff via phone, I agree to follow the rules.

_____   _____
Parent or guardian/number   Date

TEACH STUDENTS ABOUT CELL PHONE ETIQUETTE AND SAFETY

We can only expect students to exhibit appropriate behaviors when we discuss with them what behaviors are appropriate. Taking the time to teach the following lessons to students will pay off in fewer discipline issues, more fun using cell phones in future lessons, and provide them with valuable life skills of practicing good cell phone manners and good cell phone safety practices.

Etiquette

Adults often complain that cell phones are a distraction in class, but how much time have they really devoted to discussing proper etiquette? This can be woven into a general discussion around behavior and etiquette in different situations. Inviting students into the conversation about appropriate etiquette and what to say to those not exhibiting polite behavior usually works better than telling students how to best behave.

The following circumstances are good examples of when you want to address etiquette. Remember to discuss different types of cell phone use, for example, talking, texting, looking up information, photos, emergencies, and so on. For each of these circumstances ask, "What is proper etiquette in each situation?" and "What might you say to someone who is not exhibiting proper etiquette in each situation?"

- During class
  - When the instructor is addressing the class
  - When a classmate is addressing the class
  - When the class is engaging in a discussion (unless the discussion involves responding via text)
- During lunch or recess
  - When sitting with friends
  - When sitting alone
  - Passing in the halls
- At home
  - During dinner
  - During homework time
  - At bedtime

- When out
  - Movie
  - Restaurant
  - Church or temple
  - Other
- When traveling
  - In a bus, car, plane, or train
  - Waiting in line

Knowing proper etiquette of cell phone use is an essential twenty-first-century skill. We need to support students not only in developing appropriate etiquette for themselves, but also discussing with them how they may handle a situation when others are not exhibiting appropriate behavior. This lesson plan will help teachers address this topic with students preparing them for using proper manners when using cell phones both inside and outside of schools. Not only will their parents appreciate this, but also many of their future employers will as well.

The following lesson is aligned to both the National Educational Technology Standards for Students and Teachers as well as the proven and effective, research-based strategies from *Classroom Instruction That Works*, 2nd edition (Dean, Hubbell, Pitler, & Stone, 2012). The National Educational Technology Standards for Teachers were developed to help ensure that educators were innovating instruction that aligns to the needs of twenty-first-century learners. The standards for students were developed to ensure students would be prepared for success in the world of today and in the future. See Chapter Five for lessons incorporating the standards.

PHONE MANNERS: MAKING GOOD CHOICES WITH CELL PHONES

Cell Phone Tool Used
Flickr

Preparation
Set up Flickr as described in Chapter One. Share the e-mail address that students will send pictures to. Create a Cell Phone Manners tag to share with students.

Lesson Overview

Students will learn and practice good phone manners by considering good choices for public and private cell phone use. The areas addressed are choosing when to call and text, choosing where to call and text, choosing whom to call and text, choosing appropriate call and text content, choosing appropriate ringtones and signature lines, choosing appropriate pictures, and having permission to take them. Students will practice good phone manners through their role-plays.

Lesson Description

- After discussing the kinds of available cell phone use, assign groups the following categories: choices about when, where, who, and what; ringtones; signature lines; and pictures.

- Have students set up scenarios of appropriate choices (maybe comparing them to scenes of poor cell phone etiquette that we have all witnessed). The main information to be communicated in the slide show presentation is how to use *good* phone manners by making good choices.

- In designing their good phone manners slide they could stage a scene of good phone manners and bad phone manners and go around the school or community and capture real examples of good and bad phone manners (with the subject's permission).

- Have students text the pictures to your class's Flickr account. Each photo will become a part of the class's "Good Manners" slide show.

How the Use of Cell Phones Enriches This Lesson

- Cell phones make the subject matter relevant because they are using the device they are advising about.

- There is no cost of camera or video equipment for the school, no need to purchase tapes, disks, or film.

- The lesson will take less time because all groups can get started immediately.

NETS for Students Addressed

- Creativity and innovation
- Communication and collaboration
- Critical thinking, problem solving, and decision making
- Digital citizenship

NETS for Teachers Addressed

- Facilitate and inspire student learning and creativity
- Design and develop digital-age learning experiences and assessments
- Model digital-age work and learning
- Promote and model digital citizenship and responsibility

Research-Based Instructional Strategies

- Cooperative learning
- Setting objectives and providing feedback
- Nonlinguistic representations

Safety

Using a cell phone requires the same common sense that is used for using the old-fashioned home or desk phone combined with the common sense used for sending e-mails and instant messages, which are akin to texting. Here are some guidelines to consider:

- Unknown calls
    - Don't answer calls from people you don't know. They will leave you a voice mail if it's important and once you know who it is, you can determine if this is someone you wish to speak to.
- Unknown messages
    - If you receive a text from someone you don't know, it could be spam or the wrong number. Use your discretion in replying as you would if someone called the wrong number or was selling you something, such as "I'm sorry, who is this? I think

you have the wrong number." If anyone texts you something inappropriate, the text can be ignored, deleted, or the number sending it can be blocked. If they continue, the message should be shown to a trusted adult.

- Stranger danger

    - Just as in face-to-face or online communications, you should not communicate with people you don't know on your cell phone. Online and via text, it is very easy for people to impersonate someone they are not. Stick with those you know and never agree to meet someone you only know online or via text. Meeting up with strangers (even if you've communicated virtually) is dangerous.

- Block calls

    - Know how to block others from calling or texting your phone.

- Do Not Call registry

    - Avoid unwanted solicitations by registering with the National Do Not Call registry at www.donotcall.gov or call 1–888–382–1222. This is a sensible whole class activity and also something the teacher may consider sending out as a group text.

- Act appropriately and expect the same from those with whom you communicate.

    - Act on the phone as you should do in your face-to-face and online lives. Your digital identity, whether on a cell or computer, is often not private. Don't write or share (via pictures or video) anything you wouldn't feel comfortable having others know about publicly. If someone sends you something inappropriate address them as you would in face-to-face encounters. If you are uncomfortable doing this, speak with an adult you can trust, such as a parent, teacher, or guidance counselor. If messages are of a bullying or sexual tone, you and the trusted adult you are confiding in may decide to save the messages and contact the police.

- Photos and videos

    - Before taking and sharing pictures or videos you should get the consent of the subject(s). Ensure the person knows your intentions if you are sharing. Once it's uploaded to the Internet, it is public for the world to see. Never share any photo or video that contains inappropriate material.

- Protect against loss or theft

    - Place an "if lost" sticker on the phone with your e-mail and the number of someone a person could call who can notify you if your phone is found.

- Cyberbullying
  - Cyberbullying can be defined as messages or images that are mean, hurtful, or threatening. Do not respond to messages that you feel are bullying. Instead, block the sender, report the incident, and save the messages as evidence. If the message involves threats of violence, extortion, obscene messages, harassment, stalking, or other unlawful acts, they should be reported to law enforcement.
- Using cell phones to coordinate fights
  - There is a real fear among educators that students may use cell phones to coordinate fights. The reality is that students can use a variety of tools to engage in inappropriate behavior from cell phones to laptops to the good old-fashioned pencil-to-paper note or even just by talking. Instead of banning phones, clearly explain to students that using cell phones in this way will not be tolerated and that any students engaging in such activities will be referred to proper services. They should also be informed that anything on their phones can be used as evidence and will result in consequences if discovered by school staff.
- Sexting
  - Sexting is the act of sending explicit messages or seminude or nude photos via cell phones. The law outlines three categories of sexting:
    - Production or manufacturing = creating
    - Distribution or dissemination = sending or forwarding
    - Possession = keeping (receiving is not an offense, but keeping is and the longer it remains, the more serious the offense)
  - Never create or send messages or pictures of a sexual nature. If you receive such a message block the sender, share the message with a trusted adult, a teacher, or law enforcement, and delete it.

BE SMART WITH YOUR PHONE

Subject
Cell phone safety

Cell Phone Tools Used
Poll Everywhere, tool of students' choice, such as Flickr or Voki

Preparation

Go to www.polleverywhere.com and create a poll with the following questions and have the Poll Everywhere number and text-in codes ready to provide to students.

Lesson Overview

Students will learn risks and share safety tips for cell phones.

Lesson Description

Set up a poll (yes or no) with Poll Everywhere that asks students the following questions:

- Have you ever received a call or a text message from a stranger?
- Have you have ever received a call or text message that bullied you?
- Have you have ever received a call or text message that was sexual?

   Once you have your answers you can share to the tips to combat these types of unsafe situations. Tips can be generated from the group using a free text poll on Poll Everywhere. Safety tips should be similar to these:

- Do not answer calls or read text messages from strangers.
- Block unknown numbers.
- Share with adults when messages are harmful.
- Make good choices about what messages to send.
- Only take appropriate pictures or send appropriate messages.
- Only save appropriate pictures.

   When all students have had a chance to share, read through the results and as a group come up with the top suggestions. Allow students individually or in groups to use their cell phone tool of choice to create a safety tip for cell phone presentation that can be shared with others (such as with younger kids). Some suggestions for tools would be create a podcast, a Flickr slideshow, a forward text message that could be sent around school, or a Voki explaining the safety tips.

How the Use of Cell Phones Enriches This Lesson

- The use of cell phone tools demonstrates for students how, with good choices, cell phones can be used for educational purposes as well as social ones.

- Practicing on an actual phone in a safe way makes the lesson more real to students.

NETS for Students Addressed

- Creativity and innovation

- Communication and collaboration

- Critical thinking, problem solving, and decision making

- Digital citizenship

NETS for Teachers Addressed

- Facilitate and inspire student learning and creativity

- Design and develop digital-age learning experiences and assessments

- Model digital-age work and learning

- Promote and model digital citizenship and responsibility

Research-Based Instructional Strategies Used

- Cooperative learning

- Summarizing

- Nonlinguistic representations

DEVELOP AN ACCEPTABLE USE POLICY

Just like any other classroom tool, teachers need to work with students to establish acceptable use policies. In some classrooms the teacher just explains how the general policies apply to the use of cell phones, in others they create a new policy, in some schools the students help create the policies, and in some classrooms they invite parental input as well. Collecting everyone's thoughts on acceptable use is easy when you use cell phone tools such as Poll Everywhere and Wiffiti to do so. In this section you will find sample templates, actual policies from schools where cell phones are used, and links to additional policies. As you review these policies you'll be able to think about what would work best in your environment.

Cell Phone Acceptable Use Policy Templates

Template 1

Cell phones and other electronic devices may be used during [when] [where]. You will see [indicate how areas will be designated], which indicate where cell phone use is allowed and not allowed. In areas and at times when devices are not allowed they must be [explain: off, on vibrate, not visible, and so on]. Cell phone and other electronic device usage in classrooms is up to the discretion of each individual teacher. Students need to be aware of their teacher's expectations regarding these electronic devices. If a student is using a cell phone or electronic device in violation of school or classroom rules, the student will [indicate what will happen to the item]. Inappropriate use includes [indicate inappropriate use, for example, academic misconduct, messages considered bullying or sexual in nature, and so on]. Confiscated cell phones and other electronic devices may be picked up [indicate where, when, and by whom]. Failure to give the cell phone or other electronic device to a staff member on request will result in [explain disciplinary action].

Template 2

During the school day, cell phones can be used. During class time, cell phones can be used in ways that support the teaching and learning process.

Cell phones may not be used in any way that detracts from the learning environment of the school.

Cell phones may not be used to harass, intimidate, or bully anyone, at any time. Our school does not support harassment, intimidation, or bullying of any person for any reason.

Source: Courtesy of FunnyMonkey (www.funnymonkey.com/cell-phone-policy). Used with permission.

Sample School Cell Phone Acceptable Use Policies

NEW CANAAN PUBLIC SCHOOLS INFORMATION AND COMMUNICATION TECHNOLOGIES ACCEPTABLE USE POLICY & GUIDELINES

To ensure that our students become proficient in the information and communication technologies (ICT) competencies essential for success in a twenty-first century learning environment, the New Canaan Public Schools provide a variety of resources in support of our instructional and administrative programs. Students and staff may also, at times, use their own personal information and communication technologies for educational purposes. Therefore, it is incumbent upon all members of the school community to use technology responsibly, ethically and respectful for the work of others. Access to ICT resources is a privilege and not a right. To ensure that ICT resources remain available in working order, the New Canaan Public Schools has established an **Acceptable Use Policy (AUP) and Guidelines:** http://bit.ly/NCPSAUP

In order to initiate and maintain access to ICT resources, all users must submit annually assigned *Acceptable Use Agreement* (detailed below), non-adherence of which may result in loss of non-course related access and/or appropriate disciplinary and/or legal action. Violations of the AUP are deemed as violations of school behavioral expectations and codes.

ACCEPTABLE USE AGREEMENT

ICT users are permitted to use the district's ICT resources for legitimate educational purposes. Personal use of district ICT resources is prohibited. In addition, if a particular behavior or activity is generally prohibited by law, by Board policy or by school rules or regulations, use of ICT resources for the purpose of carrying out such behavior or activity is prohibited.

By signing below, ICT users (and, for students, their parent/guardian) agree to always adhere to the following standards and expectations for conduct:

1. Behave ethically and responsibly when using ICT resources

    a. Refrain from utilizing proxy gateways, or similar technologies, to bypass the ICT monitoring and filtering.

b. Handle ICT resources and equipment with care. Refrain from deleting, destroying, modifying, abusing, or moving resources without permission or accessing unauthorized ICT resources.

c. Do not breach or disable network security mechanisms or compromise network stability or security in any way nor download or modify computer software in violation of the district's licensure agreement(s) and/or without authorization from the ICT Department.

2. Use ICT resources, transmit communications or access information only for legitimate, educationally relevant purposes and to access educationally appropriate content.

a. Refrain from sending any form of communication that breaches the district's confidentiality requirements, or the confidentiality of students.

b. Refrain from sending any form of communication that harasses, threatens or is discriminatory.

c. Refrain from accessing any material that is obscene, harmful to minors or prohibited by law.

d. Refrain from using social network tools for personal use.

3. Respect the privacy of others and treat information created by others as the private property of the creator.

a. Maintain confidentiality of your username and password by not sharing it with others and not using another person's username and password.

b. Maintain the integrity of files and data by not trespassing, modifying, copying or deleting files of other users without their consent.

c. Protect the confidentiality and safety of others when sharing work and images.

d. Share, post and publish only within the context of the district *Publishing Guidelines* (see link).

e. Respect copyright and fair use laws; these policies and procedures apply in digital contexts, as well. Plagiarism is prohibited

I have read, understand, and agree to abide by the terms of the Acceptable Use Policy. Should I commit any violation or in any way misuse my access to the school district's information and communication technologies resources, I understand that my access privilege may be revoked and disciplinary action may be taken against me.

ACCEPTABLE CELL PHONE USE FROM STUDENTS

Jason Suter, a secondary school science teacher in the Hanover Public School District in Pennsylvania, had students share their ideas for cell phone rules using code names for anonymity. One way you can collect these rules is by asking students to text them into a free response poll using a service such as Wiffiti or Poll Everywhere. Jason did this during school with his students and had them share their rules using a Wallwisher, which enables students to use their computers to place digital stickies on an electronic bulletin board. The bulletin board can be shared on the class website and also e-mailed to parents, possibly as a link in the permission letter. These are a few of the rules that his science students submitted, agreed to, and successfully follow when using cell phones for learning:

- You can't use cell phones unless told otherwise, no taking pictures unless told otherwise, don't take pictures of any other students if they don't want them taken.
- Cells on corner of desk until instructed, Must be on *silent!* Can text when done with work.
- Cell phone on corner of desk, cell phone should be on silent or off while teacher is teaching. If you break rules phone gets taken away until end of day.

Following the lesson Jason said, "Students loved using their cell phones! This is sometimes an understated reason for doing things in education. How can you go wrong if the students are excited for class before you even tell them what they will be doing?" During his lesson when he let students use cell phones for learning he shared that "[e]very student's eyes were glued to the Wiffiti board to read the next posted comment. The student's eagerness to read the articles so they could send another text message speaks volumes. Every student had the opportunity to voice his or her opinion in the pre- and postdiscussion polls. The students left the classroom and raved about class and using their cell phones during the periods that followed." Many teachers who've empowered students to develop their own rules around acceptable use find that when students have ownership real learning occurs.

LINKS TO SCHOOL DISTRICT ACCEPTABLE CELL PHONE USE POLICIES

- AHS personal wireless devices. Personally owned devices use policy from the Littleton Public Schools in Centennial, Colorado (http://arapahoe.littletonpublicschools.net/forStudents/PersonalWirelessDevices/tabid/3700/Default.aspx)

- Department of Education, Melbourne, Australia. Victoria's New Primary School Internet and mobile acceptable use kit (www.eduweb.vic.gov.au/edulibrary/public/ict/Primary_Internet_and_Mobile_Acceptable_Use_Kit.doc)
- Department of Education, Melbourne, Victoria's New Secondary internet and mobile acceptable use kit (www.eduweb.vic.gov.au/edulibrary/public/ict/Secondary_Internet_and_Mobile_Acceptable_Use_Kit.doc)
- Nova Scotia cell phone policy (http://public.sisd.cc/REMC3-9/Technology%20Plans/Nova%20Scotia%20Cell%20Phone%20policy_.pdf)
- Tahoma School District electronic resources user agreement and parent permission form (www.tahoma.wednet.edu/about/technology/documents/2022F-1ElectronicUse-ParentPermissionForm.pdf)

ESTABLISH CLASSROOM MANAGEMENT PROCEDURES

As with the use of any technology in the classroom, when using cell phones in the classroom you must have classroom management procedures in place. The nice thing, however, about cell phones is that you don't have to worry about distribution, collection, storage, imaging, and charging of devices. Following is a possible classroom management protocol. You'll want to modify this to your particular classroom needs and discuss with students prior to introducing cell phones into the classroom.

- On entry and departure of class, please ensure cell phones are turned off and stored in your backpack.
- On days when we are using cell phones for learning, please ensure they are set to silent.
- Only use phones for learning purposes related to class work.
- When phones are not in use on a day we are using cells for learning, place them face down on the upper right side of your desk.
- If you notice people in the class using their cell phone inappropriately, remind them to use proper cell phone etiquette.
- If at any time your teacher feels you are not using your cell phone for class work you will be asked to place your phone in the bin in the front of the room with a sticky note indicating your name and class.
  - After the first infraction each month you can collect your phone at the end of class.
  - After the second infraction you can collect your phone at the end of the day.

- After the third infraction your parent or guardian will be asked to retrieve your phone. If you use the phone inappropriately again during the month your parent or guardian will be required to retrieve your phone.

- At the beginning of each month, you have a clean slate.

Be open to modifications or suggestions your students may have. They may have some good ideas. This should be determined and posted in advance of using cell phones in the classroom.

Following is the discipline code developed by the Center for Education Policy and Law at the University of San Diego for secondary students in the case of misuse of electronic communication devices.

SUGGESTED STUDENT DISCIPLINE RULES

October 2011

Dear Parents and Guardians:

We recognize that electronic communication devices are an important part of our everyday world and are increasingly being used in teaching and learning. However, we do not want these devices to interfere with the students' learning environment. Please read the following discipline rules with your student and return the form with your signatures. Thank you.

1. Students must follow school rules when using any of the following electronic communication devices (ECDs):

   - Cell phones

   - Computers

   - Pagers

   - Portable game units

   - Other mechanisms that enable users to communicate electronically person-to-person or through Internet social networking sites such as Facebook, Myspace, and Twitter.

2. School rules apply when students are at school or attending a school-sponsored or -related activity off campus. They apply when students are doing the following:

- Attending class

- Socializing in hallways and elsewhere on school grounds

- Using school media centers, restrooms, locker rooms, gyms, and other school facilities

- Going to and from school

- Eating lunch on or off campus

- Attending school-sponsored activities off campus such as field trips or dances

- Attending school-related activities off campus such as away football games

3. The following will result in student discipline for any of these activities:

   - Refusal to turn off an ECD when told to by a teacher, administrator, coach, counselor, or other school official

   - Damaging an ECD owned by the school

   - Causing disruption

   - Using an ECD to cheat, including getting and giving answers to tests and copying from the Internet

   - Using an ECD to bully, threaten, harass, or attack another student or school personnel whether or not communicated directly to that person

   - Sending (or asking to receive) pictures or videos of people who are partially or completely undressed or are pretending to or actually performing a sexual act

4. Additionally, the school may punish students who misuse ECDs away from school on their own time if both of the following are true:

   - The student's use of the ECD causes significant disruption at school or serious harm to the school, other students, or school personnel.

   - The student knew, or should have known, that the harm would happen.

5. When a student misuses an ECD, the school may do the following, as long as the severity of the school's action matches the seriousness of the student's misuse of the ECD:

- Search the ECD within the context of the alleged misuse.

- Warn the student verbally or in writing.

- Take away the ECD. Depending on the offense, the school may keep the ECD for the rest of the school day or longer.

- Deny the student the privilege of participating in extracurricular and athletic activities.

- Contact the student's parents, school security, or the police.

- Suspend or expel the student from school in accord with student discipline procedures.

I have received a copy of these Student Discipline Rules governing my use of electronic communication devices (ECDs). I understand that failure to follow these rules may result in discipline and affect my right to use ECDs while at school and at school-sponsored or -related activities both on and off campus.

_____   _____

Name of student (print)   Date

_____   _____

Signature   Date

_____   _____

Signature of parent or guardian   Date

Please return this form to the school office no later than _____.

Note: These rules are developed in the context of federal and California law. Whether they are appropriate for other states depends on the law in those states. It may be appropriate to have both teachers and students review these rules to see if they are understandable or should be reworded to make them so. These rules are suggestive only and are not intended to take the place of expert advice and assistance from a lawyer. If specific legal advice or assistance is required, the services of a competent professional should be sought.

Source: Used with permission of the Center for Education Policy and Law at the University of San Diego.

RULES FOR TOOLS

Cell Phone Tool Used
Wiffiti

Preparation
Go to http://wiffiti.com and create a page entitled "Rules for Tools." Have the Wiffiti number and text-in code ready to share with students.

Lesson Overview
Students will generate rules and acceptable use for using cell phones for learning in class and at home.

Lesson Description

- Ask students to discuss the rules and acceptable use for tools that already exist for the class (sharpen pencil before class, use loose leaf paper, pay for lost books, raise your hand to talk, no calculators on tests, and so on).

- Have students discuss acceptable use and the rules they think should be in place for using cell phones in class and at home to support learning. Guide the sharing by raising issues with cell phones (distraction, cheating, privacy).

- Have students privately text their ideas for rules and acceptable use in to the Wiffiti you have set up. Students don't need to sign in. They just text their answer to the Wiffiti code you share with them. For example, Text @ wif41122 + your message to 87884. Remind students to word rules in the positive: *We will turn off our phones during tests. We will have them on vibrate during instructional time. We will do our social texting outside of class.*

- The final "rules for tools" will be posted online for parents to view (linked to the Wiffiti, embedded in class website or wiki, school website, e-mailed home, and so on) and printed for the classroom. They could be included in the parent permission letter.

- You will want to share consequences for not following rules and acceptable use in place. You may choose to have students brainstorm consequences if rules are not followed or you may already have consequences in place for rules in general that you'll want to apply to cell phone use.

How the Use of Cell Phones Enriches This Lesson

- By using cell phones for the lesson you are practicing what you preach.
- By using the Wiffiti page all students can contribute anonymously. Honest sharing, valuable insight, and giving all students a voice are all the result of texting into Wiffiti.
- The rules generated will be effective because all of the students had input.

NETS for Students Addressed

- Creativity and innovation
- Communication and collaboration
- Critical thinking, problem solving, and decision making
- Digital citizenship

NETS for Teachers Addressed

- Facilitate and inspire student learning and creativity
- Design and develop digital-age learning experiences and assessments
- Model digital-age work and learning

Research-Based Instructional Strategies Used

- Summarizing and note taking
- Cooperative learning

PLAN ACTIVITIES WITH STUDENTS

A well thought-out plan for embedding cell phones into instruction is key. Create and develop lessons and activities that are truly enriched by the use of cell phones, which you can share with those who want to know what you have in store for the use of cell phones in the classroom. This plan can be shared on your class and school website as well as distributed to parents, guardians, and school community members. See Chapter Five for a lesson planning template as well as lesson ideas. For additional lesson and activity ideas visit the following sites:

- Mobile learning lesson plans (www2.scholastic.com/browse/collection.jsp?id=766)
- St Marys schools' lesson ideas (www.smriders.net/Mobile_Learning/docs/LessonPlans .pdf)

Remember the importance of celebrating and promoting the work you are doing. Invite administrators and policy makers to observe the lessons. If possible, involve them as students in the class so they can actually participate and experience first-hand an activity that promotes student engagement and achievement.

PARTNER WITH STUDENTS TO PLAN FOR LEARNING WITH CELLS

When using technology for learning, Marc Prensky's concept of partnering with students fits in well. Bring students into the conversation about ways they can meet learning goals in life, at school, and at home. The following are ideas one class came up with when they were invited to join the conversation about ways they could use their phones for learning.

Use Cell Phones for Real Life

For learning: Text an expert; set up a poll of experts, parents, and peers; or brainstorm ideas with others using a Wiffiti.

For organization: Use your phone tools for due dates in the calendar, alarms and reminders to study, notes for study on the go, calculator, and camera to capture learning and information as it happens.

Use Cell Phones for Class Outside of School

For communication: Strengthen communication with your parents by texting them about your class work, due dates, important information, and to encourage them to communicate with your school. Communicate with your teachers, coaches, and peers to stay up-to-date when absent, when you have a question on an assignment, or need to discuss an idea.

For homework: Group texts offer free ways to set up a study group. Ask questions before and review after class to extend learning. Cooperative learning helps learning and increased communication builds relationships. Here are some tools to use:

ChaCha and Google SMS offer homework help.

Google Voice and Voki offer other ways to do homework.

Using pictures and videos takes home learning into the classroom.

Use Cell Phones in Class

Invite your students to partner with you around a conversation of cell phones and learning. Capture their responses, then share the ideas mentioned in the previous section to see if there are any others students want to add. The ideas can be posted on the classroom website, blog, or wiki, with credit given to the students who are able to take more ownership of how they learn both at school and on their own. Here are some examples of student ideas:

Allows us to choose the device that makes the best sense.

Enjoy 100 percent participation in idea sharing, brainstorming, and feedback with polls and Wiffiti pages.

Have the tools we use at home available in class.

Individualize instruction for special needs, various learning styles, and availability of technology.

Taking a metacognitive approach to embedding cell phones provides a plan structure that is based on the goal-setting research in *Classroom Instruction That Works*, 2nd edition (Dean, Hubbell, Pitler, & Stone, 2012). By creating a plan as a goal-setting activity, students are given input, choice, and ownership. Once developed, these plans can be shared at the teacher's online blog, wiki, or website in slideshow format. This can be done easily by taking pictures of each plan and having students e-mail them to a teacher's Flickr account pretagged as "Cell Plans." The subject could be the student's first name or alias and the word plan (for example, "Willyn's Plan") and the subject can be a short description for the photo caption, such as "my great ideas for making learning fun with cell phones!" Once completed, these slide shows can be shared with parents, guardians, administrators, and each other. These make great testimonials for how cell phones can be used for learning. After students become familiar with the tools, you may want to repeat this activity and see how students' plans have been successful and add new ideas. The discussion could be about what worked. You could encourage students to share evidence of improvement and enhancement (such as in grades, test scores, testimonials, or pictures). The following lesson plan will guide you and your students through developing a pathway for using cell phones.

PLANS FOR PHONES (OR PLNZ 4 FONZ)

Subject
Any

Cell Phone Tool Used
Poll Everywhere

Preparation
Have the list of cell phone uses called the "Gr8 8 Top Educational Uses of Cell Phones" at the end of this lesson ready to be projected or prepare a list of your own to share with students. Go to www.polleverywhere.com and create a free text poll (open response) and have the text-in code ready to share with students. Also create a multiple choice poll for the question, "Which of the Gr8 would you most like to use for learning?" and have the text-in codes for the answers ready to share with students.

Lesson Overview
This is a planning lesson on the process of embedding cell phones in learning. Students will focus on cell phones as learning tools. With an overview of the educational uses of cell phones (see "Gr8 8" handout later in this lesson), students will determine how they will choose to use their cell phones for educational purposes. Contracts for tools will be developed by students and the result will be a plan for educational uses of cell phones that can be shared with all stakeholders.

Lesson Description

- Start with a class discussion about general tools for learning such as calculators, dictionaries, pens and paper, books, and their purposes.

- Share the "Gr8 8" to get students thinking about some ways that cell phones can be used for learning.

- Ask students if they do (or if they want to) use their phones for learning in life, for learning in school, for homework.

- Create a free text poll on a service such as Poll Everywhere to ask students to share the tools available on their phones. This captures all of the available, educational, free cell phone tools that are in students' pockets.

- Create a multiple choice poll on which of the "Gr8 8" would students like most to use for learning.
- You may want to share these poll results with parents, administrators, and other teachers.
- Students create plans explaining how they will use cell phone tools for learning using the following template.

When at school or at home, I will use my cell phone appropriately for learning in following ways:

I will use my cell phone to	The tool I will use is	This will help me learn better because	How will you know your plan is working?	Did your plan work? (To be completed at the end of a lesson or unit of study)
Example 1: Do research	ChaCha	When I don't have access to the Internet, I still have information and experts available to me.	I will turn in assignments more often because I will get stuck less.	
Example 2: Reach out to an expert when I am stuck on my work.	Text messaging or voice	I will start thinking about and collecting experts to connect with. This way I will learn more and have a lot of resources.	The quality of my work will improve because I will have a bank of expert resources to turn to. I will also use more references in my work.	

Adapted from Webb (1999).

These planning worksheets provide great evidence to make a case about the benefits of cell phones.

- At the end of each unit, teachers and students can share and learn new ways for using cells to learn.

GR8 8—TOP EDUCATIONAL USES OF CELL PHONES

1. *Engagement:* audience-response polls, Wiffitis, 100 percent participation, can be anonymous

2. *Communication:* group texting, group projects, cooperative learning

3. *Home-school connection:* group texts to parents, parent texts to teacher and student

4. *Homework:* phone rarely lost, answer questions on phone, review notes, and so on when on the go

5. *Research:* Google SMS, ChaCha, or text an expert

6. *Organization:* calendar, alarm, reminders, calculator, and notes

7. *Varied sensory instruction:* Google Voice, Voki, pictures

8. *Visual:* camera or video

How the Use of Cell Phones Enriches This Lesson

- The poll encourages all students to participate.
- Responses are collected instantly saving time that can be devoted to learning.

NETS for Students Addressed

- Creativity and innovation
- Communication and collaboration
- Research and information fluency
- Critical thinking, problem solving, and decision making

NETS for Teachers Addressed

- Facilitate and inspire student learning and creativity
- Design and develop digital-age learning experiences and assessments
- Model digital-age work and learning

Research-Based Instructional Strategies Used

- Summarizing and note taking
- Homework and practice
- Nonlinguistic representations
- Setting objectives and providing feedback

A SOLID FOUNDATION

The information, lessons, and resources in each of these building blocks for success provides you the means to lay the groundwork for the effective integration of cell phones in your classroom. It is essential that each of these areas be addressed to move from banning to embracing cells in the classroom. As the saying goes, being forewarned is being forearmed. By taking the time to address each of the building blocks, you will prevent problems, your classroom will have support from your administration, it will run more smoothly, your students will be engaged, and you will all be better prepared to harness the power of the tools of the twenty-first century.

chapter FIVE

Cell Phone–Enriched Lessons to Engage Learners

> *If we teach today as we taught yesterday, we rob our children of tomorrow.*
> John Dewey, educator and philosopher

Although integrating cell phones into instruction can be a great way to engage learners and enrich instruction, it is important to ensure you are doing both. Just using a cell phone itself will lose its appeal and value quickly if it doesn't actually enable students to either do things better or do better things. When using cell phones in instruction educators should ask themselves if the use of technology will actually enhance the unit or lesson and how. As you think about integrating cell phones into a unit of study, you can use the planning tool shown in Table 5.1. *Note:* It works best in Excel or Google spreadsheets.

Thinking of how cell phones maybe be used in general in a unit is a great place to start. The planning tool lets you think of broad ideas for cell phone use within a unit as well as ideas for support that might be helpful. Support may come from a district or school-based coach, another teacher, a leader, a parent, a student, and so on. Once you have come up with general

Table 5.1

Cell Phone Integration Planning Tool

Unit Overview	Innovative Ideas to Enrich This Unit	Ways Technology Enriches This Unit	NETS for Students Addressed	NETS for Teachers Addressed	Content Standards Addressed

ideas to enrich instruction, you can drill down to a particular lesson you want to teach. The following lesson plan format can be used for the sample lesson plans in this chapter.

Lesson Title:

Subject:

Topic:

Cell Phone Tool(s) Used:

Preparation:

Lesson Overview:
(about two sentences—-may include goals, objectives, teaching points)

Lesson Description:

How the Use of Cell Phones Enriches This Lesson:

National Education Technology Standards for Students (NETS•S) Addressed:

National Education Technology Standards for Teachers (NETS•T) Addressed:

Research-Based Instructional Strategies Used:

Assessment:
In this chapter you will find sample lessons in a variety of content areas that use tools you have learned about in previous chapters. These lessons can be modified to work with any range of grade levels. Creating a cell phone–enriched lesson generally doesn't take any longer than a traditional lesson, generally one or two class periods. If you are using cell phones for instruction for the first time, however, you will need to incorporate additional time for setting up accounts you may be using. Once the accounts are set up, using cell phones will happen quickly and easily. We know you'll enjoy implementing

lessons such as these with your students and we hope they inspire you to develop ideas for generating your own lessons as well.

The National Educational Technology Standards (NETS) for students and teachers help guide teachers to ensure they are teaching and their students are learning in ways that will ensure they are prepared for the digital world in which they live. The lessons in this chapter are written with these standards in mind. Each lesson is aligned to various NETS student and teacher standards in an effort to ensure students will have competence in the use of technology.

NETS STANDARDS FOR STUDENTS (NETS•S)

1. *Creativity and innovation:* Students demonstrate creative thinking, construct knowledge, and develop innovative products and processes using technology. Students

   a. apply existing knowledge to generate new ideas, products, or processes.

   b. create original works as a means of personal or group expression.

   c. use models and simulations to explore complex systems and issues.

   d. identify trends and forecast possibilities.

2. *Communication and collaboration:* Students use digital media and environments to communicate and work collaboratively, including at a distance, to support individual learning and contribute to the learning of others. Students

   a. interact, collaborate, and publish with peers, experts, or others employing a variety of digital environments and media.

   b. communicate information and ideas effectively to multiple audiences using a variety of media and formats.

   c. develop cultural understanding and global awareness by engaging with learners of other cultures.

   d. contribute to project teams to produce original works or solve problems.

3. *Research and information fluency:* Students apply digital tools to gather, evaluate, and use information. Students

   a. plan strategies to guide inquiry.

   b. locate, organize, analyze, evaluate, synthesize, and ethically use information from a variety of sources and media.

c. evaluate and select information sources and digital tools based on the appropriateness to specific tasks.

d. process data and report results.

4. *Critical thinking, problem solving, and decision making:* Students use critical thinking skills to plan and conduct research, manage projects, solve problems, and make informed decisions using appropriate digital tools and resources. Students

a. identify and define authentic problems and significant questions for investigation.

b. plan and manage activities to develop a solution or complete a project.

c. collect and analyze data to identify solutions and/or make informed decisions.

d. use multiple processes and diverse perspectives to explore alternative solutions.

5. *Digital citizenship:* Students understand human, cultural, and societal issues related to technology and practice legal and ethical behavior. Students

a. advocate and practice safe, legal, and responsible use of information and technology.

b. exhibit a positive attitude toward using technology that supports collaboration, learning, and productivity.

c. demonstrate personal responsibility for lifelong learning.

d. exhibit leadership for digital citizenship.

6. *Technology operations and concepts:* Students demonstrate a sound understanding of technology concepts, systems, and operations. Students

a. understand and use technology systems.

b. select and use applications effectively and productively.

c. troubleshoot systems and applications.

d. transfer current knowledge to learning of new technologies.

NETS STANDARDS FOR TEACHERS (NETS•T)

1. *Facilitate and inspire student learning and creativity:* Teachers use their knowledge of subject matter, teaching and learning, and technology to facilitate experiences that advance student learning, creativity, and innovation in both face-to-face and virtual environments. Teachers

a. promote, support, and model creative and innovative thinking and inventiveness.

b. engage students in exploring real-world issues and solving authentic problems using digital tools and resources.

c. promote student reflection using collaborative tools to reveal and clarify students' conceptual understanding and thinking, planning, and creative processes.

d. model collaborative knowledge construction by engaging in learning with students, colleagues, and others in face-to-face and virtual environments.

2. *Design and develop digital-age learning experiences and assessments:* Teachers design, develop, and evaluate authentic learning experiences and assessment incorporating contemporary tools and resources to maximize content learning in context and to develop the knowledge, skills, and attitudes identified in the NETS•S. Teachers

a. design or adapt relevant learning experiences that incorporate digital tools and resources to promote student learning and creativity.

b. develop technology-enriched learning environments that enable all students to pursue their individual curiosities and become active participants in setting their own educational goals, managing their own learning, and assessing their own progress.

c. customize and personalize learning activities to address students' diverse learning styles, working strategies, and abilities using digital tools and resources.

d. provide students with multiple and varied formative and summative assessments aligned with content and technology standards and use resulting data to inform learning and teaching.

3. *Model digital-age work and learning:* Teachers exhibit knowledge, skills, and work processes representative of an innovative professional in a global and digital society. Teachers

a. demonstrate fluency in technology systems and the transfer of current knowledge to new technologies and situations.

b. collaborate with students, peers, parents, and community members using digital tools and resources to support student success and innovation.

c. communicate relevant information and ideas effectively to students, parents, and peers using a variety of digital-age media and formats.

d. model and facilitate effective use of current and emerging digital tools to locate, analyze, evaluate, and use information resources to support research and learning.

4. *Promote and model digital citizenship and responsibility:* Teachers understand local and global societal issues and responsibilities in an evolving digital culture and exhibit legal and ethical behavior in their professional practices. Teachers

   a. advocate, model, and teach safe, legal, and ethical use of digital information and technology, including respect for copyright, intellectual property, and the appropriate documentation of sources.

   b. address the diverse needs of all learners by using learner-centered strategies providing equitable access to appropriate digital tools and resources.

   c. promote and model digital etiquette and responsible social interactions related to the use of technology and information.

   d. develop and model cultural understanding and global awareness by engaging with colleagues and students of other cultures using digital-age communication and collaboration tools.

5. *Engage in professional growth and leadership:* Teachers continuously improve their professional practice, model lifelong learning, and exhibit leadership in their school and professional community by promoting and demonstrating the effective use of digital tools and resources. Teachers

   a. participate in local and global learning communities to explore creative applications of technology to improve student learning.

   b. exhibit leadership by demonstrating a vision of technology infusion, participating in shared decision making and community building, and developing the leadership and technology skills of others.

   c. evaluate and reflect on current research and professional practice on a regular basis to make effective use of existing and emerging digital tools and resources in support of student learning.

   d. contribute to the effectiveness, vitality, and self-renewal of the teaching profession and of their school and community.

STUDENTS AS TEACHERS

Although it is customary for teachers to be responsible for lesson development, when it comes to technology, students are often the experts. The authors of this book have supported teachers in using a strategy Marc Prensky refers to as "partnering" with students in his book, *Teaching Digital Natives: Partnering for Real Learning* (2010). As you reflect on the uses of cell phones that you have read about in previous chapters and read the following lessons, we encourage you to imagine bringing your students into the conversation. Ask them how they might better learn what you plan to teach using their cell phones. This should prove enlightening for educators wanting to broaden their knowledge of cell phone uses applicable to education. It will also get the students excited about interacting with the curriculum. It is an age-old truth that when you teach, you learn. So encourage your students to partner with you as teachers. Adding texting, picture messages, or whatever else they can design on their phones will make the lesson fresh, exciting, and theirs.

STANDARDS-ALIGNED LESSONS SUPPORTED BY CELL PHONES

CELEBRATING SCIENCE FAIR PROJECTS WITH TWITTER

Subject
Science

Topic
Science fairs

Cell Phone Tool Used
Twitter

Preparation
See the previous chapters for information on using Twitter with students. Your students will need an academic Twitter account (discuss consequences for inappropriate use) and the school will need to have a tag established for this lesson. Cell phones used will need to have Twitter entered in their phone (40404) and be enabled to receive text updates, which can be set up at http://twitter.com/devices. If the school is planning to run a feed on its website or blog there are numerous ways to do this on a variety of hosts. To find what is right for you, Google "twitter feed on website." Tweets can be searched by placing the search term in Twitter or another tool like Twitterfall.com or TweetDeck.com.

Lesson Overview

Science fair judges will use Twitter tags to share meaningful feedback at a school science fair.

Lesson Description

This lesson brings science fairs into the twenty-first century using Twitter. Traditional science fairs consist of judges going around from project to project often with student creators never really knowing what those looking at their projects are thinking about their work or the work of their classmates. What's more, parents and families rarely find out what was showcased and have little opportunity to join in on the experience. This lesson changes all of that.

Student reporters with cell phones are assigned stations throughout the science fair. They may be in individual booths, certain areas, or dispersed throughout. These students are assigned to the "science fair tweet beat" where they will interview judges about the science fair projects asking questions such as the following:

"What projects had surprising findings?"

"What project made you go *wow!* and why?"

"What project made you go *hmmmm . . .* and why?"

"What project has the most potential for affecting the environment? Explain."

Work with your students and colleagues to determine other relevant questions. If student personal learning devices are banned at your school, then selected teachers could share their cell phones with the student reporters to capture the tweet beat.

When students tweet they will use the short school Twitter tag that you have created in their message as well as the Twitter username of the person's project being discussed. For example the tag for Susan B. Anthony High School in Los Angeles, California, might be "SBALA." The tweet could be, "@Innovativeedu's project at the SBALA's science fair will allow any garden to grow tropical fruit from egg shells!"

This way students can follow what is happening with their projects, the school will have an updated science fair stream that they can publish to their website, and interested parents, friends, family, can join in on the conversation tweeting feedback, reactions, questions, and thoughts. As individual students follow the tweets about them, they should be encouraged to respond and keep the conversation going.

How the Use of Cell Phones Enriches This Lesson

- Using Twitter to capture a science fair tweet beat enables students to get a deeper glimpse into the heads of attendees.
- It provides a home-school connection enabling parents and family members who can't be present at the school to follow how their child's project is going and even create their own tweets to join the conversation.
- Hosting a tweet beat science fair enables students to celebrate their work not only with the judges, but also with parents, family, and the world.

NETS•S Addressed

- Creativity and innovation
- Communication and collaboration
- Critical thinking, problem solving, and decision making
- Digital citizenship

NETS•T Addressed

- Facilitate and inspire student learning and creativity
- Design and develop digital-age learning experiences and assessments
- Model digital-age work and learning

Research-Based Instructional Strategies Used

- Summarizing and note taking
- Reinforcing effort and providing recognition
- Setting objectives and providing feedback

Assessment

Although the science fair projects will be assessed using the school's traditional methods, using Twitter provides students, the school community, and parents with an additional authentic, real-time view into the minds of those who are seeing their projects. If the school chooses, the tweet feedback could be included in the final project ranking scorecards. Scorecards typically include points for oral presentation, project presentation, clearly stated objectives, understanding of experiment, data collection, and data interpretation.

ENERGY TRANSFER LAB WITH CELL PHONE CLOCK

(Lesson created by Dolores Gende, academic technology coordinator, Dallas, Texas.)

Subject
Science

Topic
Physics

Cell Phone Tool Used
Clock

Preparation
In addition to the cell phone clocks, you will need a dynamics track and cart, pulley, hanger and set of masses, and a meter stick. The cell phone clock will be used in the stopwatch mode.

Lesson Overview
This is an inquiry activity in which students design their own experiment to determine the energy transfer that occurs in a mechanical system. The students are expected to do at least three trials to measure the time taken for the cart to move a certain distance or for the hanging mass to fall a certain distance. With measurements of time and distance the students can use a kinematic equation to calculate either the acceleration of the system or the average velocity. With this information the students determine the final velocity of the system to calculate the kinetic energy. The final calculations involve finding the

potential energy of the hanging mass. For a helpful physics labs link, including tutorials, experiments, open-ended lab ideas, and video analysis technology, see http://apphysicsb.homestead.com/labs.html.

Lesson Description

Divide the students into groups. Explain to the students that their task is to design an experiment to quantitatively measure energy transfer and the changes in energy storage.

Their experiment should include the following sections:

1. Hypothesis

   - Define the system.

   - Give the team's prediction for conservation of energy of the system.

   - What assumptions are you making?

2. Procedure

   - Identify all experimental variables.

   - Draw a neat, labeled diagram to illustrate the configuration of the equipment.

   - Write your step-by-step procedure.

   - Use symbols to clearly identify what measurements you need to make.

3. Data and analysis

   - What data need to be taken?

   - How many trials do you have to include?

   - How are data reported?

   - How do you interpret data?

   - Show all calculations as appropriate.

   - Complete an energy bar chart or energy flow diagram.

4. Conclusion

   - How well did your experiment confirm your prediction?

   - Discuss any surprising results.

   - Explain the possible source of error(s).

5. Presentation

- Prepare a report of your experiment.

6. Rubric

- Use the class-created assessment rubric.

How the Use of Cell Phones Enriches This Lesson

- The use of the stopwatch in a physics lab is ubiquitous and standard laboratory stopwatches are not always reliable. The most common problems are dead batteries, stuck buttons, delay in response, and so on.
- Using the standard clock in a cell phone has improved data collection and the cell phone interface is superior to that of a traditional stopwatch, allowing students to take better measurements with less time delay.

NETS•S Addressed

- Research and information fluency
- Critical thinking, problem solving, and decision making

NETS•T Addressed

- Design and develop digital-age learning experiences and assessments
- Model digital-age work and learning

Research-Based Instructional Strategies Used

- Summarizing and note taking
- Generating and testing hypotheses

Assessment

You can use the following rubric for assessment using a scale. Work with your students to determine what makes up each level of proficiency and empower them to do a self-assessment and peer assessment prior to the teacher assessment.

	Highly Proficient	Proficient	Developing Proficiency	Not Proficient

1. *Hypothesis*
   - The system is defined, the prediction is clearly stated, and the assumptions are identified.

2. *Procedure*
   - All experimental variables are identified and the equipment setup is neatly drawn and labeled.
   - The measurements are clearly marked with symbols.
   - An easy-to-follow, step-by-step procedure is given.

3. *Data and data analysis*
   - Data table is neatly recorded in multiple trials.
   - The analysis includes equations, calculations, and all answers include appropriate units.
   - The bar chart or energy flow diagram clearly illustrates the energy transfer and energy storage.

4. *Conclusion*
   - A reasonable judgment is made and assumptions are taken into account.
   - The possible source(s) of error is or are explained.
   - A revision is made that is consistent with all relevant evidence.

PREPARE FOR STANDARDIZED SCIENCE TESTS WITH POLL EVERYWHERE AND WIFFITI

(Lesson created by Jason Suter, teacher, grades 8–12, Hanover, Pennsylvania, with Lisa Smith.)

Subject
Science or social studies

Topic
Studying to meet tested standards

Cell Phone Tools Used
Poll Everywhere, Wiffiti

Preparation
Set up Poll Everywhere and Wiffiti accounts in advance as explained in Chapters One and Two.

Lesson Overview
The Pennsylvania System of State Assessment exams cover a wide range of science standards. Many of the topics covered come from science classes outside the physical science course taught during a student's eighth-grade year at Hanover Middle School. This lesson linked material from the Pennsylvania state standards to a current event and was intended to help keep standards taught in previous years fresh in the students' minds.

Lesson Description
This lesson is designed to help prepare science or social studies students for upcoming standardized tests by exposing them to current events that relate to material from past lessons. The following Pennsylvania state standards were considered in preparing this lesson:

- Analyze the development of technology based on affordability or urgency.

- Compare and contrast decisions to develop and use technologies as related to environmental and economic concerns.

- Explain how new technologies have resulted from the demands, values, and interests of individuals, businesses, industries, and societies.

- Explain how societal and cultural priorities and values are reflected in technological devices.

- Compare and contrast alternative sources of energy.

Have students take a closer look at a current event with a pro and con side that addresses the selected standard(s). For this lesson President Obama's decision to build new nuclear power plants in the United States was used.

Create an online poll using http://polleverywhere.com. In this example, the poll asked students whether or not they believed it was a good idea to build new nuclear power plants in the United States. The students use their cell phones to vote.

After the students take the poll they are given two articles: the first outlining President Obama's plans and the second discussing the pros and cons of nuclear power. The students read the articles in groups and are asked to write the main points from each article. After the students finish reading and writing their main points they are instructed to come to a group consensus on the topic. The group is asked to summarize their opinion in one to two sentences and post it using their cell phones to a Wiffiti board.

Once all the groups' comments have been posted, read, and discussed, the students watch a two-minute video that summarizes the discussion. For this lesson, a YouTube video clip of a news network discussing the pros and cons of President Obama's plan was used. The lesson ends with the students taking the same poll they took in the beginning of class. Poll Everywhere enables you and your students to instantly see that after doing some reading, talking, and thinking about an issue, many will have changed their opinion.

How the Use of Cell Phones Enriches This Lesson

- Even though mobile computers are a great tool in the classroom they require an extended amount of start-up time. In an activity such as this, when the Internet is only accessed for a few seconds to take a poll or post a response, the "always on" nature of a cell phone becomes a terrific time-saver.

- Having student groups text responses to Wiffiti provides an instant collection of responses in one place that can be accessed and archived for on-demand viewing by students in class, students who are absent, or students who want to review what was discussed in class.

- Using Poll Everywhere to collect responses provides an instant graphic representation of results that can be shared side by side. It also allows for anonymous collection of student opinion without requiring opinions to be stated publicly when students may feel the need to vote based on who their friends are rather than what they really believe.

NETS•S Addressed

- Communication and collaboration
- Research and information fluency

NETS•T Addressed

- Facilitate and inspire student learning and creativity
- Design and develop digital-age learning experiences and assessments

Research-Based Instructional Strategies Used

- Summarizing and note taking
- Reinforcing effort and providing recognition
- Cooperative learning
- Setting objectives and providing feedback
- Generating and testing hypotheses

Assessment

This lesson is designed to help assess student understanding. You can use the opinions posted to the Wiffiti board, class discussion, and results of the exit poll to determine if the class understands the concepts or needs additional support. It is also helpful to elicit peer feedback from students during the classroom discussion.

DEVELOPING A CITY GUIDE USING GOOGLE SMS

Subject
Social studies

Topic
My community and your community: Comparing and contrasting

Cell Phone Tool Used
Google SMS

Preparation
Review the instructions for using Google SMS in Chapters One and Two. To use the online interactive demo, visit www.google.ca/mobile/sms/index.html. The demo enables you to view the results of a query as it would look on your own mobile device.

Lesson Overview
Lead the class through an activity in which students study various characteristics of their own community using Google SMS.

Lesson Description
In class, using Google SMS simulator, work with students to find about different aspects of their school's community including population, weather, local information, such as businesses, parks, what movies are playing, and so on. Brainstorm with your class what other types of things would be interesting to look up in your community.

The Google SMS simulator allows you to use your laptop to model how students can do this work with their cell phones. After the demonstration, ask students to research another community using Google SMS in which they explore these same characteristics. Which community they explore will be dependent on your curricular focus. For example, you might want them to study the community their ancestors came from or perhaps various cities in a particular state or country of study.

Once students have used their cell phones to gather this information they should take the information they found about the community they are studying, combine it with the information the class discovered when studying their own community, and write a report sharing what they would like and wouldn't like about living in each community. Encourage students to expand on the information you asked them to find and request that they come up with at least three additional characteristics to explore in each city. For example, they may want to look up amusement parks, churches, hotels, skateboard parks, and compare the similarities and differences of each of the two communities.

The finished reports can become part of a number of larger class projects, for instance, one of the following:

- A map of the area could be posted on a bulletin board with each report pinned (in a format that gets unfolded) onto each part of the map. Sticky notes could be placed on the board so others could comment on each report. All projects could be posted on a Wikispace page that celebrates the topic being studied. A thought-provoking question to readers could be placed on the discussion tab and readers could use the tab to ask questions.

- Students could record their report using a Voki and all the Vokis could be posted on a site (such as a class wiki or web page). Students could use the comment feature on Voki to comment to one another about what they heard.

How the Use of Cell Phones Enriches This Lesson

- The integration of cell phones into this lesson provides students with resources and the flexibility to find information that is not readily available in classrooms without technology.

- The use of this tool enables students to research, explore, compare, and contrast a multitude of different topics in a city of interest on demand.

NETS•S Addressed

- Creativity and innovation
- Communication and collaboration
- Research and information fluency
- Critical thinking, problem solving, and decision making
- Digital citizenship

NETS•T Addressed

- Facilitate and inspire student learning and creativity
- Design and develop digital-age learning experiences and assessments
- Model digital-age work and learning

Research-Based Instructional Strategies Used

- Identifying similarities and differences
- Summarizing and note taking
- Cues, questions, and advance organizers
- Practice
- Reinforcing effort and providing recognition
- Setting objectives and providing feedback

Assessment

For this lesson, you should use a general writing assessment rubric containing items such as organization, sentence fluency, voice, grammar conventions, word choice, and clarity. Because this writing is comparing two communities, you'll also want to add a component such as identified similarities and differences to reach relevant conclusions or insights.

WHERE IN THE WORLD?

Subject
Math and social studies

Topics
Time, geography

Cell Phone Tools Used
Cell phone calculators, cell phone world clocks, Twitter

Preparation

Have students find the world clock in the Tools menu on their cell phones. Set up cooperative groups as needed, depending on cell phone availability. Experiment with the world clock by selecting a few cities and getting familiar with how it looks. All students will need their academic Twitter account set up and should be reminded that everything on this account should be appropriate. Discuss consequences for inappropriate use. Ensure that a tag is set up for the project so tweets can be followed. Cell phones used will need to have Twitter entered in their phone (40404) and be enabled to receive text updates, which can be set up at http://twitter.com/devices. (*Note:* Setting up Twitter is covered in detail in Chapter Two.) Have the number for ChaCha (242242) ready to provide to students as a homework help source.

Lesson Overview

Students will use cell phone world clocks to find the time in cities around the world, calculate the difference in their current time, and respond appropriately using Twitter. Students will use cell phone world clocks, tweet times, and cell calculators to determine the location of classmates. Many concepts such as military time, twenty-four-hour time, signed numbers, and global direction will be covered. The lesson could be presented like a game to the students as "Where in the World Am I?" The game element may be a fun way to motivate students in determining each others' locations.

Lesson Description

Students will work individually or in cooperative groups. Give each student or group the task of planning a multistop (number of stops determined by the teacher) trip to certain cities around the world. After providing students with either an expository or graphic advance organizer explaining the times zones of the world, have students consider the similarities and differences in the various time zones and discuss the International Date Line. Have students practice using the formulas (following) to determine times in different locations. The goal (or game objective) is to calculate each others' locations, answering the question (or playing it as a game), *Where in the world am I?* by reading each others' tweets, which will give clues to time and location. Students should tweet for each stop on their planned trip itinerary and respond to the tweets of their classmates.

Teach students the following formulas:

- The formula for determining military time: morning times are as is and afternoon times are $t + 12$.
- The formula for determining the difference in times in different locations (in military time): destination time—location time = D

After a discussion about the International Date Line, teach students the following formulas:

- If destination time—location time = D is a positive number, the destination location is east.
- If destination time—location time = D is a negative number, the destination location is west.
- If the times are on different dates, add 24 to the "next day" entry before you subtract.
  - *Example:* Tokyo 10:00 a.m. on 5–6–10 and Denver is 8:00 p.m. on 5–5–10.
  - $(10 + 24)$ and $8 + 12$ (military) so $24 - 20 = 14$, the time difference between Tokyo and Denver heading east.

Have students use the world clock on their cell phones to determine the date and time in their destination cities at various times throughout the day and text into Twitter using the assigned tag with a greeting indicative of the time of day in that city and a tweet comment giving clues to the difference in the times of day for them as compared to their home (or previous location). For example, *Good morning from Rome. How is your afternoon going in Colorado?*

Fellow students will follow the tweets, use their cell phone world clocks at the time they are reading the tweets, and respond appropriately. For example, *Still sleeping here in Rio de Janeiro. When you're having lunch in Colorado, I'll be enjoying my afternoon at the beach.* The students will be able to calculate each others' locations through the tweet time on Twitter, the world clock on their phones, and the formulas for calculating the differences. Based on the tweets (clues) the students will be able to calculate each others' locations (the city where the student is at that particular time) and win (if the game format is used).

A variation would be to have students text their responses to Poll Everywhere or Wiffiti. The next day they would come to class and see the results. To add to the competitive flavor, students who determined the correct city could win a trip to that city in the virtual world. They could then continue the game with planning an itinerary with flight times, cost, and so on.

This lesson could be an ongoing game or week-long project using various travel teams in which students are paired and thus must collaborate on their locations and times through text messaging prior to tweeting. Students could also make sure that tweets from certain locations and tweet times fit with the tweet stream based on travel times (flight, rail, boat, car). A student could not tweet from New York and then from Sydney unless the correct amount of travel time had passed. Google SMS or ChaCha could be used to acquire those flight time requirements.

How the Use of Cell Phones Enriches This Lesson

- By using real world communication devices such as cell phones and Twitter, students are able to practice curriculum in a twenty-first-century way. The formulas and lesson knowledge take on a real-world flare compared to worksheets with paper-and-pencil problems to solve.

- The use of cell phone world clocks allow students to practice their knowledge of time zones.

- Cell phone calculators allow students to do the math during the communication (tweeting) anywhere and anytime.

- With Twitter, an actual global conversation is simulated between various cities at various times. The lesson objectives are taken out of the classroom and into students' lives using the means that will be part of their future communications in our continually narrowing global community.

NETS•S Addressed

- Creativity and innovation
- Communication and collaboration
- Critical thinking, problem solving, and decision making

NETS•T Addressed

- Design and develop digital-age learning experiences and assessments
- Facilitate and inspire student learning and creativity

Research-Based Instructional Strategies Used

- Identifying similarities and differences
- Providing recognition
- Cooperative learning
- Advance organizers

Assessment

By collecting each student's or group's planned trip itinerary and then reading the Twitter feed online, the teacher will be able to determine if the time calculations were correct. The teacher will be able to see if the students accurately answered each other's tweets. A number of correct tweets could be required to pass the lesson or a percentage of required tweets that were correct could be used for a letter grade for the assignment. The use of a rubric that also considered the creativity in the planning, the correctness of the geography of the trip, and the number of and description included in tweets would be beneficial for assessing the students' learning.

BRING POETRY TO LIFE WITH A CELL PHONE AND A VOKI

Subject
Language arts

Topic
Poetry

Lesson Overview
Students use Vokis to bring their poetry to life and hear themselves reading their pieces.

Cell Phone Tool Used
Voki

Preparation

After students have written their poems, you will want to schedule a period in which students have access to computers at school to create their Vokis. (Follow the instructions for using Voki in Chapter Two.) Partner any students with computers to those without. During homework time students with a computer will program Voki to call the students without a computer so that those student can record their Vokis. Tell the students to call their partners in advance to ensure that they are available to take the call and record the message. Another option is if a student's parents, guardians, or family have access to computers at work, but not at home, they can set the Voki to call the child's phone.

Lesson Description

Voki is a terrific tool to use toward the end of a poetry unit when students are ready to publish their work. A Voki is an animated avatar whose mouth, eyes, and head move to your words. When student poetry pieces are ready for publishing, have them record themselves using their cell phones to give Voki a voice.

Select a mentor poem to model Voki creation and then have all students create Vokis with the mentor poem. This can lead to a discussion of how various elements affect how a Voki interprets and delivers.

Students will then be ready to create a Voki with their own poems. Students should create a Voki that fits the mood and style of their poem by customizing it in the following ways:

- *Character style:* Select a character; styles include classic, animals, oddballs, and more.

- *Customization:* Change the character's look, clothing, and accessories.

- *Background:* Choose a background from the Voki library or upload your own.

Next students will have Voki call their cell so they can record their poem. They can record as often as they want until they get it just right. Have the Vokis posted on a class website, blog, or wiki to share with others. Group students in pairs, threes, or fours to comment on one another's Vokis. If students are not familiar with peer review and appropriate feedback, model what is appropriate and the type of comments one might make.

The finished Vokis can also be shared with families and the rest of the school. Students may want to teach their family, friends, teachers, and administrators how to comment on their Vokis as well.

How the Use of Cell Phones Enriches This Lesson

- The Vokis serve as an engaging way for students to create and publish their work.
- It provides students with an opportunity to practice and hear themselves saying their poem in a nonthreatening way.
- It provides a medium for all students' work to be displayed and commented on by each other as well as friends, family, and other staff members.

NETS•S Addressed

- Creativity and innovation
- Communication and collaboration

NETS•T Addressed

- Facilitate and inspire student learning and creativity
- Design and develop digital-age learning experiences and assessments
- Model digital-age work and learning
- Promote and model digital citizenship and responsibility

Research-Based Instructional Strategies Used

- Providing recognition
- Practice
- Nonlinguistic representations
- Cooperative learning
- Setting objectives and providing feedback

Assessment

In this lesson, you can use your rubric for written and oral poetry assessment. This generally includes items such as creativity, follows intended form or style, sensory details, imagery, captivates audience, delivery, grammar conventions, and so on. You will also want to add a category for appearance and background that will address how well the Voki's appearance and background fit the poem.

SHAKESPEARE ON THE CELL WITH WETXT, IPADIO, WIFFITI, AND TEXT MESSAGING

Subject
Language arts

Topic
Shakespeare (or any work of a time period or culture requiring interpretation of meaning)

Cell Phone Tools Used
Text messaging, WeTxt, ipadio, Wiffiti, and ChaCha (This lesson could be done with just cell phones. The website supports are simply enhancements. You could give students the lines you want translated in class and students could text them back to you directly. The use of the websites, however, allows sharing of student work.)

Preparation
Chapters One and Two give detailed instructions on how to get started with WeTxt, ipadio, Wiffiti, and ChaCha. For the lesson enhancements you need to have your class set up as a group in WeTxt at www.wetxt.com and prepare a Wiffiti page for Shakespearean quotes and translations.

Lesson Overview
This lesson will improve students' ability to read and understand Shakespeare. Additionally, students will realize and demonstrate that some meaning can be lost in translation, that communication changes over time, that there are

varying communication needs, and that communication has many different styles.

Lesson Description

This lesson can be done when students are beginning to study Shakespeare's work after an introduction to Shakespeare and his time. Through a group text using a service such as WeTxt, send the class a couple of sentences to translate into a text message. The sentences should be from any Shakespearean work being studied, such as *To be or not to be, that is the question?* The students reply to the group text with their translations. The translations will be listed on the WeTxt page on your computer. With a quick look at the responses, you can see if there is consistency or not and choose a few to share with the class, such as I will compar u 2 a sumr day, *2b or nt 2b?* and *BB v. not BB?* The teacher could point out that even today some adults translate text messages back into regular spellings for understanding in much the same way the class is working to translate and understand Shakespeare. The discussion can then open up to modern ways love is declared and feelings are communicated. Song lyrics, music, and rap can be shared and discussed. The discussion should lead back to Shakespeare and his method of communicating.

Assign a sonnet (sonnet 18 is a favorite of students) or provide famous lines from various selections. Have students or groups of students collaborate to create a Venn diagram comparing texting, rapping, and Shakespeare's own words. The Venn diagram will focus on literal translations. The diagram should have a circle for Shakespeare, a circle for rap, and a circle for text. For example, in the Shakespeare circle, *To be or not to be, that is the question* and in the text circle, *2b or nt 2b, that is?* and in the rap circle, *To be, ya I say or not at all, that be da question?* Similarities and differences should be discussed.

Next, have students demonstrate their understanding of each line of the sonnet by putting it into their preferred method of delivery, text or rap, using today's English while maintaining the original meaning for homework and practice. Give them a choice to translate the meaning of the sonnet into a text message and text it into the teacher (or to a Wiffiti board) or into song or rap that they record in ipadio. Encourage students to use outside resources, such as their parents or other family members or the free question-answer help service ChaCha (via text message), if they get stuck on the meaning of a line. For example, if they text the question, *What does, "To be or not to be. That is the question?" mean in Shakespeare?* to ChaCha, ChaCha will text back answers from actual people (so the answers will vary). An answer might look like this: *When Shakespeare's Hamlet asks himself "to be or not to be," he is asking himself whether it is better to continue to live or to die while his life is a painful struggle. Thanks for using ChaCha.*

How the Use of Cell Phones Enriches This Lesson

The students' comfort level in reading, translating, and understanding Shakespeare is increased when they are encouraged to do it with their preferred mode of communication.

NETS•S Addressed

- Creativity and innovation
- Communication and collaboration
- Critical thinking, problem solving, and decision making
- Digital citizenship

NETS•T Addressed

- Facilitate and inspire student learning and creativity
- Design and develop digital-age learning experiences and assessments
- Model digital-age work and learning

Research-Based Instructional Strategies Used

- Identifying similarities and differences
- Homework and practice
- Nonlinguistic representations

Assessment

The rubric for the project addresses three areas: understanding of the Shakespearean lines, translation that maintains the meaning, and creativity in expression.

Measurement description	3 High Standard	2 At Standard	1 Below Standard
Understanding of Shakespeare's quote or sonnet	The understanding is true to interpretations of Shakespeare's intended meaning. Various meanings are considered. Higher-order thinking is demonstrated.	Some understanding of the meaning is demonstrated. There is little or no evidence of consideration of various interpretations or higher-order thinking.	Only a literal or flawed meaning of the lines is demonstrated.
Translation maintains the interpreted meaning of the quote or sonnet.	The text illustrates fully the meaning of the lines at a deep level.	The text maintains most of the basic understanding.	The text offers a minimal or flawed version of the original meaning.
Creativity of expression	The text shows creativity with elements such as beat, rhyme, figurative language, or alliteration. Word choice is vivid; text abbreviations are clear. The use of sound and voice are effective.	The text shows some creativity of expression. Voice and sound are used in the rap and creative line choices used in the text.	There is a literal translation only with little creativity, variation, or variety from the original.

ASSESSING SPEAKING FLUENCY AND GETTING TO KNOW CLASSMATES WITH GOOGLE VOICE

Subject
Learning English

Topic
Speaking fluency and "About Me"

Cell Phone Tool Used
Google Voice

Preparation
Review the instructions for using Google Voice in Chapters One and Two.

Lesson Overview
Students use Google Voice to record oral "About Me" reports.

Lesson Description
Google Voice is a terrific tool to use with English language learners and serves as a great way to assess oral fluency across the year. You can use Google Voice at the beginning of the year to have students share something about themselves in the form of a thirty- to sixty-second oral report. You may choose to guide the report contents with ideas such as the following:

My name is . . .

I moved here from . . .

My family is very proud of . . .

In my free time I enjoy . . .

Something I am very good at is . . .

In the future my goal is to . . .

Demonstrate how to do this in class by first recording your own oral report in front of the class. Show the students that the clearer the speaker is, the better the transcript Google Voice will provide.

To implement the lesson, either (1) ask students to click on the icon set up on a website, wiki, or blog on which you post assignments and then enter their number that will be called so they can record their report or (2) give students your Google Voice number to call into on which they can record their reports.

Once the report is submitted, you will receive a transcript of each student's report. There is also a space to write a note, make comments, add a grade, and so on for each student's recorded voice message. Additionally, you have the option to associate each phone number and recording with a student's name or nickname.

These oral reports can be posted on an "About Our Class" page of a website, blog, or wiki. The "About Our Class" page can serve as an engaging forum for students to publish their work, which can be shared with additional friends and family members and even linked to the school website. If you choose to share student work, be aware of your school's policy for doing so and student and parental preference for using their real name or an alias. The default for embedding the audio does not reveal students' names but you can add a caption so that the student's name or alias is included.

Repeat this assignment at the end of the year and let students listen to how their oral fluency has improved.

How the Use of Cell Phones Enriches This Lesson

- This gives students a safe environment in which record themselves speaking, which can be particularly important to new language learners who are shy or uncomfortable speaking publicly.

- The tool gives students the opportunity to practice recording their report as often as they like. It provides a fun and engaging way for students to get to know each other in their own voice.

NETS•S Addressed

- Creativity and innovation
- Communication and collaboration

NETS•T Addressed

- Facilitate and inspire student learning and creativity
- Design and develop digital-age learning experiences and assessments

Research-Based Instructional Strategies Used

- Homework and practice
- Setting objectives and providing feedback
- Cues, questions, and advance organizers
- Nonlinguistic representations

Assessment

You can use the same assessment you use for speaking fluency when you provide feedback in areas such as ability to understand words, interesting content, grammar conventions, words missed, words used incorrectly, and natural rate of speaking. You may want to consider the number of words converted correctly, but because voice recognition is not perfect, you may decide this is instead more of an interesting piece of information to share and consider and does not affect the students' final grade. You may also want to consider having students self-assess and peer assess with a simple rubric that includes some of the previously mentioned assessments.

ART AROUND TOWN

(Lesson created by Sandy Vickrey, art teacher, grades 7–12, Delta, Colorado, with Willyn Webb.)

Subject
Art

Cell Phone Tools Used
Cell phone camera, picture messaging, group texting, Flickr, or PowerPoint

Preparation
If you are using Flickr, set up an account to use for school-related work. Make sure that all photos sent to that e-mail address have a particular project-related tag, which might include subject name, grade, and class number, for example: art8–402. The group texting set-up can be found in Chapter One or on any free group-texting service website.

Lesson Overview

In preparation for a mural that will be painted at the school, the art class will gather evidence of other art in their community. The students will gain an awareness of the different types of art that are shared on walls and outdoor areas where the entire community can enjoy them. This will broaden their view of what constitutes art and what types of qualities must be taken into consideration when planning their mural.

Lesson Description

The assignment is to use a cell phone camera to capture at least three works of art in the community that are available for the public to view. Group students in pairs or threes so that within each group there is at least one student with a cell phone who has a camera. Each picture taken should have a caption and title that includes location as well as answers to specific questions you give them through a group messaging service such as GroupMe or WeTxt. Depending on the grade level of your students and the amount of preteaching and knowledge of art they currently have, questions might include the following:

- Does the art have a particular style?

- What is the art's particular message or purpose?

- What are the colors and dimensionality of the art?

- What is the medium used in making this art (for example, paint, spray paint, marker, chalk, and so on)?

- Why did you choose this piece?

- How did this piece of art move you?

Students can share the pictures and responses using one of the following options depending on your preference:

Option 1: Students e-mail the pictures with the title and location and question answers to your e-mail address. When the pictures come into the e-mail, open them and put them along with titles and question responses into a presentation program such as PowerPoint.

Option 2: Students e-mail the pictures to your Flickr e-mail address. The subject line automatically becomes the picture's title and the message with question answers are automatically shown in the picture's caption. Creating a specific tag for the project allows you with one click to create a slide show sorted by tags that instantly generates a URL link and embeds code that can be shared with whomever you wish. Each photo also has an option for comments, which can be used for teacher feedback as well as peer or parent feedback.

When the class reconvenes, show them the PowerPoint or Flickr presentation. Start a discussion about each example (you hope there will be a wide variety, such as community murals, graffiti, sculpture, sidewalk chalk drawings, and so on) and include the question responses. In addition to the answers to the questions, the discussion can encourage students to consider the similarities and differences in the works of art. If the class has access to computers and Flickr is used, they can note these in the "comment" section. This discussion takes the class members to a new level of understanding and awareness that now can be incorporated into planning their own mural.

How the Use of Cell Phones Enriches This Lesson

- Cell phones allow students to send in pictures of art in their community on the spot whereas a traditional camera would require downloading pictures before they can be shared.

- By e-mailing in the pictures from their cell phones, they can be easily combined in a central site to share with the entire class.

- The questions are with the students in their phones, which is more convenient than carrying a notebook, and they can be pondered about while in the presence of the art.

- The response can be texted back immediately rather than written up later.

NETS•S Addressed

- Creativity and innovation
- Communication and collaboration
- Research and information fluency
- Critical thinking, problem solving, and decision making
- Digital citizenship

NETS•T Addressed

- Facilitate and inspire student learning and creativity
- Design and develop digital-age learning experiences and assessments
- Model digital-age work and learning
- Promote and model digital citizenship and responsibility

Research-Based Instructional Strategies Used

- Identifying similarities and differences
- Reinforcing effort and providing recognition
- Homework
- Nonlinguistic representations
- Cooperative learning
- Setting objectives and providing feedback
- Cues, questions, and advance organizers

Assessment

You could use a rubric addressing the following:

- Effort: Did the group find three works of art? (See Chapter Three for an effort rubric.)
- Did the group provide complete answers to the thinking questions?
- Did the group present their chosen works of art effectively with technology?

The rubric should be made specific depending on the grade level and knowledge of art.

YOU AND YOUR STUDENTS WILL LOVE YOUR NEW CELL PHONE–INFUSED LESSONS

These lesson ideas are designed to get you thinking about ways you can spice up teaching and learning with cell phones. We hope you will try out some of them and modify the ones you like to the particular needs of your classroom. Remember, your students will be terrific partners when it comes to incorporating these tools into instruction. Share these lesson ideas with them and see what they think. Let them be your inspiration for incorporating the tools they know and love into their learning and your future lessons. Remember, whether or not you are in a school that allows cell phones, the ideas shared here can be used effectively either at school or away from school and many of these strategies can be used on a computer or cell phone. Perhaps you begin a lesson at school with computers, but with cell phone–infused lessons students have options for doing their work that doesn't require a computer or the Internet. By incorporating cell phones into instruction you are providing your students with more opportunities to learn, access, and create knowledge.

chapter SIX

The Texting School Community

Leadership should be born out of the understanding of the needs of those who would be affected by it.
Marian Anderson, singer

Cell phone technologies can benefit not only classroom teachers and their students, but also the whole school community. In this chapter we share advice for ways administrators, guidance counselors, librarians, coaches, pupil personnel secretaries, and custodians can harness the power of texting to connect with students and enrich learning. Each section serves as a useful resource for the particular audience addressed and is chock-full of ideas, uses, and how to get started.

THE TEXTING ADMINISTRATOR

Cell phones provide administrators with a powerful vehicle for connecting with parents, guardians, students, teachers, and colleagues. New Milford, New Jersey, high school principal Eric Sheninger and New York City principal Jacek Polubiec are at the forefront of harnessing the power of cell phones to do their work more effectively. Mr. Polubiec has found cell phones to be an effective tool for classroom observations and Principal Sheninger has embraced Twitter as an essential tool that has improved communications greatly, saying, "I can now easily share all the fantastic things going on in my school and have dramatically increased the amount of positive press coming out of my building. This would not have been possible just a few short years ago."

Principal Patrick Larkin from Burlington High School in Massachusetts has this advice for administrators who are considering whether to embrace cell phones as a learning tool: "Start now. If you haven't embraced cell phones as learning tools, you are missing out on a valuable resource to engage students. At the very least you can save money on the response systems that many companies are pushing in schools." Damon Lockhart, an elementary school principal, has his students' parents' numbers in his phone according to the student's name. When he is on bus duty or playground patrol, he sends texts to parents when he sees a student doing something good like being helpful or politely waiting in line. Leaders at Delta Opportunity School in Colorado use group texting with response to a Wiffiti board or a Poll Everywhere poll to gather ideas and encourage communication with students, staff, and parents. Improved input and better use of meeting time have been some helpful results.

Innovative educators know that when an administrator is on board with using technology in the classroom, it becomes much easier for the entire school to follow suit. Whether you're an administrator who wants to try these ideas out or a teacher who wants to help an administrator get on board, here are specific ways that administrators are using cell phones to do their jobs more efficiently.

Individual and Group Texting

Principal Polubiec uses texting 24/7 to communicate with teachers and administrators. Texting enables him and his staff to reach one another regardless of where they are physically. For example, it's not unusual for staff members to text him at night when they are not feeling well and might be absent the next day. This allows Polubiec to update the Google doc that his school uses to post daily announcements and enables him to get a jump start on being able to plan accordingly.

Another way Mr. Polubiec uses texting is by setting up his cell so he gets updates when teachers update their roll books in Google Docs. The teachers don't need to take time from their day to inform him and the school instantly has information delivered to all who need it via their cell phones. Polubiec and his colleagues also use cell phone calendars for meetings and text each other to send reminders about meetings, assemblies and other events. He also has all his staff's numbers stored in his cell phone in case he needs to text them to provide them with timely information or inform them of emergencies. In a nutshell, Mr. Polubiec shares, "I can't imagine my work without texting anymore."

The visitors to the academy Mr. Polubiec supervises are encouraged to text constructive feedback on the academy's hallway learning displays (bulletin boards) to Poll Everywhere. This kind of continual feedback using technology is the backbone of his staff's virtual learning walks.

At Cedaredge Middle School in Colorado the administrators feel texting supports instruction by limiting distractions. According to Principal Todd Markley, "Administratively, we text to communicate throughout the day as we are usually not in the same location in the building. Text messages can be sent to administrators from the secretary if we are needed in the office without using the school intercom, which interrupts instruction."

Another administrative use of texting comes from Alan Beam, who serves as a secondary school building administrator in Kansas. He shares that he had the students text their parents to remind them about parent-teacher conferences.

Kurt Clay, principal of Delta High School, had his secretary put his staff numbers into a group texting service so he could be in contact for emergency response notification and crisis announcements. It wasn't long, however, before he realized the service could have utility far beyond what he originally intended. Soon he was sending group texts to staff with encouragement, information on upcoming activities, scheduling updates, teaching tips, meeting announcements, and more. He found his staff meeting time to be much more productive when he could send out questions or cues before and start the meeting with a jump on the agenda. After meetings he texted key points right into his staff's hands knowing they all left the meeting with the same takeaway.

After seeing how effective this was with his staff, Principal Clay decided to use group texting to increase the home-school connection with the parents of his busiest students: his seniors. After establishing that group, Principal Clay now sends out important dates and reminders crucial to the success of these students and plans to expand this to all of the parents in his school. It also has the added bonus of saving money on printing and mailing of information that adds up significantly in the school budget each year.

Principal Lockhart has his elementary students' parents set up in groups by grade level. He can connect with each grade with a group text requesting a reply to a free response board or to ask polling questions. This allows grade-specific input for use in meetings or to replace grade-level meetings.

Free Response Boards

Principals can make parent night, staff meetings, and school assemblies a true example of two-way communication with the use of free response boards such as Wiffiti or a free text poll in Poll Everywhere. By sending out a group text with a question or request for input and the number and code to send the response to, everyone in the group has the opportunity for input prior to or during the event.

Delaine Hudson, principal of Delta Opportunity School, shares a frustration familiar to educators around the globe. Her weekly PLC meetings are always rushed and end too quickly. There's just never enough time. Principal Hudson decided she'd try seeing if creating a free response board prior to her meeting would help. Two days prior to an upcoming PLC meeting Mrs. Hudson sent everyone a text with a Wiffiti number and code and the request for input on the main agenda item for the meeting. Throughout the next two days, all of the participants were able to focus their thoughts, share their ideas, and prepare for the meeting. At the meeting Mrs. Hudson was able to display everyone's thoughtful input immediately on the Wiffiti screen. The PLC time was more focused and communication more effective with the easily referenced responses right in front of each participant. Also, the privacy of being able to text input and the anonymity of the code names Wiffiti assigns created an atmosphere of true sharing. Principal Hudson found the use of a free response board not only saved time, but it also enabled her to collect thoughtful contributions from all who wanted to share, resulting in better communication among all.

Polling Services

Polling services such as Poll Everywhere enable administrators to let those whom they want to reach out to know they value their thoughts and opinions and want their input. Jacek Polubiec has used free text and polling successfully during classroom learning walks. At Polubiec's school, learning walks serve as a professional development experience for staff who know exactly how to text observations into polls and free response observations. Their answers, which automatically populate onto the school wiki and during the debrief, allow learning walk participants to get to the thinking and discussing faster because results and data are already collected, tabulated, and ready for discussion. "Using cell phones in this way has enabled us to take learning walks to a whole new level enabling us to capture data easily using a tool all staff members already own with free technology tools," said Polubiec.

Microblogging

Principals such as Eric Sheninger in New Milford and Matt Brown in New York use Twitter as a powerful microblogging tool to help strengthen the home-school connection and give the school community a lens into what is happening in the school. Both principals feature tweets on their school website where visitors can be sure to find shout-outs to students and teachers, upcoming events, timely announcements, and more. When connecting Twitter to your cell phone, you can tweet on the go even as you are face-to-face with a student, teacher, or parent letting them know you're so excited you are going to shout (or in this case tweet) it out from the virtual school roof top. Students look forward to sharing their principal's tweets with family and friends, especially when they are the star.

Principal Sheninger's tweets now serve as a news feed for local media outlets interested keeping their fingers on the pulse of what is happening in progressive schools today. As a result Sheninger's school is regularly featured in the paper, on radio, and television celebrating the work of his students and staff. Being able to control your digital footprint in the message that is being spread about your school is powerful, and Sheninger enjoys using his phone and Twitter as a vehicle to make that happen.

Connect with Your Student Body Through Flickr

At the beginning of the year, set up a Flickr account and set up groups for each class of students you are assigned. At registration invite students to send a picture of themselves to the Flickr e-mail for their group and get a current face with a name. The school pictures from last year are rarely recognizable as students grow and styles change. This creates a connection, shows you care, and acknowledges that you know how students love to use their phones.

THE TEXTING GUIDANCE COUNSELOR

School counselors are in a unique position, without the restraints of the classroom and with a job that is based on communication and relationships with students, to start having success using cell phones and lead the way for the entire school. School counselors have many roles—from academic to career to personal and social—and text messaging provides the means for increased communication, strong relationships, and time-saving supports. Their services and programs support students in many ways from scheduling their classes; to helping them resolve emotional, social, or behavioral problems; to communicating about life issues and decisions. Effective counseling programs are important to the school climate and a crucial element in improving student achievement. They are a perfect place to illustrate cell phone enhancements and increased communication with text messaging. Before beginning to text students, make sure the agreement ("Cell Phone Agreement for Nonteaching School Personnel" in Chapter Four) is in place.

Individual and Group Texting

Being effective with students in the three areas of academic, career, and personal and social is often challenging. So many students, so little time is a frequent frustration of many school counselors. Text messaging addresses this frustration with its time-saving, private, personal method of communication, which provides school counselors the opportunity to do the following:

- Quick checks: *Did you get the job? Thinking of you. How r u? Is ur new class ok? How r u controlling the anger?*

- Quick feedback: *Great job on your ACT. Glad to c u joined volleyball. Your scholarship ap was excellent. Way to make friends.*

- Quick encouragement and support: *Do ur best 2day. Sorry abot ur grandpa. Have a good meet. Make good choices 2nite. When u need a cigarette, drink water instead.*

Group texts can be sent simultaneously to students and parent(s) to improve communication via the following:

- Reminders on dates for testing, applications, scholarships, and so on

- Links to the government's FASFA application, their students ICAP (individual career and academic plan throughout the state of Colorado), school calendars, teachers, and grades

- Encouragement texts such as *Get a good night's sleep. Ull do gr8* before *the ACT* or to say *good job its over and you survived.*

- Announcements for study groups, study tips, and available tutoring. Through the use of group text vehicles such as WeTxt, GroupMe, or Swaggle, whole sports teams, the freshman class taking a field trip, any club, the staff, support groups, and so on can receive these types of messages at the same time.

Whether it is because teens' preferred method of communication is texting or because there is safety, privacy, and distance in texting, when no other efforts at communication work, texting often does. Also, whether you get a response or not, the statistics show that your text message will get read, and sometimes just getting your message read is very important. It is important for our students to know we care, to know that we noticed they were absent, to remember that their family was evicted last night, to ask how court went, to support them before the interview, and so on. A text message will get the job done and in a timely, noninterruptive manner.

Using Poll Everywhere to Gain Input and Plan Better

Gathering information about what classes students would like to have offered, what classes teachers would want to teach, and what parents would like to see available at school is often an overwhelming task. Once all courses are set, registering students is a time-consuming activity. The following cell phone tools will provide time-saving, fun ways to gather input and plan better. By providing all stakeholders the option of using their cell phones, more input is likely to be gained and more effective plans made.

For Course Offerings

Using an audience response system such as TextTheMob or Poll Everywhere provides an effective means of gathering input regarding opinions for course offerings from staff, parents, and students:

- Poll students on what courses they would like teachers to offer.
- Poll teachers on what courses they would like to teach.
- Poll students on what courses they would choose to take when making schedules.

This quick method of audience response allows everyone to have a voice and gives counselors valuable insight into the school set-up and the needs of students and teachers so that they can make informed decisions.

For Career and Academic Plans

Audience response can be a valuable tool in gaining input regarding career and academic planning for students and can get parents involved:

- Poll parents on the best times for conferences, college visits, and so on.
- Poll students on interest for college field trips or guest speakers.
- Poll students on career day desires for presentations, featured careers, and willingness to help.

Schedule Changes Made More Smoothly

Class change lines can be long and frustrating, keeping students out of classes where they need to be in order to connect with the counselor to make a change. Encourage students to text their change request and go to class. This will empower you to look into it, if needed talk to the student, communicate with the teacher and parent, and do it all with less disruption. Also, with text requests, the counselor can get a feeling for how many students want in or out of a certain class prior to meeting with each one face-to-face. By giving a little time to review the texts before responding, valuable information can be gleaned and used. Maybe another section needs to be added, maybe requests to get out of a challenging class will have to be denied before a flood takes place, and so on. Counselors will be able to help more students in less time with the use of text messages.

Test Prep via Text

Rather than paying for an expensive online ACT or SAT study program that sends sample test questions (about three per day) to your student's phone, use a free guide with sample questions that can be accessed at your school or local library, from your teachers, or websites such as www.studyguidezone.com/ or www.testprepreview.com/. Text some of the questions from that guide to students each day or give them to study groups, who could divide them up and text each other, with all involved reviewing the questions and answers, whether sending or receiving. The partnership, the support, and the content for study are all enhanced for free.

Organization and Study Skills for All

During parent night, orientations, school registration days, or in study skills and test-preparation classes, school counselors can offer helpful cell phone tools for organization, study, and test prep that students will quickly embrace. Table 6.1 provides a workshop and curriculum outline that overviews the areas in which cell phone tools will help students be better organized, study more effectively, and prepare for tests.

Wiffiti for Anonymity

School counselors can provide students with more opportunity to share through the use of Wiffiti boards, which provide engagement and anonymity. When students text into the Wiffiti board they are given code names that consist of a color, an animal, and a number. They can be silly, such as AvocadoHyena5, TopazDuck2, or LemonSnipefish3. and even high school students get a laugh out of them. This allows students to ask questions, share ideas, set goals, and have input without embarrassment. Previously teacher-heavy discussions become fun-sharing sessions with all students engaged. More accurate, honest sharing happens, especially with discussion topics such as drug and alcohol use, cheating, or bullying, when done with a Wiffiti.

Table 6.1
Workshop Agenda: Organization, Study, and Test Prep with Cell Phones

Time	Activity	Facilitator Notes
00:00	**Welcome, Introductions, Objectives** Participants will do the following: • Understand the use of cell phone tools as organizational and study aids. • Discover free and easy mobile learning activities that will engage students outside of the classroom and improve their performance in all subject areas. • Try out the tools by putting important dates into their phone calendars, setting up reminders, taking cell notes, texting an expert with ChaCha, and answering a poll question.	Welcome. Introduce why you are interested in the topic. Depending on group size, you can poll the participants for types of members or have each do introductions. Explain objectives.
00:05	**Background for the Workshop** It's not *if* we should use cell phones, but *when:* • Ninety-four percent of Americans under age forty-five have a personal learning device that could greatly enrich the way teachers teach and students learn (Marist Poll, 2010). • Organization and study can be enhanced by cell phones outside of school. • Play the video clip of the U.S. secretary of education in his discussion of using cell phones for learning (Duncan, 2009).	Use any supportive statistics that you have regarding cell phone use in your area.
00:15	**Calendars** Make it a habit to put in assignment due dates, test dates, deadlines for applications and scholarships, and so on. • Let's try it. Everyone get out your phone and go to your calendar. Different phones have different avenues. Look for words such as *menu, tools, calendar.* • When you've found it, enter a new date, for example, ACT test on January 8. • It may ask you if you want a reminder, which is a good idea, especially for assignment and project due dates. Set it so that that the reminder will give you enough time to do the assignment or study for the test.	Have a master calendar of dates for the school year ready to try a few entries. Have some student volunteers go around and help the parents find the calendar function. Examples of story types of students' use of these tools are great. *(continued)*

Table 6.1 (*continued*)

Time	Activity	Facilitator Notes
00:25	**Reminders and Alarm** • A good study and homework tip is to do it the same time every day. As students are increasingly active and mobile, cell phones can be an aid. • Set the alarm in your phone to beep you for homework or study time each evening. Having notes in your phone will remind you of the tasks. No matter where you are, you can text in some notes, read some material, and make plans to get to your homework. • Let's try it. Find the alarm function in the phone and set it for study and homework time or add a reminder for an upcoming project.	Have helpers to float around the room and assist with questions. You may want to mention that having a clock in your pocket is also helpful for being on time.
00:40	**Notes** • Cell phones can be excellent for note taking (in and out of class). If they are not allowed in class, use them for studying on the go. By putting your notes in your phone, you are reviewing material, making it available for studying anywhere, and using a research-based strategy of summarizing and note taking. • Let's try it. Find the note function in your phone and put in a fact, a vocabulary word, a math formula, or something you need to study. • You could text notes to your e-mail when you need to compile and print them. There are also group texting sites that offer note taking through texting. Send notes to WeTxt, for example, and they are organized by date and can also be organized by subject. You can print them when you are at a computer.	Get a WeTxt account and create some notes. Show your notes as an example. You could also have a handout for participants on how to set up WeTxt or text them the directions.
00:50	**Study Tips and Homework Help** • You can text an expert when you are stuck on homework, even when you are not home. Have a personal learning network of experts or use a free service called ChaCha. • Let's try it. Text 242242 (ChaCha) and ask these two questions: "What is the formula for the area of a circle?" and "What does 'to be or not to be that is the question' mean?" • Text the questions to an expert of your choosing. Build support systems within students' own networks. • Review the calculator and conversions tool. • Show the virtual phone that Google SMS has set up online at www.google.com/mobile/default/sms.html and translate a few words or try any feature.	Choose questions for ChaCha that you have already tried out. You may want to alert the participants that there will be some advertising as part of the responses but that as informed users they can simply disregard them.

Table 6.1 (*continued*)

Time	Activity	Facilitator Notes
01:05	**Test Preparation** • When preparing for tests you could have a friend, your parent, or your teacher text you practice questions. • When preparing for the ACT or SAT you and a friend could text a question a day out of the study guide to each other. This makes preparation quick and on the go. One question per day does not burden you when you have homework in other classes. • You could use Google Voice to record the information you need to review for a test and then listen to it on your phone wherever you are. Or set up minitutorials about topics by leaving yourself a Google voice mail and listening to it later. • If you use Twitter, you could tweet test questions and use the answers for review—all through your phone. • When you know the basic questions that will be on the test or have a study guide with sample questions, set up polls of the questions and answers, which is great review, then practice with friends by texting in your answers. • Let's try it. Take a poll question from an ACT study guide such as, "What words should be capitalized in the following sentence—"Lisa and george went to the museum to see the king tut exhibit." Text 22333 and vote for your answer (www.polleverywhere.com/multiple_choice_polls/MTU0MjAxODg1Ng).You will want to have set-up directions for Google Voice, Twitter, and Poll Everywhere on your handout or have them sign up to get texted directions.	You will want to have set-up directions for Google Voice, Twitter, and Poll Everywhere on your handout or have them sign up to get texted directions. Show students more about how Google Voice works by viewing Google's video channel demonstration (www.youtube.com/googlevoice).
01:15	**Questions and Conclusion** • Sharing your cell number, group texting number, or e-mail so you can be texted would be a great way to end the workshop. Having a phone list of educators in your school who would be willing to support students with homework questions, studying, or for test prep via text message would be even better.	

The Intervention of the Emoticon

A common counseling intervention, especially with adolescents is to ask for a picture or word to illustrate feeling, which provides better communication and understanding, encourages acknowledgment of the feeling, and provides for release of emotion. Text messaging incorporates this very intervention. Through the use of emoticons, students label their text messages with a feeling. Now that is clear communication and built-in intervention!

Support Groups Support by Text

School counselors know the primary benefit of a support group comes not from an excellent group leader or a savvy facilitator, but from the support the members provide each other through understanding, empathy, listening, and caring. Oftentimes the most frustrating component of support groups is not having enough time or having enough carry over into daily life. Text messaging takes the support of the group into daily life. Whether set up as a group with the facilitator sending out encouragements, reminders, and helpful tips or just the group connecting and supporting each other, texting improves support groups. For example, if the group members worked on visualizing a positive place in their minds to go to as a coping skill when the anger starts, the counselor can easily text them later and encourage them to visualize that place right then, to practice going there in their minds, to text other members of the group, and encourage them. A face-to-face group activity can be to create a message or forward based on the current subject of the group. Then members can send it out to each other when needed. Whether the group is convened for grief, divorce, quitting smoking, or any other group common to schools, with proper guidelines and boundaries in place, text messaging can be another useful tool of support.

Home-School Counselor Connection

Many school counselors have wanted to involve parents more in supporting the personal and social growth of students, in resolving conflict, and in problem solving, but because they don't have hours to spend on the phone and parents' busy schedules often prevent them from coming in, valuable opportunities are lost. However, with text messaging, even during student-counselor conversations, parents can be more involved. For example, when a student is in the counseling office dealing with an issue that involves a parent, rather than wasting time or trying to problem solve without all involved parties, the parent is often just a text message away. Misunderstandings, questions, and feelings can be communicated by a student with his or her parent(s) or family members via text while the counselor provides support, direction, and clarification. Parents will be able to respond and be part of the resolution in the moment from work or wherever with a minimal amount of disruption. Other examples include course selection, college planning, scholarship applications, or schedule changes. When a student needs to get input or confirmation from a parent, just text them together and decisions can be made on the spot, saving the need for further conversations.

Forwards for Support in Times of Crisis

A forward is simply a text message, usually with a picture and sometimes with music, that is sent out with the request to "keep it going" or to "forward to all of your friends." They are the same as the e-mail forward but most likely a little shorter. Forwards are something students are used to sending to groups and they realize the value. When you don't have a set group and need to reach many of your students in times of crisis, a forward may be your best option.

In certain situations, carefully creating a text message with a purpose, including sound and pictures as desired, can have a beneficial, ripple effect of spreading desired information, encouragement, and support among students, staff, and parents. Make sure that you plan on anyone and everyone possible reading the forward prior to sending. Make sure any involved parties are aware of it and its potential influence and that nothing that could be misunderstood is included. In times of crisis, when a comforting message needs to be spread throughout the school and community, a text forward is a powerful communication tool.

Safety Plan via Text

Reporting to the proper agencies and authorities is the legal and ethical duty of all school staff when there is risk of self-harm or suicide. Getting professional help is always advised. A safety plan is a viable tool used by school counselors, mental health professionals, and emergency response workers. Creating a safety plan with students at risk can be helpful but it is not a replacement for reporting. Additionally, beyond suicide prevention, the components of a safety plan can be beneficial for addressing other types of risk behaviors such as drinking, stealing, sexual activity, drug use, cutting, or anything that needs a plan to prevent. When a school counselor is working with a student on a safety plan, a copy of the safety plan is shared when the appropriate agency responds to the report and with parents.

Safety plans are most often done in person but when the situation does not allow that and phone conversation is not happening, text messaging can be used. For example, asking who should be contacted first when there is an at-risk situation could be sent by text. The responses of names, numbers, hotlines, and 911 can be texted back. Helpful activities, instructions, and coping skills could be shared, requested, and texted back and forth. Because teens are so used to expressing themselves and communicating via text message, using text messaging to create a safety plan cannot be ruled out in the event that a safety plan is required. The requirement to carry the plan with them is more likely to occur when it is on their phone rather than on paper. Follow your school's procedures for crisis management but remember that texting may provide an additional tool for communication, support, and a life line.

THE TEXTING LIBRARIAN

Although for some, libraries bring to mind microfiche, card catalogs, and dusty stacks, today's innovative librarians are shattering these stereotypes by using technologies to provide engaging and relevant learning spaces for students. Tamara Cox, Heather Loy, Tracy Karas, Joyce Valenza, and Gwyneth Jones know that to engage twenty-first-century readers, researchers, and writers, they need to use the tools and technologies students love. The following is a collection of ideas these librarians have implemented to successfully engage learners and empower students with the freedom to use their cell phones as personal learning devices.

Phone Basics

There are many standard features in most phones that make librarians more effective and efficient. Heather Loy, librarian at Wagener-Salley High School in South Carolina, uses the notes or memo pad feature on her phone to record meeting notes, outlines, and even taking roll at the graduation ceremony. The benefit of this over paper is that it doesn't have to be transcribed. It can instantly be shared and it is searchable.

Students also enjoy using the notes or memo pads on their phones to write short book reviews that they can submit to their teacher right from their phone for posting on the library website.

Texting

Even though her school has a significant low-income population, librarian Tamara Cox says many of her students have cell phones and in the last few years she has seen cell phone use skyrocket among her students. She felt it would be a great idea to reach out to her students via text. and started with school library notices. Today, students at Palmetto Middle School in South Carolina can sign up to receive text notifications from the library.

Ms. Cox can text overdue and hold notices, which not only gets information directly into the hands of students, but it also enables her to stop wasting paper.

Another way Ms. Cox tapped into this technology was by placing her book club students in a group so that she can text them reminders of book club meetings and other club news. Her students love being in contact with her in this way.

Phonecasting

Book talks are one of the favorite tools in a librarian's bag of tricks. The purpose of book talking is to get students excited about reading books, telling them just enough to whet their appetites, then setting them free to explore on their own. Innovative librarians are using phonecasting to create book talks and make them available for students anytime, anywhere. A phonecast enables you to use your phone to record, capture, and share audio. There are a number of free services that allow you to record audio from a phone including Google Voice, Voki, and ipadio.

Librarians can set up an online space such as a wiki or website to list books in the library and use their selected phonecasting service to embed an audio recording of the corresponding book talk. Many librarians have also had success inviting students to create book talks as well. Not only do students like to hear about books from their peers, but creating a book talk can also be a great project for students. In schools where librarians organize buddy reading (upper grade students read to younger buddies), having the older partners record their book talk with their buddies in mind provides a built-in audience and perhaps even someone who can provide useful insight if the talk inspired the buddy to want to hear more.

Twitter

Librarians love Twitter not only because it provides an instant and easy window into what is happening in their libraries, but also because it serves as a tremendous professional development resource as well as a tool to globally connect teachers and students.

Using Twitter right from their cell phones enables librarians to provide the entire school community with a window into their library. Tracy Karas, a librarian in New York City, uses her phone to tweet updates about new books that have come in, to celebrate student successes, to provide reminders about upcoming events, and more. All these tweets are embedded directly on her school library page from the school's website.

Other librarians use Twitter to help their students connect or reach out for on-demand professional development using the hashtag #TLchat (T for teacher, L for librarian) started by the popular librarian Joyce Valenza. Using and following the hashtag provides viewers with a wealth of ideas, resource sharing, and networking. For example, here are some possible librarian tweets:

- 13-yr-old male who luvs skateboarding. Book ideas? #TLchat
- Looking for a student(s) who's reading or luvs Catcher in the Rye to join our book talk. #TLchat
- Looking for someone to Skype with our class abt creating a digital footprint. #TLchat
- Anyone have a resource for free eBooks? #TLchat

Using this tag brings your message to innovative librarians across the globe. Your thirty-second investment results in a payoff consisting of plenty of ideas and responses on demand and for free!

Librarians should also be aware of the many notable librarians that tweet. By following #TLchat, you'll quickly see popular names appear time and again including @buffyjhamilton, @shannonmiller, @joycevalenza, @keisawilliams, and @gwynethjones. You can tag tweeps (tweeting people) like these librarians in your tweets giving them a virtual tap on the shoulder when you think they may have something to contribute. For example, you may tweet, "Wondering what folks like @joycevalenza think about iPads as a replacement for books in the library?"

Group Response

In Tamara Cox's library, students are often asked to bring their cell phones when they come to the library. She uses the group response site Poll Everywhere to get the students involved. One way she does this is after viewing book trailers. Ms. Cox has her students use their phones to vote for their favorite book. Not only does this engage the students, but it also illustrates to classroom teachers that cell phones can offer an effective way to collect and capture students thoughts, opinions, and feedback. When teachers see their librarian modeling the use of phones with students they are often more open to the idea of using them in their own classroom. This is especially important in schools that have limited or no access to student response systems (clickers). Cell phones provide the same opportunity for student involvement without the cost.

Ms. Cox has also had success in using cell phones as an audience response system during teacher professional development when she has engaged participants by introducing a topic and polling them. She'll have the question shared on the board with directions on how to respond. This involves the teachers immediately while also giving them a relevant topic to discuss as they wait for the meeting to begin.

The globally connected, digitally savvy librarian of today empowers students to be independent learners, connected to an infinite amount of resources to meet their interests, passions, and learning needs. Harnessing the power of cell phones is a free and easy way to bring this reality to life.

THE TEXTING COACH

Physical education teachers are realizing the simple power of cell phones for administrative purposes and to enrich coaching. Here are ideas for texting coaches.

Group Texting

Group texting is the perfect way to reach the entire team with the ease of one text: when practice schedules change, when the team needs a motivational message, and with training tips for stretching in the evening, eating a healthy breakfast, or taking a day off. By creating a group of the team and the team parents at the first meeting of the season, you are set for great communication, increased coaching time, and a way to bond with your team in the way they love to connect. You also will have a written record of all of the texts sent throughout the season.

Video Capture

A proved coaching method is the use of film, video, and now cell phones. It is often too time consuming and equipment too burdensome to video and watch practices and games of the whole team, much less individual athletes. With cell phones, individual videos can be taken during practices. Just put your athletes in groups of two or more with at least one cell phone with video capabilities. Have the athletes video each other doing key skills such as serving a volleyball, starts in track, or free throws in basketball. The replay can be watched immediately and improvement can be tracked, corrections made, and practice time fully used. It is like putting a coach into every group's hands.

THE TEXTING PUPIL PERSONNEL SECRETARY

The pupil personnel secretary is responsible for ensuring all students are accounted for. When a student is absent, attendance calls are made. This can be time consuming, but is a very important part of the attendance secretary's day. Keeping track of students holds them accountable and shows that the school cares when they are absent. Texting has become a tool that some pupil personnel secretaries are finding useful.

By using text messaging, secretaries can reach out to both parents and students quickly and easily and with a better chance of being connected. The result is better responses, more information coming back, and improved communication. The secretary can respond appropriately, share what is needed with the counselor, and have more of an opportunity to encourage the student to return the next day, to offer to have the teacher text the homework or notes, and support the student in the situation.

THE TEXTING CUSTODIAN

Communicating is essential for running a school. Leo Beltran, custodian for a large multifaceted facility, commented that he has been a school custodian for twenty years and his job is so much easier, better, and more time efficient now than ever because of text messaging.

Texting on the Run

According to Leo Beltran, his cell phone has become his life line. It is impossible to be everywhere at once, but that is often what everyone expects. By having his cell phone handy, Leo can receive texts, prioritize the needs, and respond to each quickly and efficiently even while walking from one area of the campus to another. This makes better use of his time by not having to go talk to everyone who needs him, deal with frustrated individuals, or waste time going in person. He often only has to deal with something that just needs to be adjusted, cleaned up, or fixed.

Group Texting for Parts Saves Time and Money

An increase in communication among district maintenance personnel regarding parts could save time and money. Whenever a part is needed a first step could be to send out a group text asking if another school in the district has the part on hand. An exchange, borrow, or give-away could be arranged.

Be Available Without Being Disturbed

Custodians are often the first person called whenever something goes wrong, somebody needs some equipment, or facilities need attention. This can be at all times of day or night, which can be very disruptive to home and family life. Text messaging has alleviated some of the disruption with the quiet, private manner that texts can be addressed.

THE TEXTING SCHOOL COMMUNITY

When everyone involved in the school community uses the tools available from cell phones to improve communication, enhance relationships, and model twenty-first-century skills, a school climate will result that fully supports students and student achievement. By being proactive and taking the time to conduct or attend the example workshops, secure the agreements, and learn the tools, the whole school community can have success with cells.

chapter SEVEN

How to Use *Teaching Generation Text* for Professional Development

> *The more I learn, the more I realize what I don't know. The more I realize I don't know, the more I want to learn.*
> Albert Einstein

Although many educators want to begin using innovative strategies such as incorporating texting into instruction, the reality is that most need the jump start and support that professional development provides. In this chapter you will discover ways to provide professional development to help educators who just need a hand to help them get on board through workshops, your personal learning network, and an online course. You will want to consider providing these workshops at your school, for your district, or at conferences. When you do, please credit this book. You may want to consider providing books to your participants, too.

Before you give each workshop, you will need to be familiar with and understand the tools referred to in Chapters One and Two. If you are not, you can refer back to them.

WORKSHOP ONE: USING CELL PHONES OUTSIDE THE BAN

Description

Participants discover free and easy mobile learning activities that will engage students outside of the classroom. Workshop participants will collaboratively design mobile learning activities that they will share with the group and be able to begin implementing in their schools.

This can be completed in one to two class periods.

	Workshop Agenda	
Time	**Activity**	**Facilitator Notes and Resources**
00:00	**Welcome and Introductions** Participants will do the following: • Understand the issues surrounding school bans. • Discover free and easy mobile learning activities that will engage students outside of the classroom. • Collaboratively design mobile learning activities that can be used even in schools where cell phones are banned. • Share these activities with the group.	Welcome the class. Introduce why this is an important topic. Consider creating an open response poll for participants to text name, title, and how they believe this workshop will enrich their work. Provide an overview of what participants will be doing in the class.
00:05	**Issues Surrounding School Bans** • District that bans phones (http://weblog-ed.com/2007/i-lost-something-very-important-to-me) (Richardson, 2007) • District that embraces phones (www.edweek.org/dd/articles/2010/10/20/01mobile.h04.html) (Quillen, October 15, 2010)	Share these two stories of districts on either side of the spectrum.

Time	Activity	Facilitator Notes and Resources
00:10	**Share Free and Easy Ways to Use Mobile Learning Activities to Engage Students** • Student response systems such as Poll Everywhere, TextTheMob, and Wiffiti encourage collaborative discussion and reflection. • Photo-sharing sites such as Flickr help to develop and present work. • Tweeting can strengthen the home-school connection by connecting what's going on in school with the world outside of school. • Audiocasts such as Voki help create and publish student work. It enables your students to share a message using an animated avatar that talks with their own voice recorded right from their phone. Students design their avatar's appearance, add their voice, and can pop it into any Web 2.0 compatible site (wikis, blogs, Facebook, websites). The avatar moves and speaks based on what you say.	These are some activities you can share. Share as few or as many as time allows. Chapters One and Two have all the directions participants need to get started. Provide a brief overview of each, then have participants pick the one they want to explore and create a lesson plan around using your school's lesson plan format or the one provided in Chapter Five.
00:20	**Participants Break into Groups, Pairs, or Work Individually to Design a Lesson Based on Technology Selected**	Have participants complete your school's lesson plan format or the one provided in Chapter Five. You can capture results on paper or via Google forms. *(continued)*

Time	Activity	Facilitator Notes and Resources
00:40	**Participants Share**	Have one person from each group or pair share a one- to two-minute overview of the lesson.
00:55	**Questions, Answers, and Lessons Are Distributed as Takeaways**	If using Google forms, distribution is automatic. If using paper, make copies or scan documents.
00:60	**Adjourn**	

WORKSHOP TWO: CELLS IN THE CLASSROOM: FROM BANNING TO EMBRACING (A FIVE-STEP PLAN)

Description

According to a 2010 Marist Poll, 94 percent of Americans under age forty-five have access to a personal learning device that could greatly enrich the way teachers teach and students learn. Unfortunately, many schools and districts ban student-owned learning devices such as cell phones. In this session we'll reveal a sensible and progressive five-step plan that will enable all stakeholders (parents, teachers, administrators, and students) to embrace these powerful learning tools and discover how doing so can enrich student learning and strengthen the home-school connection. This can be completed in about two class periods.

Workshop Agenda

Time	Activity	Facilitator Notes and Resources
00:00	**Welcome and Introductions** Participants will do the following: • Understand why integrating cell phones into their work is important. • Discover a progressive five-step plan to begin integrating cell phones into their work. • Receive examples that can be used with each part of the plan.	Welcome the class. Introduce why this is an important topic. Consider creating an open response poll for participants to text name, title, and how they believe this workshop will enrich their work. Provide an overview of what participants will be doing in the class.
00:05	**Why Are We Here** • Because students *love* their cell phones! • We can make the school world better match the real world. • We can bridge the digital divide! • We can teach proper cell phone behaviors and educational uses that are free, easy to use, and engaging! • We can open up global resources, use a ubiquitous device, and better prepare our students for their future.	You may want to find comics that illustrate these points.
00:10	**Five-Step Plan to Begin Harnessing the Power of Cells** • Ask participants to share successes they've had, what they are doing, or what they might try in each step.	Set up a Wiffiti board or Twitter tag to collect participants' feedback. You will want to check in on this in the middle and at the end of the five steps.

(continued)

Time	Activity	Facilitator Notes and Resources
00:15	**Step One: Teacher Use of Cell Phones for Professional Purposes** • Share the uses then discuss. • Use Poll Everywhere to conduct staff surveys that would be useful and interesting to share with students and the school community. • Use group texting to inform colleagues and staff rather than disrupting instruction with announcements. • Set up Google Voice to serve as your personal secretary, which will transcribe your messages and enable you to easily share with others.	Explain the importance of learning to use and be comfortable with this technology. You can use these examples of how teachers employ cell phones, but consider personalizing this to ways that you have used your cell phone.
00:25	**Step Two: Teacher Models Appropriate Use for Learning** • Share the uses then discuss. • Model for your students how your cell phone supports your work when you use the phone for basic features such as alarm clock, calendar, calculator, stop watch, note taking. • Demonstrate how you can use your phone to gain information instantly using ChaCha (242242). • Ask participants a question here (such as "What was the birth date of the person our school was named after?") and give a reward to the winner who gets the answer right first.	Explain the importance of being able to model once you are comfortable with this technology. You can use these examples for how teachers might model the use of cell phones, but consider personalizing this to ways that you have used it.

Time	Activity	Facilitator Notes and Resources
	• Use your cell phone as a camera to capture student work and events and load them to Flickr so they can be embedded in your class or school website, wiki, or blog.	
00:35	**Step Three: Strengthen the Home-School Connection with Cell Phones** • Share the uses then discuss. • Show parents, families, and guardians their thoughts and opinions matter. Poll them or request an open response using a tool such as Poll Everywhere. • Use Twitter and have the updates feed into your blog, school website, or wiki to reinforce the home-school connection and build class and school pride. • Text home individually or to groups of students (using a service such as WeTxt or one from your service provider) to celebrate student success or reach out via text if there is an area of individual concern. (*Michael is absent. I hope everything is okay.*) or group concern (*Tomorrow may be a snow day. Stay tuned.*). This can be done quickly with minimal disruption to either party. Added benefits include the following: • Environmentally friendly • More likely to make it into parent's hands	Explain the importance of getting buy-in from parents. Using cell phones with parents shifts the thinking of the tool from a distraction to a valuable connection to the school and teacher. You can use these examples or your own.

(*continued*)

Time	Activity	Facilitator Notes and Resources
00:45	**Step Four: Students Use Cell Phones for Homework** • Share the uses then discuss. • Use ChaCha to connect your students to a free network of thousands of guides who can help them when they get stuck or have no one around to help. • Use Google Voice to set up a widget and have students record oral reports or other assignments of your choosing. • Test prior knowledge of a unit your class is about to study by using Wiffiti or Poll Everywhere to have students share one thing they know about the subject. Added benefits include the following: • Can be done anywhere, anytime. • More likely to be completed.	Discuss how supporting students in using cell phones for homework builds a strong foundation, case, and understanding for using them in the classroom. It also provides students with the opportunity to see the devices as a learning tool. Address ideas for accommodating students without phones, such as buddying up students; connecting them with businesses or mentors whose phone they could use and who could provide support in such work; or enabling students to come early, at lunch, or after school and use a teacher phone.
	Banned or Embraced? If cell phones are banned in your school or district, this is the conclusion of the workshop and you will want to consider breaking the ban with a six-part plan as outlined in the Appendix. If cell phones are not banned in your school or district you will want to ensure you have the building blocks for success before moving to the final step.	If cell phones are banned in your school or district, the workshop can conclude here as you work to break the ban. If they are not, proceed to the final step.

Time	Activity	Facilitator Notes and Resources
00:55	**Ensure You Have the Building Blocks for Success** Even in districts where cell phones are allowed, it is beneficial to follow the previous steps first as you move toward and get comfortable with step five. If you are ready to take the next step, you must ensure you have the building blocks for success in place that are addressed in Chapter Four. The six building blocks are as follows: • Get your school's approval to use cell phones. • Secure parent and guardian and student agreements. • Teach students about cell phone safety and etiquette. • Develop an acceptable use policy. • Establish classroom management procedures. • Plan activities with students. *Note:* If the building blocks are not adequately addressed, do not move to step five. Instead, come up with a plan to ensure the building blocks are in place to take the next step.	Discuss the building blocks and how they are addressed where you teach. If you are providing this workshop in your local school or district, have all the policies on hand during the workshop and use samples from Chapter Four to compare different policies. *Discuss:* Are they each adequately addressed? How was the acceptable use plan derived? Do they have a laptop appropriate use plan? How are these plans generally conceived? Does this work? Could it be improved? How? *(continued)*

Time	Activity	Facilitator Notes and Resources
00:65	**Step Five: Students Use Cell Phones for Class Work**	

- Share the uses then discuss.
- You're going on a field trip. Ask students to determine how they might want to use cell phones to meet the learning goals of the trip using the tools most phones have. They may decide to tweet for a scavenger hunt, send reflections to Wiffiti or Poll Everywhere, or capture pictures and send to an album on Flickr.
- You're about to learn about a new country or explore your own neighborhood. Ask students for ideas to meet learning goals using their cells. Maybe they can use ChaCha or Google SMS to collect data about the area.
- Invite students to use cell phones to create a Voki character or Google Voice to make audio recordings of short stories, personal narratives, or poems.

Time	Activity	Facilitator Notes and Resources
00:75	**Wrap Up**	Explain to participants that this plan along with this video, with its call to action from the U.S. education secretary, are strong resources they can use to begin harnessing cell phones as a teaching and learning tool.

- This five-step plan allows you to begin embracing cells and leading your entire school into the future.
- This video from the U.S. education secretary Arne Duncan (2009) will provide back up for support: www.pbs.org/wgbh/pages/frontline/digitalnation/learning/schools/school-theres-an-app-for-that.html

Time	Activity
00:85	**Questions, Comments, Reactions**
00:90	**Adjourn**

WORKSHOP THREE: SUPPORTING RESEARCH-BASED INSTRUCTIONAL STRATEGIES WITH CELLS

Description

In this session you will gain a wealth of lesson ideas to support the nine instructional strategies in the classic *Classroom Instruction That Works* by Dean, Hubbell, Pitler, and Stone (2012), all using free cell phone technologies. Participants will focus on cell phone technologies for the strategies they're most interested in exploring.

Time	Activity	Facilitator Notes and Resources
	Workshop Agenda	
00:00	**Welcome and Introductions** Participants will do the following: • Receive an introduction to nine research-based strategies for effective learning. • Discover tools that can be used to support each research-based strategy. • Receive hands-on demonstration and practice using the tool to support the strategy(ies) in which they are most interested.	Welcome the class. Introduce why this is an important topic. Consider creating an open response poll for participants to text name, title, and how they believe this workshop will enrich their work. Provide an overview of what participants will be doing in the class.
00:05	**It's Not If We Should Use Cells, but When . . .** • Watch *Nokia: Go Play—Fourth Screen* (www.youtube.com/watch?v=XpeNk3E36YU&feature=player_embedded)	Explain that in life outside school, cell phones have become our personal connecting and learning devices. The world inside school needs to move closer to what is experienced in the real world lest it moves toward irrelevance. *(continued)*

Time	Activity	Facilitator Notes and Resources
00:10	**Overview of Dean, Hubbell, Pitler, and Stone's Research-Based Strategies** • Set objectives and provide feedback: Wiffiti, Voki • Reinforce effort and provide recognition: Voki, polling, Wiffiti • Cooperative learning: Group texting, Google SMS, ChaCha • Cues, questions, and advanced organizers: Group texting, Google • Nonlinguistic representations: Cell phone cameras, video, Flickr • Summarize and take notes: Twitter, Google Voice, notepad, camera • Homework and practice: Group texting, polling • Identify similarities and differences: Polling, phonecasting • Generate and test hypotheses: Phonecasting, Twitter, Flickr, polling	Provide a general overview of Dean, Hubbell, Pitler, and Stone's research-based strategies and how each can be enriched with the use of cell phones (see Chapter Three for details).
00:25	**Audience Poll** • Respond to a poll indicating the strategy you are most interested in enriching with cell phones.	Assess what your participants are most interested in and display the results via a Poll Everywhere poll.

Time	Activity	Facilitator Notes and Resources
		Explain that for this session you will focus on the strategies for which there is most interest.
		This is to whet their appetites. Once they've tried these tools, a follow-up session could introduce others.
00:27	**Supporting Research-Based Strategy with Cells** • Share one thing you have tried or might try to support one of the strategies. • Text your thoughts to Wiffiti. • Discuss.	Set up a Wiffiti board for participants to brainstorm what they might try. Discuss the results to get the audience excited about learning how to get started.
00:40	**Overview and Discussion of the First, Second, and Third Most Popular Strategies** Note: Depending on the allocation of time for this workshop you can include fewer or more strategies.	Provide an overview of the sections participants are interested in from Chapter Three. Share possible ideas for each strategy then show participants how to implement the idea in which they are most interested. Have participants take out their cells so they can engage in hands-on participation. Pause after each strategy to discuss and answer questions.
00:55	**Questions, Comments, and Reactions**	
00:60	**Adjourn**	

USING *TEACHING GENERATION TEXT* IN YOUR PERSONAL LEARNING NETWORK

Although professional development and classes are a great way to learn, personal learning networks are quickly picking up momentum as the learning platform of choice for innovative educators and leaders. A personal learning network provides individuals with ongoing, on-demand, personalized support anytime and anywhere they want it with others they meet in platforms such as Twitter, Facebook, Classroom 2.0 or face-to-face. Because cell phones are banned in many schools and districts, it's often difficult for educators interested in harnessing the power of cell phones in education to connect with others who share their interest. Here are ideas for getting started with developing your own personal learning network that will enable you and others to stay connected with the best ways to remain in the know about using cells for education.

Blogs

Read and comment on blogs that cover the topic of cell phones in education. As you come across blogs you like, add them to your Google RSS reader. Here are a few blogs to get you started:

- *The Innovative Educator* (http://theinnovativeeducator.blogspot.com)
  - Sharing ideas about educating innovatively, including information on using cell phones in education
- *From Toy to Tool: Cell Phones in Learning* (www.cellphonesinlearning.com)
  - A conversation about integrating student cell phones into classroom curricula
- *Living in the 4th Screen* (www.livinginthe4thscreen.com)
  - Exploring the use of mobile technology in education and life
- *Learning with Mobile Technology* (http://blogs.cellularlearning.org)
  - A blog about technology in the classroom
- *Teaching Generation Text* (http://teachinggenerationtext.blogspot.com/)
  - A blog sharing success stories, lessons, and ideas for using cell phones to enhance learning

Twitter

Use Twitter to find others who are interested in the same topic. You can do this using search terms such as *education cell phones, mobile learning, phones education,* or this commonly used Twitter hashtag, #mlearning. Once there identify tweeps (Twitter peeps) who are saying things you like and follow them, reply to them, or retweet what they are saying. When you have questions or want feedback about a particular topic, use "@" (example @ innovativeedu) to tag people in your tweet and they'll directly receive your tweet. Twitter will instantly provide you with a terrific on-demand network just waiting to support your personal learning.

Facebook and Google+

Facebook and Google+ are great vehicles to expand your personal learning network about topics of interest. As you begin following blogs, Twitter, and meeting people face-to-face and at conferences who are interested in the same topic, request their friendship on Facebook or add them to your Google+ circle. Both provide some benefits over Twitter in that you can link to other web pages and tag the people who you want to see using "@" (example @Lisa Velmer Nielsen). All those tagged will have your post show up on their feeds and they can comment and see one another's posts—the makings for a great conversation indeed. Others who may be interested can also chime in.

Another option on Facebook is joining a page about an area of interest. Just type the topic in the search box and see what comes up. A page that exists for cell phones in education is *Teaching Generation Text* (www.facebook.com/home.php?sk=group_12205345787 4137&ap=1). On such pages you'll see information about the topic and you can share posts, thoughts, and questions. Again, you can tag specific people if you want what you write to appear on their wall.

Classroom 2.0

Classroom 2.0 (www.classroom20.com) is a terrific resource with tens of thousands of members available all the time. Once there you can join the Cell Phones in Education group (www.classroom20.com/group/CellPhonesinEducation), start your own conversations, or join conversations that are already in progress. You can also share any of these conversations on Classroom 2.0 with your Twitter network, Facebook network, as well as a number of other sharing platforms. Those you connect with here also become a part of your personal learning network. You can friend these folks on Classroom 2.0, follow their blogs if they have them, introduce them to yours (if you have one), and connect with them on Facebook, Twitter, and beyond.

Google Docs

Google docs provides a collaborative environment that supplies an amazing opportunity when combined with the power of your personal learning network to think, build, and grow. You can increase and solidify your learning and knowledge as you work on creating a document, such as a comparison chart, a curriculum map, a lesson plan, a collection of ideas, and so on. When you invite your PLN to join you, you all grow and create together. All you need to do is sign up for Google docs, create a Google doc, and make it public and allow anyone with the link to edit. Then share what you are doing via a tweet, status update, e-mail, and so on. Your learning partners will have the opportunity to learn and grow with you . . . and, don't forget the chat feature available on the page, so you can communicate with your collaborators.

Face-to-Face

We all know the old fashion face-to-face connections work really well. The problem for some is finding others in their physical space who share their interests. Of course a solution is taking a class or attending a conference. Those of us who have had the pleasure of connecting in online environments appreciate how such relationships can deepen and grow when face-to-face and online connections are married.

If you're ready to begin building your personal learning network of others interested in using cell phones in education, pick one or two of these ideas and get started. When you do, not only will you learn a lot, but you will also contribute to the learning of others as well.

PROFESSIONAL DEVELOPMENT THROUGH PROFESSIONAL LEARNING COMMUNITIES

Many schools use professional learning communities (PLCs) for professional development. A professional learning community is characterized by an environment fostering mutual cooperation, emotional support, personal growth, and a synergy of efforts. Growth, change, and development happen when school staff study, work, plan, and take action together on behalf of improved learning for students. Being part of a PLC reduces teacher isolation, increases commitment to the mission and goals of the school, creates shared responsibility for the total development of students, creates powerful learning that defines good teaching and classroom practice, and enhances understanding of course content and teacher roles (Hord, 1997).

A PLC can be created around using cell phone technologies to enhance research-based instructional strategies by learning new tools, applying cell phone enhancements to lessons, and discussing results. To develop a community of learners, pull interested, willing people together, engage them in constructing a shared vision, develop trust and relationships, and nurture a program of continual learning (Hord, 1997).

Enhancing PLCs with Cell Phone Tools

PLCs can address how to use cell phones to enrich learning and also enhance themselves with cell phone tools. Doing this enables educators to experience firsthand the communication, logistical, and learning benefits from cells. You can start by collecting your PLCs' numbers and placing them in a group text distribution list. From there you could text out reminders, updates, or questions to the group. You might want to set up a poll on Poll Everywhere and have members text in their responses to a polling question or set up a Wiffiti page and have them text in their thoughts about a discussion question. The polls can be done to instantly collect and graphically show the representation of data that PLCs may have collected. The Wiffiti board discussion can make productive use of time by sending out discussion topics prior to the meeting. This way during meetings you can skip past idea collection and move on to making meaning of ideas as they relate to the work at hand. It can also be a useful way to collect info if your PLC has break-out groups. Each group can submit its feedback to the Wiffiti board where it is captured and collected in one place. Having the Wiffiti boards is great because discussion topic responses are archived for group members to refer back to and it provides a way to keep the conversation going even after the meeting has ended. Collecting information via cell phone tools such as Poll Everywhere and Wiffiti provides a way for members who may not be able to attend a meeting to give input. Additionally, by using the response tools, all participants will be free to respond, not just those who tend to dominate the discussion or for all to answer even when time runs out or an idea happens at another time. Using cell phones to enrich PLCs is a great way to model effective uses of texting.

USING *TEACHING GENERATION TEXT* IN AN ONLINE COURSE

An online course is a great way to support educators and administrators interested in learning more about teaching generation text. To follow are guidelines for an online course that enables participants to dive deeper into the wealth of cell phone enhancements to support research-based instructional strategies. Regardless of their school's or district's cell phone policy, participants of this class will be able to explore and experience cell phone activities that support teaching and engage students.

If you are interested in providing an online course to those in your district or personal learning network, the following overview of the modules could be included in a self-paced, online course. In the course participants are encouraged to build PLNs to enable the availability of ongoing support beyond the course.

This course is modeled after one available at Colorado Mesa University in Grand Junction, Colorado, which earns two continuing education credits. You can use the outline below as a guide to deliver your own course or you can take this course yourself by visiting www.mesastate.edu/online/gentext.html. The introductions to the modules provide an overview of the content, learning activities, and course progression. The modules are followed by a quick guide for all of the links required to set up the class, which are ready to go and include input from previous participants.

Overview of the Course

Teaching Generation Text will empower you to move from fighting student cell phones to using student cell phones to enhance teaching and learning. Not only are cell phones the most ubiquitous device, but they are also the method of choice for communication by our secondary students. Based on research-based teaching and learning strategies, using a simple text-capable phone, free web-based tools, and your open mind, this class will be easily applied to your teaching and make it better. You will progress through six modules. Each module provides content and instruction through reading, experience with cell phone tools, and a progression of activities that culminate in teaching and reflection on a cell phone–enhanced lesson. Continued practice, support, and experiences using the cell phone tools and lessons will be provided through the networks of support established during the course.

Each module is organized by providing a brief overview, an outline of what participants will complete, and steps on how to complete activities in each module. There are also facilitator notes and a resources section that includes tips and considerations for facilitators along with links to resources. Following all six modules you will find a course assessment checklist on which participants can indicate if each activity is complete and provide a link to the completed work. As noted in the facilitator notes and resources, participants might need guidance in how to create documents so that links can be shared.

Module One: From Banning to Embracing—the Five-Step Plan

In this module participants learn why other educators and schools embrace the use of cell phones for learning and they share the reasons behind their interest in doing so as well. They will discover and join learning networks with others who share their interest. They learn to embrace cell phones as powerful learning tools and they discover a simple and progressive five-step plan they can use to support teaching and learning even in schools where they are banned. The following steps will take you through this module.

Step	Activity	Facilitator Notes and Resources
1	**Read** • Introduction of this book	The facilitator will want to determine where course materials will be shared, for example, a wiki, website, blog, or content management system (CMS).
2	**Answer** Text in your answer to these two polling questions: • *What step of the five-step plan are you currently on?* • *What step do you want to be on by the end of the course?*	Determine where you want to publish the poll results.
3	**Read** • "6 Ideas for Developing a Personal Learning Network of Others Interested in Using Cell Phones in Education" (Nielsen, 2010)	Article link: http://theinnovativeeducator.blogspot.com/2010/10/6-ideas-for-developing-personal.html
4	**Expand Your Personal Learning Network** These groups will be great resources as you engage in the assignments. Contribute to each. • Join Classroom 2.0. • Become a member of the group "Cell Phones in Education." • Join Facebook. • Become a member of the group "Teaching Generation Text." • Follow your class blog.	Classroom 2.0 Group: www.classroom20.com/group/CellPhonesinEducation Facebook Group: www.facebook.com/pages/Let-Students-Use-Cell-Phones-to-Learn/311313147415 The class facilitator will need to create a blog for class participants to share their responses. Ideally this will be a blog that will have interest beyond this class and will be named accordingly. You may want to draw inspiration from the names of existing blogs that were shared in the "Blogs" section of this chapter. When you do start a blog, don't forget to share it with your PLN as well as on the Facebook page and Classroom 2.0 group.

(continued)

Step	Activity	Facilitator Notes and Resources
5	**Read** • Preface of this book • "Get Smart About Phones" (Ullman, 2010)	Article link: www.techlearning.com/article/32470
6	**Respond to Why Are You Interested in Using Cell Phones for Education** • In the Preface you read about why the authors of *Teaching Generation Text* became interested in using cell phones for learning. In the article you read about several schools that also use cell phones for learning. Write an article or create a video or audio explaining (1) why you became interested in using cell phones for learning and (2) how your school policy is or is not in alignment with your vision for using cell phones for learning. • Submit this article for inclusion on the class blog. • Invite members of your PLN to respond. You should have at least three comments and respond to at least two of your classmates.	If you are teaching preservice teachers have them explain the policy at a school where they are student teaching or where they wish to teach. You will need to establish a protocol for submission. Some options include the following: • Set up a class account and share the username and password with all students. • Invite each student as a contributor. • Have students submit posts to you and you share on the blog.

Module Two: Breaking the Ban with a Six-Part Plan

In this module participants will find and discuss local policies and, if necessary, develop a plan to break the ban where they teach. They will also survey parents, students, and teachers to determine their attitudes and access to technology. The following steps will take you through this module.

Step	Activity	Facilitator Notes and Resources
1	**Read** • The Appendix, "Breaking the Ban with a Six-Part Plan," of this book	
2	**Conduct Surveys** • Conduct the parent, student, and teacher surveys from the Appendix to gain insight into each group's attitudes, access, and more. • Distribute the surveys to all parents, students, and teachers and do your best to get as many responses as possible. Teachers may want to set calendar invitations with the survey link to track who has and has not completed the survey. • Write a summary of your findings and ensure you have a link to the results. • This will be used as a part of your action plan.	Electronic survey collection is easier and more efficient than paper. If you decide to go this route there are free tools you can use such as Google forms or SurveyMonkey. Ensure your participants know how to create a link to their survey results, for example, a link to where they're published on a school or class website, or a Google doc.

(continued)

Step	Activity	Facilitator Notes and Resources
3	**Locate Your Local Policy on the Use of Cell Phones and Other Electronics** • Share this by replying to the acceptable use post at Classroom 2.0. If none exists for your school, share that. This will enable classmates and others interested in the topic to see the range of possibilities currently implemented in various schools and districts.	Facilitators may want to use the following discussion or create a new one for their class on their own CMS or at Classroom 2.0. Classroom 2.0 acceptable use policies discussion: www.classroom20.com/group/ CellPhonesinEducation/forum/ topics/acceptable-use-policies
4	**Create an Action Plan** Use components of the Appendix to draft either (1) a short plan for addressing policy or (2) if you have a policy that works share why it works. You should include the following: • Cite the assigned readings, the discussion from the PLN groups, and your survey results. • Indicate who is responsible for your plan (for example, principal, school board, superintendent, mayor, and so on). • Indicate who is responsible for updating your plan. • Share the appropriate audience for your plan and how you plan to submit it. • Share your plan in the "action plan" post on the Classroom 2.0 Cell Phones in Education group discussion forum.	Action plan: www.classroom20.com/group/ CellPhonesinEducation/forum/ topics/ action-plans-for-policy- change

Module Three: The Building Blocks for Success with Cell Phones in Education

In this module participants will learn about the six building blocks for success with cell phones in education:

1. Get your school's approval to use cell phones.
2. Secure parent and guardian and student agreements.
3. Teach students about cell phone safety and etiquette.
4. Develop an acceptable use policy.
5. Establish classroom management procedures.
6. Plan activities with students.

They will do this by starting to put some of these building blocks together beginning with a parent and student agreement letter that they share for feedback with their PLNs, followed by addressing current concerns regarding cell phone use, and then developing a plan to address them. The following steps will take you through this module.

Step	Activity	Facilitator Notes and Resources
1	**Read** • Chapter Four, "The Six Building Blocks for Success with Cell Phones in Education," of this book	
2	**Create Parent and Student Agreement Letters** • Using what you read in Chapter Four develop parent and student agreements that will work best with your class. • Ask for feedback from your PLN.	Facilitators may want to use this discussion or create a new one for their class on their own CMS or at Classroom 2.0. Classroom 2.0 parent and student agreements discussion forum: *(continued)*

Step	Activity	Facilitator Notes and Resources
	• Share your agreement in the parent and student agreements discussion forum in the Cell Phones in Education group on Classroom 2.0 post on the class blog.	www.classroom20.com/group/ CellPhonesinEducation/forum/ topics/parent-student -agreements
3	**Student Acceptable Use of Technology Strategy**	
	• Using what you read in Chapter Four explain how you plan to teach students about cell phone safety and etiquette, develop an acceptable use policy, establish classroom management, and plan activities with students	
	• Draft your explanation in the form of an article and submit it to the class blog.	
	• Share your post with members of your PLN and elicit at least three comments to your explanation.	

Module Four: Tools of the Trade for the Texting Learner and Teacher

In this module participants will discover how they can use cell phones as tools as explained in Chapter One. Participants will try out one tool selected for the class and two tools on their own. Then they will explore ways they can empower their students to use cell phones to learn in Chapter Two and will try out one tool selected for the class and two tools on their own. Participants will engage in global conversations on what works with cell phones in schools and classrooms currently having tremendous success. The following steps will take you through this module.

Step	Activity	Facilitator Notes and Resources
1	**Read** • Chapter One, "The Texting Teacher," of this book	
2	**Trying the Tools: The Texting Teacher—Whole Class** • Flickr • Take a picture of yourself in your learning environment on your cell phone and send it into the class Flickr e-mail. Put your first name and subject or grade you will teach in the subject and share the teaching tools you plan to use in the body. • These will be autopublished on the class blog in a post called "These Teachers Text" enabling all those interested to see innovative teaching practices educators are trying using cell phones.	Create a Flickr account as explained in Chapter One. You'll need to get a Flickr e-mail at www.flickr.com/account/uploadbyemail and set up your account so the pictures come in with a tag you have determined, for example, the class identification number. You will then get the slide show embed code to place in your class blog post. Create a class blog post called "These Teachers Text." In it explain a little about the class and perhaps provide links to some of their online spaces where discussions and work is published. Embed the Flickr slide show that captures the teachers along with the tools they plan to use for teaching.
3	**Try and Share Experiences** • Try the tools indicated in your Flickr response and share your experience using the tools by commenting in the class blog in the "These Teachers Text" post.	Be sure to plan to respond to the teachers' experiences in the blog comments. *(continued)*

Step	Activity	Facilitator Notes and Resources
4	**Read** • Chapter Two, "The Texting Learner," of this book	
5	**Trying the Tools: The Texting Learner—Whole Class** • Wiffiti • Text the learner tools you would like to try to Wiffiti at **87884** include the @wif code for your screen + your tools as the message. See what your classmates and others will be trying by viewing the Wiffiti page at the screen you set up for the class.	Make a Wiffiti board as explained in Chapter One. You may want to call it something like "Teachers Get Smart About Cell Phones for Learning." You will use the embed code in this board for your blog post in the next step.
6	**Try and Share Experiences** • Try the tools indicated in your Wiffiti response and share your experience using the tools by commenting in the class blog in the "Texting to Learn" post.	Create a blog post for participants to respond to that can be called "Texting to Learn." This explain about what the teachers are doing and that you can see the tools they're trying on the Wiffiti board and read about their experiences in the comment section. Be sure to plan to respond to the teachers' experiences in the blog comments.

Module Five: Cell Phone–Infused Lessons

In this module participants will review research-based instructional strategies and discover how cell phone technologies support and enhance them by reading Chapter Three of this book. Class members will select a strategy and become familiar with the example lessons for enhancing the strategies with cell phones. Participants will discuss the strategies and enhancements in the "Supporting Research-Based Instructional Strategies Using Cell Phones" discussion in the Cell Phones in Education group at Classroom 2.0.

Participants will also read Chapter Five for ideas on lessons they may use once the building blocks are in place to use cell phones in the classroom. Using the lesson format from Chapter Five, participants will create their own cell phone–enhanced lesson plan based on their selected research strategy and customized to their needs using content that they are or will be teaching.

Participants will select lessons in this module that will be implemented in the following module. Participants should plan to deliver lessons in which the students are using cell phones outside of school and that don't involve direct teacher-student texting. This provides a foundation and a level of comfort as you work to put the building blocks in place for success in using cell phones in school. If your school or district allows the use of cell phones for learning at school, you may want to write future lessons incorporating the devices into the classroom. This should only be done after you and your students have developed experience and achieved a level of comfort for using the devices as learning tools outside of class. The following steps will take you through this module.

Step	Activity	Facilitator Notes and Resources
1	**Read**	
	• Chapter Three, "Supporting Research-Based Instructional Strategies Supported by Cell Phones," of this book	
		(continued)

Step	Activity	Facilitator Notes and Resources
2	**Choose** • Select one research-based strategy around which you would like to create a lesson.	You may want to suggest students review the nine research-based strategies in the second edition of *Classroom Instruction That Works* (Dean, Hubbell, Pitler, & Stone, 2012).
3	**Read** • Chapter Five, "Cell Phone–Enriched Lessons to Engage Learners," of this book	
4	**Create** • Draft a research-based lesson using the lesson plan template in Chapter Five or the one used in your school.	You should accept lesson forms of their choosing but encourage students to consider the NETS standards as well as using a research-based strategy and a cell phone tool.
5	**Share** • Share the lesson with members of your PLN and ask for feedback. It might be easiest to send out a link to your lesson, which means you might want to use a tool such as Google docs or just upload the lesson to your class webpage or wiki if you have one. • Incorporate the feedback from your PLN.	You may want to standardize how students obtain lesson links. You might consider creating one Google account for the class and enabling them to create their lessons using that account. This way all students will have access to a bank of lessons that could be placed in a folder and made public for use by others.

Module Six: Application and Reflection

In this module participants will teach the lessons, write a reflection, and share it at the Cells in Education group on Classroom 2.0. The following steps will take you through this module.

Step	Activity	Facilitator Notes and Resources
1	**Teach** • Teach the researched-based lesson you created.	You may want to suggest that students select a peer to observe or have their students provide feedback after the lesson.
2	**Write a reflection** • Include (1) a link to the lesson; (2) links to lesson artifacts, for example, phone casts, Vokis, free response screens, Flickr slide shows; (3) relevant photographs; (4) student testimonials; and (5) video clips (optional). • Share. What worked? What could be improved? Were learning objectives met to your satisfaction? Did the cell phone tool increase engagement and enhance learning (how or why not)? What worked well? What were the obstacles? Describe student reactions, feedback, and experiences.	Facilitators should have exemplary samples of their own to share that include each of the pieces mentioned.
3	**Share** • Submit the reflection as a contribution to the blog. • Invite members of your PLN within or outside the class to comment. You should have at least three responses. • Comment on the posts of at least two of your classmates.	You will want to have a method established for contribution.

This is a pass or fail course. Participants must complete *all* the deliverables with links to their work for a passing grade.

Assessment Checklists

Module One Deliverables	Complete	Incomplete	URL
Five-step plan answers texted to Poll Everywhere			N/A
Read "Why Are You Interested in Using Cell Phones for Education?" article			

Module Two Deliverables	Complete	Incomplete	URL
Parent, teacher, student survey results			
School policy			
Action plan			

Module Three Deliverables	Complete	Incomplete	URL
Parent and student agreement letters			
Acceptable use of tech strategy			

Module Four Deliverables	Complete	Incomplete	URL
Create "These Teachers Text" Flickr photo			
Create "These Teachers Text" comment			
Create "Teachers Get Smart About Cell Phones for Learning" Wiffiti submission			N/A
Create "Texting to Learn" comment			

Module Five Deliverable	Complete	Incomplete	URL
Cell-phone infused lesson			

Module Six Deliverables	Complete	Incomplete	URL
Lesson implementation reflection			
Lesson implementation reflection: Comment one			
Lesson implementation reflection: Comment two			

This overview of the modules, lessons, and links to teach this book, *Teaching Generation Text*, should serve as a springboard for anyone wanting to share this knowledge in a formal manner. Practice all of the tools, make sure all of the links are still active, and review each module and step prior to offering the course. All of the instructions are available in this book. Getting ready and making the course fit the needs of the participants will be a fun review of the material for the instructor. In addition to offering the course as is to educators in general, the instructor could offer it face-to-face or to a special population (for example, special education staff, school counselors, administrators, math teachers, and so on). If you need assistance when setting up and offering the course, e-mail teachinggenerationtext@gmail.com.

THE MANY ROADS TO HARNESSING THE POWER OF CELLS THROUGH PROFESSIONAL DEVELOPMENT

Professional development takes many forms, from workshops and courses to the development of PLNs and PLCs. Any time an educator, school, or district purchases and reads a book, professional development begins. It is up to educators themselves to pursue how much they will learn and apply. These options for professional development will enhance the learning and continued development of the tools, lessons, and ideas for using cell phones in education, thus benefiting the students of generation text, which is the goal of this book. Happy texting!

Appendix
Breaking the Ban with a Six-Part Plan

> *Let's admit the real reason that we ban cell phones is that, given the opportunity to use them, students would vote with their attention, just as adults would "vote with their feet" by leaving the room when a presentation is not compelling.*
>
> Marc Prensky, author

High school assistant principal Kevin Bals knows firsthand the power of breaking the ban. Mr. Bals was so impressed with the power of cell phones for learning he started the *Living in the 4th Screen* blog (www.livinginthe4thscreen.com) and knew it was time to be a force in lifting the ban at his school. When the cell phone policy in his school was updated in 2009–10 allowing students to use their cell phones during the day he fully expected the number of cell phone violations to increase somewhat during the first year of a new policy and he expected more conduct reports dealing with cell phone violations. That did not happen. Instead he saw cell phone violations at his school decrease. The students say because they had opportunities to use their cell phones throughout the day it diminished the temptation to use them at inappropriate times. He notes that students are certainly happier with the new policy and parents have also shared they are pleased with the change because it allows them to connect with their children during the day if they need to. Though administration agonized over the decision to update the school's policy, Mr. Bals realizes now that the change in policy was really no big deal.

If you are not fortunate enough to work in a school that has a policy enabling you to harness the power of cell phones to enrich learning, you may need to educate your department, principal, parents, and district leadership. Educators know that student learning and achievement are the basis for all efforts in education. You first need to realize that leadership begins with example. There are those who are threatened by transitions and change. To break the ban, you will need to present yourself in ways that do not make your colleagues uncomfortable about their instructional methodology.

The following six steps will show how to build relationships with stakeholders, illustrate how cell phone use for education is progressing, provide research-based reasons, equip you to get supportive data in your school and district, set you up to run a pilot program, and summarize the key points for meetings:

1. Build relationships
2. Catch the momentum
3. Give reasons with research
4. Rally support through surveys
5. Plan a pilot
6. Know how to talk the talk

Look at this as an opportunity. Just think: you could be the one who starts the process of changing policy in your school or district, paving the way for educators to use cell phone technologies to enhance their lessons. This is what innovative educators such as George Engel, Rob Griffith, Scott Newcomb, and Jason Suter did. They were key to lifting the ban where they teach in an effort to empower students with the freedom to use cell phones as personal learning devices. This six-part plan includes ideas they used to change the minds of key players in their school community about the use of cell phones for learning. It all starts with the building of relationships with key constituents.

STEP ONE: BUILD RELATIONSHIPS

With students

- Let students know you care about making learning fun and relevant and ask them if they'd like the option to be able to do work using their cell phones. Most likely, the answer will be yes! If they are interested, provide them with homework options that enable them to use cell phones.

With parents and guardians

- Start with the parents by using the cell phone as a tool to bridge the home-school connection. You can have a text of the day to update parents on what's happening in the class. You can text parents individually to share information about their child. You can poll parents with Poll Everywhere to get their input and show their opinions matter. Once parents are on your side and see the value personally, your job convincing other stakeholders becomes much easier.

With colleagues

- Try to establish yourself as an innovative leader when it comes to empowering students and teachers with technology. A focus on student-centered learning is key. At grade or subject meetings offer to support teachers in harnessing the power of cell phones for themselves, and if they're ready, with their students. Get them started and model for them. Perhaps have a polling question in a meeting or gather input with a Wiffiti board.

With administration

- Start by working within the system to bring about technological change. Become known as someone who works with what your school has on hand and is flexible with administrative needs. When the opportunity presents itself, respectfully present the need for change and recommendations to update your school's technological teaching processes.

With the district

- Become known as a tech leader. Offer to participate in school and districtwide technology decisions. Offer to collaborate with the district technology coordinator and others to help establish a new acceptable use policy that will allow the use of cell phones as a learning tool. (The acceptable use policy is a critical step toward technological change. Many districts are still working with acceptable use policies developed in the late 1990s.) Keep in mind that in most cases, what is acceptable in the physical world applies to the online world as well.

STEP TWO: CATCH THE MOMENTUM

We need to know where we've been to know where we're going. The second step in lifting the ban takes a further look at the progression of school policy in conjunction with the development of cell phones and their increasing popularity. While the policy makers have been debating, educators across the country are realizing the value of cell phones, in varying degrees, from texting a single reminder to a single student to whole class uses both in and out of the classroom (regardless of policy). The research-supported time line in Table A.1 shows the trends and gives you solid background. This will assure leaders that they will be moving with the momentum of success in schools across the country.

Table A.1
Time Line of the Cell Phones-for-Learning Movement

When	What
Early 1990s	Schools banned all electronic devices (pagers, beepers, cell phones) that tended to be associated with drug dealing or gangs.
Late 1990s	Cell phones became commonplace, smaller, and cheaper. Text messaging became popular, especially with teens.
1999–2002	After the Columbine High School shootings and other acts of terrorism on our country, parents wanted to be able to communicate with their children at any time. Cell phones, parents argued, were necessary for safety, and the ban was relaxed in many schools.
	As stated on the *Education World* website in an article on school issues in 2002, "[m]ore than a decade after many school systems and states prohibited students from carrying and using cellular phones in school, state lawmakers and administrators are rethinking their positions. The widespread use of the devices and parents' concerns about their children's safety are prompting new policies that allow student use" (Delisio, 2002).
	The National School Safety and Security Center (2002) acknowledged that schools were looking into this issue and "some have reversed their past positions of prohibiting cell phones in schools."

Table A.1 (*continued*)

When	What
Mid-2000s	Technology advanced and the industry exploded making phones no longer a luxury item. Many school districts allowed phones but they had to be off during the day. Some tried to ban camera phones or ones that had text messaging.
	Many parents are using cell phones not just for emergencies and text messaging daily to communicate with their children, keep track of them, and manage busy schedules. More and more, cell phones are seen in the elementary grades. Recently out-of-college teachers (those who spent their own teens texting), innovative teachers, and teachers who are parents of teenagers themselves are using cell phone technologies as tools for teaching. According to Georgia senator Richard Marable, chairman of the education committee, "[t]imes change," he told *Education World.* "Certainly we can protect the educational integrity of schools and still utilize this high technology" (Delisio, 2002).
	Most major school districts (twelve out of the fifteen largest) allow phones at school. "It is the policy in Los Angeles, Chicago, Miami, Houston, San Diego, and Dallas" according to Gotbaum (2006). Articles such as "Become a Ringleader" (Smith, 2006) and "SMS is Top of the Class" appear (ClickPress, 2006).
By 2007	Across the country in schools and in families, cell phones are seen as important in learning, communication, and safety. In Connecticut cell phones were seen as "serious educational tools, and the results are already impressive" (Whamond, 2007). In Nevada, "[i]nstructors at University of Las Vegas are now using text messaging as a tool to teach students" (Sheneman, 2007). In Pennsylvania, "Penn State uses text messaging to communicate with students" (Glazer, 2007). In Tennessee, administrators handed out phones (up to fifty) to a student advisory council made up of average students with leadership qualities so that they could communicate with principals in order to keep the school safe (Pytel, 2007). Cingular Wireless released a survey indicating that "63% of parents who use text messaging believe it improves their communication with their children" (McCarthy, 2007).
By 2008	Brooklyn schools doled out 2,500 cell phones to students (Medina, 2008).
	International Society for Technology in Education published the book *Toys to Tools: Connecting Student Cell Phones to Education* (Kolb, 2008).
	"According to a Nielson Mobile Survey, more American cell phone users are using text messages than using cell phones to make calls" (Reardon, 2008).
	Many colleges were using cell phone technologies in educational practices. Individual teachers were incorporating them into their classrooms and lesson plans across the country.

(continued)

Table A.1 (*continued*)

When	What
By 2009	Changes in school policy begin again. "The Collier County School Board recently voted to change the student code of conduct regarding cell phones and, in the process, expanded the code to allow schools to petition to allow students to use their phones in the classroom—to some extent" (Albers, 2009).
	"Florida schools allow cell phones to be used in class" (Solochek, 2009).
	"Suzette Kliewer, the teacher who administered the Digital Millennial program at Southwest High School in Jacksonville, N.C., said the phones excited her students and made them collaborate and focus on their studies, even outside of school hours. 'They took average-level kids and made them into honors-level kids'" (Richtel & Stone, 2009).
	It was stated in the *Charlotte Observer*, "some teachers in Charlotte are seeking to harness [texting's] power. Researchers back this approach with new evidence that texting teaches some positive language skills, and pragmatists argue that a war on texting is unwinnable" (Elder, 2009).
	According to a *Times Daily* article, "The Lauderdale County school board changed its policy on student cell phone usage this year to allow students the freedom to not only have them at school, but to use them at specified times during the day." This policy change reportedly reduced cell phone violations by 85% and according to superintendent Billy Valentine, "'[i]t's working so far' because 'it's not practical to eliminate cell phones altogether.' A principal in the district says he's seen a renewed sense of responsibility from his student body since the new policy went into effect" (Singleton-Rickman, 2009).Text messaging for teaching is a hot topic at many educational conferences.
By 2010	Cell phones and the technologies they provide for educational enhancements, especially text messaging, will be so obvious that school policy allowing them within classrooms and for educational purposes have begun to be adopted throughout the country. Additionally, "[t]he only difference now between smart phones and laptops, they say, is that cell phones are smaller, cheaper, and more coveted by students" (Richtel & Stone, 2009). As cell phone technologies continue to improve, become more available, and have more computer connections, their use as educational tools will continue to grow.
	"But with cell phones tucked in the book bags and pockets of three-fourths of today's teens, many high schools are ceding defeat in the battle to keep hand-held technology out of class and instead are inviting students to use their phones for learning" (Malone & Black, 2010).
And beyond	More than half of the world's population now owns a cell phone and children under twelve constitute one of the fastest-growing segments of mobile technology users in the United States according to The Joan Ganz Cooney Center at Sesame Workshop (Shuler, 2009).

STEP THREE: GIVE REASONS WITH RESEARCH

The next step is to address the critics with positive reasons and evidence. The most common arguments against cell phone use are that it is unfair to students who cannot afford them, that they are a distraction, that text abbreviations are ruining the language, or that they are tools for cheating. When these comments are made, the best response is your own use of the ideas in this book and the success of your students. However, when there is not enough time to compile your own evidence, the following reasons, with research support, will combat some of the common arguments against cell phones. Also, because data and examples that are up-to-date are the most convincing, we encourage you to continue to follow the research as new studies continually become available in support of using cell phones in education.

Cell Phones Can Bridge the Digital Divide in Cash-Strapped Times

Anyone interested in embedding cell phones into the curriculum has heard the argument, "but what about the students who don't have a phone?" Answer: You do the same thing as you do when your class doesn't have enough textbooks or computers. You don't say, "I guess we can't do our work." You find workarounds, partner or group students, get some extra phones on hand for those who don't have them, and reach out to the community for support to see if there are companies or groups who would be able to donate cell phones. Whereas many schools are spending money on expensive clickers, interactive white boards, proprietary software and trainings, cell phones are a piece of educational technology that most students already have access to so they represent no extra cost to a school or district.

Supporting Evidence

- Most students have text messaging even when they do not have minutes for talking.
- Most educators already own a phone and are familiar with its capabilities. By harnessing the power of cells, they can enhance their teaching strategies and increase student achievement without additional training, which is expensive and time consuming.
- Creative educators can find ways to get phones to students when access is an issue. When the desire is there, schools can investigate developing programs similar to the "four North Carolina schools in low-income neighborhoods, where ninth- and tenth-grade math students were given high-end cell phones running Microsoft's Windows Mobile software and special programs meant to help them with the algebra studies. The students used the phones for a variety of tasks. The study found that students with

the phones performed 25 percent better on the end-of-the-year algebra exam than did students without the devices in similar classes" (Ritchtel & Stone, 2009).

- Develop a plan to work with students who do not own cell phones or a plan that allows unlimited texting. Ensure to include them in all activities. Possible solutions include the following:
  - Connecting students with mentors who could ensure students had access to technology
  - Creating partnerships with local library
  - Reaching out to cell phone providers or the community to donate minutes or equipment for students in need
  - Setting a place in the school (for example, library, lab, classroom) for after- or before-school access to school technology
  - Partnering or grouping classmates who can share technology
  - Providing an alternate assignment
  - "Relying on features that are more common on less-expensive phones will help ensure that mobile technologies can help close rather than amplify the digital divide" (Shuler, 2009).
  - "[M]ore educators are concluding that cell phones may be the only realistic way their schools can offer the one-to-one computing experiences that better-funded schools provide with laptops" (Trotter, 2009).

Cell Phones Can Enrich Instruction, Motivate Students, and Decrease Discipline Issues Around Cell Phone Use

Whereas some critics see cell phones as distractions, many innovative educators are seeing the benefits. When cell phones are accepted into classrooms, appropriate behaviors, etiquette, and class procedures can be established. Because students love their phones, using them in instruction increases motivation. By embracing the power of cell phone technologies and using it, educators can spend their time enhancing lessons rather than taking phones and writing referrals.

Supporting Evidence

- Texting is an efficient and effective note-taking tool. Text abbreviations provides advantages for phonemic awareness and spelling.

- Students should be using the devices they use in the real world in school where they practice proper boundaries and etiquette. This better prepares them for their future.

- "Students, regardless of community demographics, socio-economic backgrounds, gender and grade, tell us year after year that the lack of sophisticated use of emerging technology tools in school is, in fact, holding back their education and in many ways, disengaging them from learning. In many communities and states, this hard realization that today's classroom environment does not mirror the way today's students are living their lives outside of school or what they need to be well prepared to participate, thrive and compete in the twenty-first century economy is actually exacerbating the existing relevancy crisis in American education" (Project Tomorrow, 2010).

- "In fact, when asked to identify the major obstacles that prevent use of technology at your school, the #1 response from the students in grades 6–12 was 'I cannot use my own cell phone, smart phone or MP3 player' in school, beating out for the first time since 2003, school filters and firewalls as the students' top obstacle" (Project Tomorrow, 2010).

Text Messaging Encourages Writing and Literacy

Whereas some critics feel that text messaging and the abbreviations used in texts are ruining the language, communication, and writing skills of our youth, there is a growing body of research illustrating the benefits of texting on writing and literacy.

Supporting Evidence

- Students engaged in multiple methods of communication are writing better than ever before.

- *The Times,* October 31, 2005: "Fears that text messaging may have ruined the ability of teenagers to write properly have been shown to be unfounded after a two-year study revealed that youngsters are more literate than ever before. Alf Massey, head of evaluation and validation at Cambridge Assessment, the department at Cambridge University that conducted the study, said 'The most comprehensive comparison made of exam papers of the past 25 years has discovered that the writing ability of 16-year-olds has never been higher'"(Fresco, 2005).

- In England as far back as 2006 researchers Plester and Wood presented findings of their research to the British Psychological Society's developmental section annual conference at the University of London: "Contrary to popular belief, the use of text message abbreviations is linked positively with literacy achievements. In fact, the children who were the best as using 'textisms' were also found to be the better spellers and writers. 'We are interested in discovering whether texting could be used positively to increase phonetic awareness in less able children, and perhaps increase their language skills, in a fun yet educational way'" (Smith, 2006).

- Another benefit was found by T. Wolsey, who stated that "[y]oung writers who know how to effectively use iTap and related technologies may be learning letter order as part of the English orthographical system" (2009).

- ". . . a new study from California State University researchers has found that texting can improve teens' writing in informal essays and many other writing assignments" (Miners, 2009).

- Donna Metke, head of the English department at Juanita High School in Seattle, agrees. "If anything, students seem to be better writers. Any type of writing that gets thoughts down, I don't see as a negative. They're more comfortable with the written word and it doesn't frighten them" (Dunnewind, 2003).

- Chrisitina McCarroll, staff writer at *The Christian Science Monitor* states, "Though plenty of adults grumble . . . the text messages that send adolescent thumbs dancing across cell phone keypads, many experts insist that teenage composition is as strong as ever—and that the proliferation of writing, in all its harried, hasty forms, has actually created a generation more adept with the written word." She also quotes Al Filries, director of the Center for Programs in Contemporary Writing at the University of Pennsylvania, who deals with high school writers as well as college students. In the past twenty years he's seen, ". . . the quality of student writing at the high school level [go] way up, and this is explained by the fact that they do more writing than they ever did." In fact Dr. Filries goes on to state in the interview that overall whatever the worries that teens are morphing into fleet-fingered, e-mail happy robots, there's a genuine writing renaissance under way. "We lost it in the '50s and '60s as telephones and TVs poured into American homes and daily writing dwindled to grocery lists and office memos. I think we've gained it back. After a period of formal writing went away, the Internet revolution brought back writing in the daily sense" (McCarroll, 2005).

- Students can distinguish when to use text lingo and formal language. According to *The Christian's Science Monitor's* Christina McCarroll (2005), "As for the much-maligned lexicon of IM—'ru there?' and 'wuzup?'—teens insist they haven't forgotten formal English, and are undaunted by transitioning between the two."

- "Writing is good. Writing is expressing thoughts. Expressing thoughts is good. We just don't like their modality," argues Larry Rosen, an author and researcher at California

State University, whose book is titled *Rewired: Understanding the iGeneration and the Way They Learn.* Rosen and four colleagues surveyed more than seven hundred teens and aggregated multiple findings in a new study that suggests texting may help teens' writing in informal essays and other assignments. In a conversational essay, teens who used more texting shortcuts performed better than colleagues who did not (Elder, 2009).

When Phones Are a Learning Tool, They Cease to Be a Cheating Aid

Whereas the media and many schools have had problems with students using cell phones for cheating, with acceptance of them as a learning tool information access can be encouraged and assessments can become a true measure of learning. When cells are part of the classroom, proper testing procedures can be developed. We must remember that books, paper, even our palms can be used for cheating. The answer is not banning but instead instilling responsibility and enforcing consequences. It might also mean rethinking our assessments. If students can find the answer in a device that's accessible to them all the time, perhaps they should be assessed on questions they have to think about instead of things that are easily answered with a cell phone? Using cells as learning tools brings them out where they can be used to empower learners and proper boundaries can be put in place.

Supporting Evidence

- "In terms of preparing them for the world, we need to redefine our attitudes towards traditional ideas of cheating. Unless the students have a conceptual understanding of the topic or what they are working on, they can't access bits and pieces of information to support them in a task effectively. In their working lives they will never need to carry enormous amounts of information around in their heads. What they will need to do is access information from all their sources quickly and they will need to check the reliability of their information" (Patty, 2008).

- "Marc Prensky threw out the following challenge to educators in a British Educational Communications and Technology Agency publication: 'What if we allowed the use of mobile phones and instant messaging to collect information during exams, redefining such activity from 'cheating' to 'using our tools and including the world in our knowledge base'? I have begun advocating the use of open phone tests. . . . Being able to find and apply the right information becomes more important than having it all in your head" (Patty, 2008).

Fighting Cell Phones Is a Losing Battle

Many schools are now realizing that they are fighting a losing battle. Schools across the country are allowing cell phones in various degrees. The momentum of the progression is toward total acceptance and use of cell phones as educational aids.

Supporting Evidence

- Be ahead of the curve and begin using these powerful devices today.
- Shaw (2005) sums up the situation and states the need like this: "It's not clear when—or even if—the controversy regarding cell phones will be resolved. What is clear is that cell phones have become a permanent part of society. Some teachers argue that trying to ban student cell phones is as futile as former efforts to ban calculators from classrooms. Cellular technology has improved drastically in the last few years. Even more drastic improvements and changes are just around the corner. Keeping up with technological advances is not easy, particularly when benefits and drawbacks may not be clear, but it is necessary. Well-thought-out cell phone policies enable schools to continue to reflect the society they serve."
- Easily half—46 percent—of U.S. "tweens" (those age eight to twelve) use a cell phone, and safety is the primary reason that parents cite for their children's having a mobile phone, according to Nielsen's newly launched Mobile Kids Insights survey (Nielsen, 2008).
- The survey also estimates that U.S. tweens—a population segment of twenty million—get their own cell phone between age ten and eleven, on average.

STEP FOUR: RALLY SUPPORT THROUGH SURVEYS

The next step in getting prepared is conducting surveys for support. Surveys for students, teachers, and parents (examples follow) can provide you with valuable insight regarding the availability of cell phones for use in education, the attitudes of those involved, and how they might be incorporated in the classroom. Using surveys such as the following examples will help you assess the potential use of cell phones in your classroom. You can copy and use these survey forms or create your own.

STUDENT CELL PHONE USE SURVEY

As a student you are the most important person in school and we want to hear from you! Please share your feelings about the idea of being able to bring cell phones to school.

Student name:

What grade are you in?

Do you have a cell phone?

Yes, No, I share one, Other:

How many cell phones are in your home?

If you have a cell phone, please describe your plan. Check all that apply.

☐ Free evenings and weekends

☐ Unlimited texting

☐ Unlimited minutes

☐ Camera

☐ Video

☐ Unlimited data and Internet

☐ Other:

Which of these ways that cell phones can be used do you think would help you learn better and be fun to use? Check all that apply.

☐ Record an oral report spoken by an avatar

☐ Text a number to help with research

☐ Tweet on your phone to respond to important news events

☐ Use your phone to define unknown words

☐ Use your phone to translate unknown words

☐ Share your vote or input on things you are learning with a poll like on *American Idol*

☐ Receive your homework via text message

☐ Put test dates into your calendar

☐ Other:

Would you like it if you and your teacher came up with ways that you could use cell phones *during class* to help you learn better?

Yes

No

Would you like it if you and your teacher came up with ways that you could use cell phones *for homework* to help you learn better?

Yes

No

Does your teacher allow you to use your cell phone to learn in class or for homework?

Yes

No

Explain how you can or would use a cell phone to help you learn better.

Please share any ways your cell phone currently helps you.

If you could use your cell phone, would you be more motivated to do any of the following? Check all that apply.

☐ Go to class

☐ Participate in class

☐ Study

☐ Complete homework

☐ Enjoy learning

Do you think you could be trusted to use a cell phone responsibly and respectfully in school?

Yes

No

Make a statement for or against using cell phones to learn. Explain why.

PARENT SURVEY FOR CELL PHONES IN EDUCATION

As parents, you are the most important supporters of your children's education. We are interested to learn how you would feel about cell phones being used for educational purposes. Thank you for your input.

Does your child have a cell phone?

Yes No

Comments:

If yes, do you allow him or her or them to take the cell phone to school?

Yes No

Comments:

If no, would you if you knew the cell phone was being used for educational purposes?

Yes No

Comments:

Do you pay the cell phone bill?

Yes No

Comments:

Does the plan have unlimited texting?

Yes No

Comments:

Do you allow your child(ren) to use a cell phone for homework?

Yes No

Comments:

If not, would you if the teacher was incorporating it as a learning tool?

Yes No

Comments:

Do you feel students need instruction on cell phone etiquette?

Yes No

Comments:

Do you feel incorporating cell phone technologies for educational purposes will help prepare students for the twenty-first century?

Yes No

Comments:

Do you think your child(ren) would be motivated to use his, her, or their phones for learning?

Yes No

Comments:

TEACHER CELL PHONE USE SURVEY

Please share your feelings about using cell phones to engage learners and enrich instruction.

What grade do you teach?

Do you have a cell phone?

Yes, No, I share one, Other:

How many cell phones are in your home?

What percentage of your students do you think have cell phones in their households?

☐ 95 percent or more

☐ 86 to 94 percent

☐ 75 percent or less

What percentage of your students do you think own cell phones?

☐ 95 percent or more

☐ 86 to 94 percent

☐ 75 percent or less

If you have a cell phone please describe your plan. Check all that apply.

☐ Unlimited texting

☐ Free evenings and weekends

☐ Unlimited minutes

☐ Camera

☐ Video

☐ Unlimited data and Internet

☐ Other:

Which of these ways do you think cell phones could be fun for your students to use and help them learn better? Check all that apply.

☐ Record an oral report spoken by an avatar

☐ Text a number to help with research

☐ Tweet on their phone to respond to important news events

☐ Use their phone to define unknown words

☐ Use their phone to translate unknown words

☐ Share their vote or input on things they are learning with a poll like on *American Idol*

☐ Receive their homework via text message

☐ Put test dates into your calendar

☐ Other:

Would you consider coming up with ways that your students could use cell phones *during class* to help them learn better?
Yes
No

Would you consider coming up with ways that your students could use cell phones *for homework* to help them learn better?
Yes
No

What ways would you consider using cell phones to help students learn?

Please share any ways your cell phone currently helps you as an educator.

If your students could use cell phones how much more motivated do you think they would be to participate in class?

☐ Much more motivated

☐ Somewhat more motivated

☐ Wouldn't make a difference

If your students could use cell phones, how much more motivated do you think they would be to go to class?

☐ Much more motivated

☐ Somewhat more motivated

☐ Wouldn't make a difference

If your students could use cell phones, how much more motivated do you think they would be to study?

☐ Much more motivated

☐ Somewhat more motivated

☐ Wouldn't make a difference

If your students could use cell phones, how much more motivated do you think they would be to do homework?

☐ Much more motivated

☐ Somewhat more motivated

☐ Wouldn't make a difference

If your students could use cell phones, how much more do you think they would enjoy learning?

☐ Much more

☐ Somewhat more

☐ Wouldn't make a difference

Do you think your students could be trusted to use a cell phone responsibly and respectfully in school?

Yes

No

Do you have any concerns about working with your students to use cell phones for homework?

Do you have any concerns about working with your students to use cell phones for work at school?

Make a statement for or against using cell phones to learn. Explain why.

STEP FIVE: LAUNCH A PILOT PROGRAM

When working to lift the ban, be willing to start small, demonstrate success, and work from there.

- Meet with key members of your school and district decision makers to map out an acceptable pilot program, for example, the district technology coordinator, building principal, and assistant principals.
- Ensure that the pilot program includes all teachers interested in participating.
- Make sure to invite administrators to observe and participate when you are incorporating cell phones into the curriculum. This can be one of the fastest ways to build relationships and get key stakeholders on board. Film videos of what you and your students are doing. Publish on online spaces to celebrate the work your students are doing, for example:
  - Culbreth Middle School's collection of videos (www.youtube.com/user/greyculbreth) featuring the use of iTouches
  - Video of a student field trip to the Chesapeake Bay (www.youtube.com/hanoverscience#p/u/13/Gs12DUGrdFQ). Twitter updates at the end of the video were posted by the students during the trip via cell phones.
- Indicate alignment to the National Education Technology Standards. Indicate how the use of cell phones is aligned to Dean, Hubbell, Pitler, and Stone's (2012) nine research-based strategies. You can think of your own or use the ideas shared in Chapter Three.

The following is a sample pilot program format that you can use and modify to the particular needs of your school or district.

Pilot Program

[School Name] is piloting the use of cell phones to investigate our hypothesis that the use of this tool will better serve the needs of our students. The following steps outline how our pilot is being implemented.

1. *Identify how cell phones will be used to improve teaching, learning, and leading.* The school principal will allow the use of cell phones to support our efforts for school improvement. Cell phones will be used to communicate to and teach students using group texting to combat the following issues at our school:

   - Lack of homework supplies
     - Students do not have paper and pencils at home and they lose their binders when they take them out of the building. Many live in various places, get rides from anyone, go to jobs, take care of children, all which makes keeping track of homework a problem. They never lose their phones, so putting the teaching and learning into their hands outside of school is a chance to increase learning.
   - Poor attendance and getting behind on make-up work
     - Students often miss school for many reasons such as no ride, had court, sick kids, had to work (survival comes before school for our students). Group texting the day's lesson points, the assignment, the homework, the review, the test date reminder, and so on would help combat inconsistent attendance and help keep students in the learning loop.
   - Minimal involvement from parents and guardians
     - Getting communication from school to parents is a struggle with frequent changes in address, jobs, and family make-up. By having parents' cell phones in a group texting site, increased communication can happen without additional expenses of mailing home reminders, announcements, calendars, or surveys. Parents are more likely to read a text than a letter. Texting is free; mailing is not.

2. *Select the right tool.* We are starting a pilot with the most commonly used cell phone tool. Texting! By starting simple, we selected a tool everyone already knows how to use. We are focusing on the basic skills of peer-to-peer texting and group texting. Group texting has almost no learning curve for students, teachers, leaders, or parents if they already know how to text.

3. *Tie to research-based teaching and learning strategies.* By providing the research base, we alleviated concerns of administrators, parents, and colleagues. Group texting would enable us to enhance the following of Dean, Hubbell, Pitler, and Stone's (2012) research-based strategies:

- Setting objectives and providing feedback
  - Group text prior to a lesson to let students know what the day's objectives will be and invite them to come to class with thoughts about how to best meet them. After a lesson send a text to individual students or the class with feedback you may not have had an opportunity to address during the lesson.
- Reinforcing effort and providing recognition
  - The first and main reason for getting student cell phone numbers and texting students (individually and as a group) is to send shout-outs that celebrate their successes. Texting makes this a simple and easy practice. When appropriate the student's parents, friends, and principal may be included on the text, too.
- Cooperative learning
  - Once students and teachers are familiar with group texting, subgroups for cooperative learning can be set up.
- Cues, questions, and advance organizers
  - Use group texting to send out lesson cues, questions to get the thinking started, and build schema prior to class.
- Nonlinguistic learning
  - Have students video themselves exercising to support their PE logs.
  - Have students video their science projects done at home.
  - Use video within the class to partner students in practicing speeches.
- Summarizing and note taking
  - Have students use your class or assignment Twitter tag to summarize today's lesson in 140 characters or less. Not only is this a great research-based skill, but the classroom teacher could also have the responses posted on the class website so parents know what their children learned that day.
- Homework and practice
  - Homework is rarely assigned in our school as many of our students go to jobs, are taking care of children, or have home lives and living conditions that are unstable and inconsistent. Lost books, notes, assignments, and not completed homework

have been the norm (lost cell phones never happen). A group text puts the information in students' hands and minds at home, encouraging practice. Any tool or idea to increase student learning and practice outside of school is valued.

- Identifying similarities and differences

  - Teacher group blasts students and they text back answers to Poll Everywhere. The teacher has a list of responses to grade rather than a stack of papers.

- Generating and testing hypotheses

  - Have students use Twitter to access experts to assist them in generating and then testing their hypotheses.

  - Use cell phone cameras and a Flickr account to measure and document results and test hypotheses for science experiments.

4. *Prepare.* Prior to launching our pilot program make sure the following has been completed:

- Student cell phone plan surveys are completed and summarized.

  - Alternative plans for access or alternate assignments are created for students with no personal, friend, or family cell phone availability.

- Parent and student agreements are signed.

- Acceptable use contracts are developed and signed by students.

- Lessons plan are developed incorporating research-based strategies and standards alignment.

Completion of these items ensure students will be on task and prepared for engaging instruction using the tools they love.

5. *Evaluate the pilot.* The upcoming unit will be taught to three language arts classes but only one class will have the group texting enhancements. The learning outcomes of the three groups will provide comparisons of the effectiveness of the tool. The one-unit time frame allows timely feedback. In addition to the outcome measures for the learning objectives of the unit, the following questions will be helpful:

- For the teacher:

  - Did the outcomes between the cell phone and non-cell phone groups vary significantly? In what ways?

  - Were the students more engaged in the cell phone or non-cell phone class? Explain.

  - What worked? Explain.

- Did you notice increased learning outcomes when cell phones were used or when they were not used? Explain.
- What did you learn? Explain.
- What suggestions do you have for improvement?
- What do you want to continue?
- What might you change?
- For students:
  - How did you feel about the use of your cell phone during the unit?
  - What was helpful? Explain.
  - Were you more motivated? Explain
  - What suggestions do you have for improvement?
  - What did you learn?
  - What do you want to continue?

STEP SIX: TALKING POINTS FOR TEXTING

After having used many applications yourself, reading the research in support of cells, reviewing the movement toward cell phone acceptance for education, preparing your survey results, and investigating the possibility of doing a pilot, you will be motivated, educated, and inspired. You have the pieces in place to lift the ban, prepare your talking points, and start the discussion. By opening up conversations with the powers that be, you will begin the process necessary to eventually lift bans on cell phones, create acceptable use agreements, and change school policy.

In the following section you will find a ten-talking-points worksheet designed to be customized for your particular situation. If you are talking with (or happen to be) your building principal, your district administration, your school board, a policy review committee, or any combination of these, you will want to be prepared. By taking the time to insert data from your school or district that will support the main points for cell phone use, you will present a convincing case. Even if you do not have the time to compile the data or copy the suggested handouts, the points are still valuable to go forward and start the discussion. The policies, procedures, management strategies, and templates included in Chapter Four can be put in place when you get agreement and policy changes to happen.

Ten Talking Points to Lift the Ban and Begin Using Cell Phones for Learning

1. **Harness the power of the tools already in student's pockets.**

   The ubiquitous use of cell phones by our students illustrates the reason why we should allow cell phones, with an acceptable use agreement, and use the tools available on them for learning purposes inside and outside the classroom. Students are motivated to use them! The majority of our secondary students are sitting in classrooms with cell phones in their pockets regardless of the ban. Integrating cell phones is a student-desired educational enhancement, making it very likely to be successful due to the bottom-up approach.

   [Insert your school's teacher, student, and parent cell phone survey results here.]

2. **Cell phones have educational capabilities built in.**

   Cell phones have many educational capabilities: calculator, clock, calendar, picture and video, stopwatch, text messaging for communication and writing, Internet, polling, and so on. Cell phones are used to support and enhance current research-based instructional strategies.

   [Insert examples from this book that you personally feel will be valuable for the students in your classroom, school, and district.]

3. **Save money for your school.**

   Using student cell phone capabilities as educational tools is *free;* no hardware or software purchases required.

   [Insert your school's or district's technology budget from previous years and projections of cuts, which cell phones do not require.]

4. **There is little to no learning curve.**

   Most educators already own and are familiar with cell phone technologies; thus, integration would not require a large amount of time-consuming and costly training. All it would take is an open mind. Students can teach educators how the tools can be used for learning.

   [Insert your school's or district's training, in-service, and workshop expenditures from previous years and projections of cuts, which cell phone use will not require.]

5. **Decrease discipline issues.**

   Using cell phones for educational purposes should reduce phone-related discipline issues. Working with students to establish appropriate and inappropriate uses is useful in developing proper etiquette for use at school and in the community. It teaches self-control, boundaries, and compliance.

[Insert your school's statistics on referrals, detentions, and so on from cell phones, which can be reduced through acceptance of use and establishment of protocols.]

6. Reduce cheating with cell phones.

With acceptance of cell phones in classrooms and established policies and protocols in place, students will know what is acceptable. During assessment students and teachers will have established if cell phones should be out on their desks, under their desk, collected in a basket, or, just maybe, used as part of assessment. *Consideration:* If the answer is already available in a student's pocket, on demand, are we really assessing what is relevant in the twenty-first century?

[Provide a sample of classroom procedures addressing cell phones during testing, such as the example feature in Chapter Six.]

7. Cell phones can be used to support research-based strategies.

Cell phones can support research-based educational strategies while engaging learners and enhancing instruction. As we shared in Chapter Three, there are numerous research-based instructional strategies that can be enhanced with the use of cell phones.

[Provide some examples from Chapter Three of this book.]

8. Help your school go green with the tools students already own.

Cell phones and text message communications are environmentally friendly and fit the trend of many schools to decrease paper. There are even a few schools across the nation that have become paperless (Francis, 2000).

[Insert your school or district's paper and copy machine budget from previous years and projections of cuts, which can be positively affected by cell phone use.]

9. Establish a positive educational environment.

An acceptable use agreement developed with the educators and students and shared with the school community can help establish a positive educational climate.

[Provide a sample agreement such as the ones in Chapter Four.]

10. Many educators are already having success with cell phones in their classrooms.

Use some of the examples given throughout this book of teachers who are having success with cell phones in the classroom.

[Tell a few of your own touching or motivating success stories. Use the results of your pilot program here!]

PUTTING THE PIECES TOGETHER TO LIFT THE BAN

Now you are well equipped with a feel for the momentum of the movement, the research for reasons to use cell phones in education, the results of your surveys, the talking points plan, and are possibly even ready to launch a pilot. With all this in place, you are well positioned to take on the task of helping your local policy makers think outside the ban and embrace the technology most students already have access to for learning. By being prepared, you will open minds and start the ball rolling to lift the ban so cell phone technologies will be available for all. When policy is supportive of cell phones, educators will have more choices, students will have more tools, and we will all move into the twenty-first century better prepared.

REFERENCES

Albers, K. (2009, July 20). *Texting in school? Not quite, but school district adjusting cell phone policy.* Naplesnews.com. Retrieved from www.naplesnews.com/news/2009/jul/20/texting-school-not-quite-school-district-adjusting/

ClickPress. (2006, November 21). *SMS is top of the class.* Retrieved from www.clickpress.com/releases/Detailed/22141005cp.shtml

Cohen, M. (2009, September 23). Text message marketing. *New York Times.* Retrieved from www.nytimes.com/2009/09/24/business/smallbusiness/24texting.html

Dean, C. B., Hubbell, E. B., Pitler, H., & Stone, B. (2012). *Classroom instruction that works* (2nd ed.). Alexandria, VA: ASCD.

Delisio, E. R. (2002, February 7). Schools, states review cell phone bans. *Education World.* Retrieved from www.education-world.com/a_issues/issues270.shtml

Disney Corporation. (2007). *Disney mobile survey: Teen and tween cell phone calls rise during the summertime.* Retrieved from www.highbeam.com/doc/1P1-141706505.html

Duncan, A. (2009, July 28). *School: There's an app for that?* PBS Frontline's Digital Nation. Retrieved from www.pbs.org/wgbh/pages/frontline/digitalnation/learning/schools/school-theres-an-app-for-that.html

Dunnewind, S. (2003, April 29). *Generation text: Teens' IM lingo evolving into a hybrid language.* Knight Ridder/Tribune News Service. Retrieved from http://community.seattletimes.nwsource.com/archive/?date=20030412&slug=immain12

Elder, J. (2009, October 27). Teachers putting texting to use. *Charlotte Observer.* Retrieved from www.newsobserver.com/2009/10/27/159701/teachers-putting-texting-to-use.html

Francis, R. (2000). The paperless school of the future is here now. *Education World.* Retrieved from www.educationworld.com/a_tech/tech059.shtml

Fresco, A. (2005, October 31). Texting teenagers are proving "more literate than ever before." *Times.* Retrieved from www.timesonline.co.uk/tol/life_and_style/education/article584810.ece

Glazer, E. (2007, May 3). More schools use text messaging since shootings. *Daily Northwestern.* Retrieved from www.dailynorthwestern.com/2.13894/more-schools-use-text-messaging-since-shootings-1.1923993

Gotbaum, C. (2006, June 14). *Statement for city council hearing on department of education cell phone policy*. Retrieved from http://publicadvocategotbaum.com/news/CellPhonePolicy.html

Haury, D. L., & Rillero, P. (1994). *Pathways to school improvement: Perspectives of hands-on science teaching*. Columbus: OH: North Central Regional Educational Laboratory. Retrieved from www.ncrel.org/sdrs/areas/issues/content/cntareas/science/eric/eric-2.htm

Hord, S. (1997). *Professional learning communities: Communities of continuous inquiry and improvement*. Austin, TX: Southwest Educational Development Laboratory.

Johnson, D. W., & Johnson, R. T. (2009). An educational psychology success story: Social interdependence theory and cooperative learning. *Educational Researcher, 38*(5), 365–379.

Kaiser Family Foundation. (2010). *Generation M2: Media in the lives of 8- to 18-year-olds*. Retrieved from www.kff.org/entmedia/upload/8010.pdf

Kolb, L. (2008). *Toys to tools: Connecting student cell phones to education*. Washington, DC: ISTE.

Lenhart, A., Ling, R., Campbell, S., & Purcell, K. (2010, August 20). *Teens and mobile phones: Summary of finding*. Retrieved from www.pewinternet.org/Reports/2010/Teens-and-Mobile-Phones/Summary-of-findings.aspx

Malone, T., & Black, L. (2010, October 11). Cell phones increasingly a class act. *Chicago Tribune*. Retrieved from http://articles.chicagotribune.com/2010-10-11/news/ct-met-cell-phones-in-class-20101011_1_class-act-students-reporter-tara-malone

Marist Poll. (2010, June 12). *Cell phone nation*. Retrieved from http://maristpoll.marist.edu/612-cell-phone-nation/

Marrero, T. (2010, March 1). Hernando County schools consider rules on student-teacher text messaging. *St. Petersburg Times*. Retrieved from www.tampabay.com/news/education/k12/hernando-county-schools-consider-rules-on-student-teacher-text-messaging/1076541

Marzano, R., Pickering, D., & Pollock, J. (2001). *Classroom instruction that works: Research-based strategies for increasing student achievement*. Alexandria, VA: ASCD.

McCarroll, C. (2005, March 11). Teens ready to prove test-messaging skills can score SAT points. *Christian Science Monitor*. Retrieved from www.csmonitor.com/2005/0311/p01s02-ussc.html

McCarthy, M. (2007). *Text messaging your teenager*. Retrieved from www.suite101.com/content/text-messaging-your-teenager-a35917

Medina, J. (2008, February 28). For "A" students in some Brooklyn schools, a cellphone and 130 free minutes. *New York Times*. Retrieved from www.nytimes.com/2008/02/28/nyregion/28cellphones.html

Miners, Z. (2009, October 29). Could texting be good for students? *U.S. News*. Retrieved from www.usnews.com/blogs/on-education/2009/10/29

National School Safety and Security Center. (2002). *Cell phones and text messaging in school*. Retrieved from www.schoolsecurity.org/trends/cell_phones.html

Nielsen. (2008). Mobile kids insights. *The Nielsen Company survey report*. Retrieved from http://ca.nielsen.com/content/dam/nielsen/en_ca/documents/pdf/fact_sheets/Nielsen%20Mobile%20Kids%20Fact%20Sheet.pdf

Nielsen, L. (2010, October 24). 6 Ideas for developing a personal learning network of others interested in using cell phones in education. *The Innovative Educator*. Retrieved from http://theinnovativeeducator.blogspot.com/2010/10/6-ideas-for-developing-personal.html

Partnership for twenty-first Century Skills. (2009). *P21 framework definitions.* Retrieved from www.p21.org/documents/P21_Framework_Definitions.pdf

Patty, A. (2008, August 20). Phone a friend in exams. *Sydney Morning Herald.* Retrieved from www.smh.com.au/news/national/phone-a-friend-in-exams/2008/08/19/1218911717490.html

Pickering, D. (2010). *Technology workshop.* Retrieved from www.marzanoresearch.com/professional_development/events.aspx

Prensky, M. (2004). *What can you learn from a cell phone?—Almost anything!* Retrieved from www.marcprensky.com/writing/Prensky-What_Can_You_Learn_From_a_Cell_Phone-FINAL.pdf

Prensky, M. (2010). *Teaching digital natives: Partnering for real learning.* Thousand Oaks, CA: Corwin Press.

Project Tomorrow. (2010). *Creating our future: Students speak up about their vision for twenty-first century learning.* Retrieved from www.tomorrow.org/speakup/pdfs/SU09NationalFindingsStudents&Parents.pdf

Pytel, B. (2007, January 9). *Limited cell phones permitted.* Retrieved from www.suite101.com/content/limited-cell-phones-permitted-a10979

Quillen, I. (2010, October 15). Schools open doors to students' mobile devices. *Education Week.* Retrieved from www.edweek.org/dd/articles/2010/10/20/01mobile.h04.html.

QWASI Research. (2009–2010). *2101 mobile access survey shows "more people doing more things on their cell phones."* Retrieved from www.qwasi.com/news/tag/text-message-statistics

Reardon, M. (2008, September 23). Text messaging explodes in America. *CBS News Online.* Retrieved from www.cbsnews.com/stories/2008/09/23/tech/cnettechnews/main4471183.shtml

Richardson, W. (2007, June 1). *I lost something very important to me.* Retrieved from http://weblogg-ed.com/2007/i-lost-something-very-important-to-me

Richardson, W. (2009, August 22). *What did you create today?* Retrieved from http://weblogg-ed.com

Richtel, M., & Stone, B. (2009, February 16). Industry makes pitch that smartphones belong in classroom. *New York Times.* Retrieved from www.nytimes.com/2009/02/16/technology/16phone.html

Shaw, K. (2005). *Students and cell phones: Controversy in the classroom.* Retrieved from www.associatedcontent.com/article/4903/students_and_cell_phones_controversy.html?cat=9

Sheneman, K. (2007). *Teaching through text message.* [Web log post] Retrieved from www.protexting.com/Teaching_through_text_message-faq-106.htm

Shuler, C. (2009). *Industry brief: Pockets of potential—using mobile technologies to promote children's learning.* Retrieved from http://joanganzcooneycenter.org/Reports-23.html

Singleton-Rickman, L. (2009, November 2). Lauderdale finds compromise in student cell phone war. *Times Daily.* Retrieved from www.timesdaily.com/article/20091102/articles/911025026?Title=Lauderdale-finds-compromise-in-student-cell-phone-war

Smith, R. (2006). *Become a ringleader: Teaching with text messaging.* Retrieved from www.edutopia.org/ringing

Solochek, J. S. (2009, October 4). Students get out phone. *St. Petersburg Times.* Retrieved from www.tampabay.com/news/education/k12/some-tampa-bay-high-schools-allow-cell-phones-to-be-used-in-class/1041399

Trotter, A. (2009). Students turn on their cell phones for classroom lessons. *Education Week, 26*(16), 10–11. Retrieved from www.edweek.org/ew/articles/2009/01/07/16cellphone.h28.html

Ullman, E. (2010, September). Get smart about phones. *Tech & Learning.* Retrieved from www.techlearning.com/article/32470

Uses of cell phones in education. (n.d.). Link to Classroom 2.0 social network discussions. Retrieved from http://wiki.classroom20.com/Cell+Phones

Webb, W. (1999). *The educator's guide to solutioning.* Thousand Oaks, CA: Corwin.

Whamond, K. (2007, April 4). Text messaging is transforming education. *Connecticut Post.* Retrieved from http://m2m.tmcnet.com/news/2007/04/14/2508874.htm

Wolsey, T. (2009). *Spell check and writing tasks in high school: Spell checkers and texting promote accurate spelling.* Retrieved from www.suite101.com/content/spellcheck-and-writing-tasks-in-high-school-a118299

INDEX

Page references followed by *t* indicate a table.

Student response systems–enhanced lessons: American history (Civil War generals), 80–82; math (multiplication tables), 101–102; physical education (knowledge of sports), 105–106; social studies (women in history), 103–104. *See also* Audience response systems (ARS)

Student understanding development: using cell phones for cues, questions, and advance organizers for, 84–89; using cell phones for generating/testing hypotheses, 106–111; using cell phones for homework and practice, 99–102; using cell phones for nonlinguistic representations for, 89–93; using cell phones to identify similarities and differences, 102–106; using cell phones to summarize and take notes for, 93–99

Students: accessing their love of mobile technology, 2; cell phone camera to learn faces and names of, 30; cell phone–enriched lessons to engage, 147–183; partnering to plan for learning with cells, 141–146; planning cell phone activities with, 140–141; securing cell phone agreements from parents and, 114–122; as teachers, 153–154; texting as communication method of choice, 5; Tweets celebrating success of individual, 26; Voki used to facilitating English fluency of ELL, 61. *See also* Communication tools; Digital natives; Teacher-student texting

Students with special needs, 45–46

Stumpenhorst, J., 27

"Success with Cells for the Texting School Community" workshop, 5

Summarizing practice: language arts (summarizing books) lesson on, 96–97; rule-based strategy, 94; summary frames, 95

Supporting Research-Based Instructional Strategies with Cells workshop, 215–217

Suter, J.: cell phone agreement sent out by, 116; general technology use/publishing agreement sent out by, 117–118; Prepare for Standardized Science Tests with Poll Everywhere and Wiffiti lesson by, 161–163; sharing ideas for cell phone rules with students, 134

Swan, C., 5

T

Teacher-student texting: appropriate use of, 15–19; boundaries, privacy, and safety workshop on, 40, 41*t*–45*t*; concerns about, 37; creating effective, 36–37; emoticons for enhancing expression, 38–39*t*, 65*t*, 196; to enhance instruction, 64; getting started with, 37–38; for hands-on activities, 62, 64; ideas for communication with students, 39–40; popular texting abbreviations, 37–38; postlesson activities, 63*t*; prelesson activities, 62*t*; supporting students with special needs, 45–46; supporting students through, 40, 45; texting learner resources quick guide, 64–65*t*. *See also* Students

Teacher-student texting tools: intro to audience response systems (ARS), 23, 24, 33*t*; intro to cell phone cameras, 29–30, 50–51, 89–90; intro to cell phone notepad, 20–21, 88–89; intro to ChaCha, 12, 52–53, 65*t*; intro to Flickr, 31–32, 88–89, 89–90, 91–92, 108–110; intro to Google SMS, 12, 28–29, 54, 65*t*; intro to Google Voice, 12, 21–23, 49–50, 65*t*; intro to group texting, 12, 17–19, 33*t*; intro to phonecasting, 27–28, 33*t*; intro to Poll Everywhere, 12, 23–24, 52, 65*t*; intro to student response systems, 80–82, 101–106; intro to Textnovel, 55–57, 65*t*; intro to TextTheMob, 23, 24, 52, 65*t*; intro to Twitter, 13, 24–26, 54–55, 65*t*; intro to

Voki, 13, 60, 65*t*; intro to WeTxt Notebook, 48–49, 65*t*; intro to WeTxt used for group, 46–49, 65*t*; intro to Wiffiti, 13, 19, 33*t*, 57–58, 65*t*. *See also specific tool*

Teachers: appropriate use of texting by, 15–19; developing your personal learning network, 218–220; embracing cell phones in the classroom, 4–5; mobile learning resources for, 3–4; texting by physical education, 201; using texting for professional development, 205–235; Texting Teacher Resources Quick Guide for, 33*t*. *See also* Communication tools

Teaching: integrating texting into, 32–33; NETS Standards for Teachers (NETS*T), 151–153; students as teachers and role in, 153–154. *See also* Cell phone instructional strategies

Teaching Digital Natives: Partnering for Real Learning (Prensky), 153

Teaching Generation Text: cell phone workshops using, 206–217; developing your personal learning network through, 218–220; online course for using, 221–235

Teaching Generation Text (blog), 218

Technology skills: NETS*S technology operations and concepts, 151; as professional job competency, 6

TeleParent, 19

Templates: basic cell phone permission letter, 120–121; cell phone acceptable use policies, 131

Test preparation tools, 192, 195*t*

Text lingo/abbreviations: 18r (later), 38; asap (as soon as possible), 37; b4 (before), 37; BF (boyfriend), 37; brb (be right back), 17, 37; btw (by the way), 37; cos (because), 37; cya (see ya), 37; fyi (for your information), 37; GF (girlfriend), 38; gtg (got to go), 38; idk (I don't know), 38; jk (just kidding),

38; kk (okay), 38; Ling2Word service for translating, 38, 65*t*; lol (laugh out loud), 17, 38; omg (oh my gosh), 17, 38; oxox (hugs and kisses), 38; pos (parent over shoulder), 38; rofl (roll on floor laughing), 38; sup (what's up), 38; thx (thanks), 38; tml (text me later), 38; ttyl (talk to you later), 17, 38; w/ (with), 38. *See also* Emoticonszzzz (sleeping or bored), 38

Texting: among school staff, 16, 17*t*; appropriate use by teachers, 15–19; between teachers and parents, 16–19; as communication method of choice among students, 5; efficiency of, 16; English language arts (common and proper nouns—capitalization) lesson, 79–80; integrating into teaching, 32–33; learner resources quick guide for, 64–65*t*; school administration use of, 186–188; by school librarians, 198–199; student-teacher communication through, 36–65*t*. *See also* Communication tools; Group texting

Texting guides: Learner Resources Quick Gide, 64–65*t*; Texting Teacher Resources Quick Guide, 33*t*

Textnovel: description of, 55–56; how to get started with, 56–57; ideas for using with students, 57; quick guide on, 65*t*; safety note about using, 56

TextTheMob: description of, 23; how to get started with, 23; ideas for educators using, 24; life skills or advisory (peer pressure) lesson using, 110–111; quick guide on, 65*t*; teacher-student communication using, 52

Theft of cell phone, 127

TTYL (talk to you later), 17

TurningPoint, 51

Twitter: description of, 13, 24, 54; developing your personal learning network through,